A History of the Jews
Since the First Century A.D.

A HISTORY
OF THE JEWS
SINCE
THE FIRST
CENTURY A.D.

Frederick M. Schweitzer

THE MACMILLAN COMPANY, NEW YORK, NEW YORK

COLLIER-MACMILLAN LTD., LONDON

The Macmillan Company
866 Third Avenue, New York, N.Y. 10022
Collier-Macmillan Canada Ltd., Toronto, Ontario

Library of Congress Catalog Card Number:
76–144818
4-30-74
SECOND PRINTING 1972

Printed in the United States of America

Contents

"All Israel will be saved."
St. Paul, *Rom. 11:25*

"Judaism's preservation and presence in the world was a basic part of God's plan of salvation and therefore could not be without significance for the Church. Christians ought not to leave this present reality out of account, nor should they look at it from a purely human and political point of view, as do those who are not believers. They should rather draw nourishment for themselves from the Jewish world, with the insight and respect due to its past, its faith, and its trials. The Church expects it of her children that they leave nothing undone to tear down the walls of division between herself and the Jews, a wall which the misunderstandings of centuries have rendered almost impenetrable; and that they leave nothing undone to establish brotherly relations with the Jews, and to show them, at last, by their conduct the true face of the Church."
Study group of priests and laymen from Apeldoorn, Holland, preparing for Vatican II

"Nothing is more difficult, even for the best-intentioned student, than a detached view of Jewish-Gentile relations."
Gerson D. Cohen

"If any imaginative work combines intellectual content with pure form, everyone is satisfied. If a scholarly work penetrates its materials and explains them in an arresting interpretation, nothing else is expected. The task of the historian, however, is simultaneously literary and scholarly; history is both art and science. It has to meet all the postulates of criticism and scholarship like any philological work. Yet at the same time it must give the intelligent reader the same pleasure as the most excellent literary piece."
Ranke

Introduction

THE FOLLOWING SKETCH of Jewish history in the post-biblical period has its origin in the stimulus to new and better feelings, thought, and knowledge to which Vatican Council II has given rise. It is one of the works of *Aggiornamento* commissioned, as it were, by Pope John XXIII. More specifically, it owes its inception to a cooperative effort by the Archdiocese of New York and the Anti-Defamation League of B'nai B'rith to act upon the imperatives set forth by the Second Vatican in its "Declaration on the Relationship of the Church to Non-Christian Religions"; the joint efforts of the League and the Archdiocese have already produced a remarkable set of films for public and educational use, one series on the image of the Jew in Western literature and society and another on Jewish religious life, particularly in America.

In Vatican II's Declaration (Part 4) it is recalled that Jews and Catholics share the fatherhood of Abraham, that the beginnings of the Church's "faith and her election are already found among the patriarchs, Moses, and the prophets" of the Old Testament, that the Church "draws sustenance from that good olive tree onto which have been grafted the wild olive branches of the Gentiles." In the Council's "Dogmatic Constitution of the Church" (Part 16) further reference is made to the Jews; they are related in a special way to "the people of God," for it was to them that "the covenants and the promises were given and from whom Christ was born of the flesh. On account of their fathers, this people remains most dear to God, for God does not repent of the gifts He makes nor of the calls He issues." The Council reminded us also that, on the one hand, the Apostles, those "foundation stones and pillars of the Church" were Jews, as were most of the first Christians. On the other hand, according to the New Testament, it appears that some Jewish leaders and those who listened to them demanded the death of Jesus. It hardly follows that the Jews, as a people, were guilty of Jesus' death; in fact, the Council expressly repudiates any such notion of collective guilt, then or at any time in history; anti-Semitism is a sin and a heresy.

In the view of many observers, whether Protestants, Catholics, or Jews, Vatican II did not go far enough in its repudiation of ancient errors. They note, e.g., that at one time it was proposed that the wording be "to deplore and condemn" in the strongest terms the notion of "deicide," "collective Jewish guilt," etc., but that the final version was considerably weakened. Paradoxically, in the same Declaration or elsewhere, the Council expressed regret and a desire for forgiveness of Protestants, Greek Orthodox, and Moslems, yet there is no statement of contrition or repentance for the sufferings and persecutions Jews have undergone in the Christian West and frequently under Christian auspices. The sardonic criticism of the Declaration by a few Jews as too little and too late is quite understandable: "How many more million Jews have to suffer before a word of contrition is heard in the seats of Christendom?" they ask.

Yet as Msgr. John M. Oesterreicher has observed, the Declaration is disappointing only in comparison to the earlier drafts, only on the principle that "the good is the enemy of the best." In the light of two millennia of the

Jewish-Christian encounter and particularly in the light of
Arab pressure on the Council—when for a while "politics
held theology in chains," it has been said—the promulga-
tion of the Declaration on October 28, 1965, must be seen
to have been, in Msgr. Oesterreicher's word, a "miracle."

Many important Jewish spokesmen have, in fact, recognized the Declaration as a milestone, stating with great
satisfaction that we are now "in the post-Vatican II era."
Dr. Joseph L. Lichten of B'nai B'rith's Anti-Defamation
League recalls how "that historic Thursday, October 28,
1965, left many of us with a feeling, above all, of relief that
the fundamental ground for disharmony between the two
communities had been swept clear. Many are deeply convinced that a powerful instrument has been forged which
will give impetus to intergroup cordiality. . . . [The
Declaration] decries the great injustice of the past and
rejects anti-Semitism in all its myriad forms. And it presents these statements as the defined doctrinal guide for the
Church, present and future." At the very least, no person
or government can ever again believe, assume, or proclaim
that there is a Christian sanction for persecution or discrimination against Jews.

Those who have been somewhat hesitant in acting upon
the imperatives of the Declaration have been Catholics
themselves, whether clergy or laymen. One may still hear,
as I did in an up-country parish on Passion Sunday last
spring, a sermon on the Gospel of St. John (8:46–59) that
makes one's hair stand up on end, as though Pope John had
never lived, Vatican II had never met, and biblical exegetes
of the last half century did not know what they were talking
about. As Father Donald W. McIlvane of Pittsburgh
complained in a letter to *The New York Times* for Febru-
ary 24, 1969, "There are very few parishes where sermons
[reflecting the Declaration] have been preached. Parish-
ioners who did not read the press would never know that
it existed." I.e., the old curse of Christian-Jewish rela-

tions, "the silence of Christians," whether to speak out in the recent difficulties between Jews and Negroes in New York City or to proclaim the message of the Declaration from the pulpit and in catechetical instruction, is still with us.[1]

I am aware, as I sometimes say to my students, that inertia is the strongest force in history. How else can one explain the insane proposals, anonymous but putatively Christian in origin, that circulated on the periphery of the Council? These included, among other ancient rubbish, the demand that Jews be confined to ghettos, wear the infamous yellow badge, acquire only books which have been censored, be barred from celebrating their rites in public or from playing, eating, drinking, speaking with Christians— on pain of fines, flogging, etc.! What is needed is not merely a new thinking cap, which is relatively easy to come by, but a new set of feelings, which is much more difficult and slow in coming. I dare say one sovereign reason for the protracted deliberations, not much short of four years, before the Council could come to agreement, was that the bishops and theologians themselves had to enter into a new frame of mind.

I am confident, though it will take a generation or more, that the letter and the spirit of the Declaration will triumph. For one reason and another, I have reread the Declaration perhaps twenty times, and each time it seems to open greater and more promising vistas. I have come to be particularly impressed by that passage in Part 4 that reads: "the Church ever keeps in mind the words of the Apostle [Paul] about his kinsmen," that to them belong the sonship, the glory, the covenant, the giving of the law, the worship, and the promises; it appears to me to be the ideal point of departure for the "dialogue" between Jews and Catholics that the Declaration called for.

The assertion by the Council of the affinity of the Church with the chosen people of the Old Testament is not, however, a new theological conception. Far from it, for the idea that Judaism and Christianity form a deeply interrelated religious community is as old as Christianity itself. The metaphor of the olive branch, invoked by the Council and referred to above, comes from the eleventh chapter of St. Paul's Epistle to the Romans. The greatest of the Apostles here was teaching that the Gentiles who had been converted to Christ have become members of a community of believers which has existed from ancient times among the Hebrew people. He characterizes this community as the olive tree, the root of which is Abraham and the other patriarchs, the natural branches of which are those Jews who accepted Christ; the Gentiles who have become members of it are called engrafted branches. (Precisely what Paul's metaphor signifies, whether this view is consistent with his doctrine of the Body of Christ—these are problems of theological interpretation which need not concern us here.)

Suffice it to say that had the relations of Jews and Catholics (and Christians generally) over the past two millennia been guided to any significant degree by the theological views reiterated (and extended) by the Council, the story of Jewish-Christian relations would have been radically different from the macabre tales of massacre, expulsion, robbery, and ill will that are the staple of that history. As it is, we are presented with the paradox of a theology that is right and a history that is wrong. That is to say, seen from the vantage point of Vatican II's statements on relations with non-Christians, two millennia of Jewish-Christian history become an enormous aberration. Given these theological assumptions, nothing of the order of the inhumanity and agony that loom so large in the following pages should ever have occurred. Somehow—and we shall have to examine the reasons for it—a mistaken or misinterpreted theology was substituted for the right one, with the consequence that the history of Jewish-Christian relations is much more a chronicle of one community's inhumanity to its neighbor than of the love, kindliness, and respect which ought to obtain between two peoples who share and revere the same sacred book. Given this long and saddening chronicle, it was appropriate for the Council to direct that Catholics and Jews seek mutual understanding by joint biblical and theological studies, by "brotherly dialogues," and, what is implied in the document, by Catholic education that refrains from depicting the Jews as in any way "repudiated or cursed by God." In the Council's debates several bishops referred to the evil consequences of bad teaching of Jewish history and emphasized that proper religious and theological formation require great care for the accurate and unprejudiced rendering of Jewish history. More positively, for our present purpose, we must render and interpret the history of the Jewish people so as to give full scope to their contribution to the Catholic faith and to Western civilization; equally, it must measure up to the professional historian's canons of objectivity and empathy.

The present work is a modest step in the right direction. The task, even on the small scale attempted here, is no easy one. Catholic or Christian histories and Jewish histories of the same events and eras have very little in common; neither in selection of material and emphases nor in generalizations and conclusions do they concur, as though the authors came from the intellectual antipodes. In my own reading and reflection on Jewish history I have come to call this phenomenon "historiographical antithesis." That is, what is taken to be a great and golden age of the Church or Christendom by Christian scholars is seen by Jewish historians to have been a dismal one for Jewish life. And vice versa, what Father Edward Flannery points up in *The Anguish of the Jews* when he says that "most Christians have torn out of their history books the pages that Jews have memorized." E.g., the era of the French Revolution and Napoleon is for Catholics one of the bitterest periods of persecution and massacre, of disestablishment, loss of property, and destruction of education centers, of a floodtide of destructive criticism and skepticism, and of humiliation of the Papacy; for Jews it is the age of their Emancipation—the Revolution was the cause and source of their attainment of political and civil equality for the first time since the fourth century, when the Emperor Constantine inaugurated anti-Jewish legislation.

The age of the Crusades presents a historiographical antithesis of the opposite sort. For the Christian scholar, it is the expression of so much that was best in the medieval world: of Christian courage, faith, generosity, vision, selflessness, devotion for the redemption of the Holy Land; it was the turning of the tide when the Church could go over to the offensive against the Islamic enemy that had long threatened her existence, etc. But to the Jewish historian his sources present a grim picture of fanatical crusaders running amuck in pillaging, murdering, expelling, robbing, forcibly converting Jews; of ecclesiastical legislation requiring Jews to wear distinctive insignia humiliating them as a pariah people and making them the obvious target of any mob, of the onset of the rigorous enforcement of ghetto isolation, etc. In short, what appears as the Christian high middle ages is simultaneously the Jewish dark ages.

Almost every period in the two millennia of the Jewish-Christian encounter exhibits—in greater or lesser degree—historiographical antithesis. The age of the Renaissance, however, is something of an exception to the rule. For it was a time when, tentatively at least, a considerable degree of toleration prevailed, and also of cordial cooperation between Christians and Jews in the great intellectual and cultural enterprises of the day, particularly in biblical exegesis and philosophical studies. Hopefully, the present age, once we have properly resolved the ambivalences and contradictions between theological professions and historical facts, will see great achievements of both (indeed of all) peoples. Hopefully, too, the time will then have arrived when Christian and Jewish historians can come together to write a cooperative history of the Jewish-Christian encounter, one that has no pages "torn out" and includes everything that is true and significant.

In the meantime I, a Catholic and a historian writing a history of the Jews, have tried to reckon with those historiographical antitheses as best as I could. I have the consoling thought, no matter what the deficiencies of the present narrative may be, that I have lit one candle to dispel among Catholics some of our immense ignorance about the Jews and Judaism in the period since the "proto-schism" of the first century. The virtual ignoring of Jewish history, whether in the elementary, secondary, or university institutions, is the worst lacuna in Catholic education, not excluding Negro history, which has not nearly the same richness of content or significance for the history of the Church, of the United States, or of Western civilization.

It will be noticed that the larger context of this book is, in considerable degree, the Catholic-Jewish encounter. I have been much concerned to point up the sins of omission and commission of my Church. Interestingly, in this post-Vatican II era, it has been Jewish readers of my manuscript who have sought to warn me off certain subjects as being "highly sensitive" to Catholics, whereas it has been Catholic colleagues who have tried to steer me away from subjects about which Jews are "touchy." Except in those instances where my facts were shown to be wrong or my emphases misplaced, I have not accepted such advice. I have indeed tried to write a history with a purpose, one to which all the readers of my manuscript have been decidedly sympathetic. Yet I have thought throughout that our purpose will be best served by presenting as accurate and full an account as is possible in less than three hundred pages, let the chips fall where they will. I say with Lord Acton, whose

Catholicism and idea of history have long been an inspiration to me, "Whatever we think of the faith, we must condemn the [evil] works" to which the Church has in any way been a party.

The relative stress here on Catholic-Jewish relations should not be taken, however, to mean that Protestantism is exempted as unblameworthy. This needs to be said, because I have given much attention to the philo-Semitism in the seventeenth and eighteenth centuries of Calvinism on the Continent and Puritanism in Old and New England. There is, clearly, a striking parallel in the Reformation re-emphasis on the Hebraic heritage of the Old Testament, and that of Vatican II; both provide a secure theological foundation for Christian tolerance and friendliness toward Jews. Yet all the Protestant churches and sects (the Mormons are one of a very few exceptions) bear a common responsibility with the Roman Church for anti-Semitism. (I do not, of course, mean to say that either the origin or development of anti-Semitism is exclusively Christian.) Protestants were heirs, whether unwittingly or not, to the medieval heritage of contempt and persecution of Jews. In those countries where one form of Protestantism became the national or established religion, e.g., some of the Lutheran states of Germany, a more virulent anti-Semitism, political as well as religious, frequently emerged.

In other countries, such as the United States, where Protestants have been in the majority and set the tone for the national life and culture, Protestant anti-Semitism has appeared in the form of a dislike of Jewish immigrants—as strangers, a minority, economic competitors, etc. Should a second edition of this book ever be issued, I would be more concerned to heed Professor John Higham's injunction not to underestimate anti-Semitism in the history of our country, and I would wish to explore its essentially Protestant origin. American Catholics, as a minority, have tended to be more conciliatory toward Jews than they might otherwise have been. I may be permitted to observe that the flurry of anti-Semitism among some Negro groups in New York City last spring (though in retrospect it begins to look like a tempest in a teapot) was, to the extent that it was religious in character, essentially Protestant. But as a Catholic I am hardly one to cast stones, beyond saying that the Christian churches, including my own, share much of the blame for anti-Semitism and have a common responsibility to make such amends as are possible.

I have not written, although I am much concerned with it, a history of anti-Semitism, in its Catholic, Christian, or any other variety; that has been done and better than I could do it. In the course of the work on this book I have come to detest the very word *anti-Semitism*. As a pseudo-scientific, Latinizing term, it seems to me to confer too objective an existence on the phenomenon it designates and even to legitimize the inhuman attitude it expresses. I sometimes wonder whether attempts to combat anti-Semitism by pronouncing it wrong, immoral, sinful, undemocratic, etc., and writing its history in what must be rather abstract terms do not have the opposite effect from that intended. Out of sheer contrariness or a perverse sense of daring, the response of human nature to such exhortation frequently can be to adopt just the attitude that is condemned. One reader of Father Flannery's fine book on anti-Semitism left me flabbergasted by saying, quite innocently I think, "Oh, but the Jews have always been persecuted," as though that—even if it were correct—were explanation or even justification! A book which chronicles the crime of anti-Semitism, by its very concentration, tends to leave the impression that there is nothing else to tell but persecution, and to lead to such bizarre conclusions as the one I have quoted. It may be the illusion of the historian, but I think the aim of diminishing prejudice and laying a basis for mutual respect is more likely to be attained in a work of history that tells a story, that depends less on sociological and psychological analysis and leaves the reader

to draw the moral instead of presenting him with an advo-
cate's brief.

In writing the present work, I have avoided the temptation, which I have certainly felt, to idealize the Jews, for
that would be historically as misleading (though not so
dangerous) as the opposite and more common error of
vilifying them. The great majority of historians dealing
with the plague of anti-Semitism set out not only to narrate, analyze, and explain, but also, and very properly, to
discredit it; in so doing they have, Professor Higham has
said in his important essay "Anti-Semitism in the Gilded
Age," "a common tendency to clothe the Jew in innocence
—to concentrate almost entirely on the anti-Semite's need
for a scapegoat." But for a fuller understanding, he argues
and I concur, it is also necessary to reckon with those
factors within Jewish life that have tended to rouse or
attract antagonism rather than that cheery human attitude
summed up in the phrase, *"Vive la différence!"* Certain
supposedly invidious characteristics—whether a peculiar
manner of dress, accent, business success, clannishness, or
other innocent peculiarities—in few or many Jews have
served frequently as the lightning rods to draw down the
lightning of prejudice on the whole community.[2]

What must be insisted upon, however, is that these or
other traits apply only to *some* Jews: There is no such
thing as a typical Jew, still less is there a typical American
Jew, since American Jewry is a melting pot of world Jewry
and represents such a variety of national origins and cultural backgrounds that it is virtually impossible to general-
ize about it. To say that all Jews or all American Jews
are short is likely to be as accurate and as inaccurate as any
other all-inclusive statement about Jews. Generalizations
can, in fact, do great harm, since repetition transforms
them into stereotypes. Stereotypes have a life of their own;
they can go on and on, giving rise to great evil and
suffering, although they may be the antithesis of truth. It
is the lesson which a scholar would have us understand

when he writes, "for centuries, the Jewish people have suffered because of generalizations. We have only to glance through the books of Jewish history to realize that the most popular weapon of anti-Semites has been to attribute to a whole people the faults of individuals."

Some people today dislike Jews because, they say, Jews are "pushy and aggressive" (reminiscent of some of those remarkably successful Jews referred to by Professor Higham), or because Jews have what they take to be a very acute capacity for business (dealt with at length in chapter 8), or because they find them to be too "exclusive and unforthright." To adopt such attitudes is to fall into the generalizing trap, and is as absurd as disliking apples after biting into a couple of sour ones. Theoretically, one might be willing to grant the right or propriety of a person to dislike a whole people, whether the Jews or others. The trouble with disliking Jews is that, unlike, say, disliking the Swiss, it leads too readily, if not automatically, to a revival of the ancient pattern of hatred and discrimination and even to violence; "dislike" is too often a fig leaf for anti-Semitism, and what may be mere dislike in one person all too naturally becomes anti-Semitism in his children or pupils. Anti-Semitism runs so deep in Western civilization as to be a habit of which we are only dimly aware, and it is still far too easy—sometimes despite the best intentions—to fall back into that hateful mental posture.

Until that ugly habit (I use the term in the sense intended by William James when he said that habit is the great flywheel of our social life) has ebbed away completely, the writing of Jewish history will be extremely difficult. It requires of the historical scholar the highest canons of accuracy and truth, proportion and completeness, and objectivity. He must take infinite pains if he is not to fall into the error or oversimplification that supports—or can be used to support—some old or generates some new prejudice.

I have adhered to the convention of B.C. and A.D. in

the matter of dating, partly because I am addressing myself principally to non-Jews and partly because it is the standard practice of historical writing. I am aware, however, that to many Jews these abbreviations are repugnant. And though it is perhaps slightly impractical, I should welcome the general adoption of B.C.E. (Before the Common Era) and C.E. (of the Common Era), since they do not require anyone to use an abbreviation conveying a theological doctrine he does not accept. In another matter I have tended to be conventional also. I have tried to write as fresh a synthesis of Jewish history as possible; yet a friendly critic of the manuscript complained that, in contrast to the rest of the work, my biographical sketches of Maimonides, Rashi, and others are pre-potted affairs on the model of encyclopedia articles. That is true in the eyes of an expert on Jewish history, but I see no way out of the difficulty in a short work that will be the first book of Jewish history for most of its readers. The outstanding figures of Jewish cultural and intellectual history would have to be given, I concluded at an early stage, something more than a mere mention. On the other hand, to treat them fully would lengthen the book disproportionately. Having steered clear of both Scylla and Charybdis, I may have fallen into the conventional, and I can only hope that my readers will be induced by what I have said to consult some of the numerous full-length studies of the great figures who have made the Jewish cultural tradition.

In writing the present work I have lapsed into the red ink, having incurred debts, intellectual and other, that I can never repay. Especially is this true of the professional staff of the Anti-Defamation League. Dr. Joseph L. Lichten has been a perceptive critic and fertile source of suggestions. Judith Herschlag Muffs, particularly in the first discussions of the scope and purpose of the book, was most kind and encouraging; she also made it possible for me to work far from the madding crowd of New York by sending along books and Xeroxed materials. To Irwin Feder I owe thanks for much editorial help. Oscar Cohen was most generous in his confidence in me and the book, and always gave the green light when obstacles of expense or judgment threatened to stymie the project. Stanley Wexler I must thank for a hundred things, not least of all for his suggestions and help on the question of publication.

Dr. Sidney Z. Lieberman, Headmaster of the upper division at Ramaz School, has had a large part in the work from its inception almost to the finish line. His expertise, his easy mastery over the whole range of Jewish history, is most remarkable. Several lengthy discussions with him, many written comments and observations, and his indispensable "flow charts of Jewish history" have been fascinating and extremely useful to me.

To that ecumenical spirit Father George B. Ford, long pastor in the good old days of Corpus Christi Church, a word of thanks is due for the intellectual tone he preserved in the parish and for his encouragement on the occasion or two that I have seen him since his retirement. To Msgr. Myles M. Bourke, pastor in the good new days of Corpus Christi, I am indebted for having brought his expertise in biblical exegesis to bear on several parts of the manuscript and saving me from errors I blush to think about; he also very kindly made his dissertation available to me.

Several of my colleagues at Manhattan College have given me assistance on special points. I should like to acknowledge Professor Joseph Wiesenfarth (now lamentably gone to Wisconsin) for his help on George Eliot, Professor Walter Stojko for his discussion of the Jewish question in independent Ukraine in 1917, and to Professor Edmund Tolk and Father Bruno Tausig for clarification of various aspects of German-Jewish history.

Msgr. Edward M. Connors, then Associate Superintendent of Schools in the Archdiocese of New York, presided at an early meeting on the project and gave it his blessing. I should like to thank Brother Patrick S. McGarry, F.S.C., my chief as Head of the History Department at Manhattan, for choosing me as the author when the joint project of the Archdiocese and the Anti-Defamation League was under consideration. Anne McCabe, as so often, has made books galore available to me. Estelle Miskin generously helped with typing additions and changes, and also commented helpfully on the manuscript. My wife and son had to put up with many periods of prolonged silence when the work was in hand. My thanks to The Macmillan Company for taking on the venture despite the credit crunch, and to their editor and reader for their highly professional assistance.

It goes without saying that I alone am responsible for errors, mis-emphasis, and so on.

Finally, I should like to express my gratitude to my teachers over the years. They are not responsible at all for what I say here, but that I should be saying anything at all is in some indefinable way their doing. Professor Carl F. Strauch of Lehigh University is the greatest teacher and nearest realization of Socrates I have ever known, and it is with much pleasure that I recall his launching me off on the course I have followed ever since. From my graduate mentors at Columbia I learned something of the art of research and writing: my thanks go especially to Professors Herman Ausubel, Jacques Barzun, Shepard B. Clough, and R. K. Webb (now managing editor of the *American Historical Review*). Let me also mention Salo W. Baron, although I do not know him personally: his work on Jewish history is as profound as its scale is grand, and I have mined it like a rich vein of ore. Except within his own field and among his co-religionists, he is the great unrecognized master of the vast realm of Jewish history; by any standard he is one of the half dozen or so greatest historians of our time.

F.M.S.

Providence Lawn
Spring, 1970

NOTES

1 Speaking to Vatican II, Cardinal Cushing of Boston asked, "How many [Jews] died because Christians were indifferent and kept silent? . . . If in recent years, not many Christian voices were raised against those injustices, at least let ours now be heard in humility. . . ."

2 Professor Higham furnishes an example in his characterization of American anti-Semitism in the 1870's. It focused on the German Jews who had arrived twenty years earlier as poor as they were uneducated; noting that from rags and the peddler's sack many of them rose to riches and education, he writes, "It seems highly unlikely that in any other immigrant group so many men have ever advanced so rapidly. Many of them bore the marks of this experience in the form of assertive manners and aggressive personalities." Thus a view of Jews "as rude, ostentatious parvenus took form, both distorting and reflecting their ambition and success."

There is a parallel in the prejudice that fastened itself on Polish and Russian Jews, who began to arrive in great numbers after 1881. Many of them, too, rose from rags and ignorance to affluence and education, though less dramatically than the previous immigrants. The more important fact was that they derived from East or East Central Europe's downtrodden masses. It is an area which, as Professor Halecki demonstrates in his book *Borderlands of Western Civilization,* has been subject to numerous conquerors and despotic taskmasters; its native population, Jews among them, has often been beggared into servility. Having been exploited and mistreated for centuries, Eastern Europeans acquired certain characteristics, unattractive surely, but which frequently enabled them to survive persecution and massacre. And when Eastern European Jews came to the United States, they inevitably brought some of those traits along. The new lightning rods for prejudice against Jews in America became, variously, that they were "secretive," "mistrustful," "deceiving," "clannish and exclusive," "so tight knit no outsider is admitted among them," etc. But, again, the only appropriate stance to take in such circumstances is *"Vive la différence!"* (Times of danger and persecution place a premium on such modes and attitudes; it becomes sheer necessity to distrust strangers and outsiders or even neighbors, to stick together, and to mislead officials; the capacity to deceive, trick, bribe, cajole

S.S. officials and informers, saved some Jews from the Nazi gas chambers.)

To the extent that such seemingly invidious adjectives did apply to American Jews—a minority of them—it is an illustration of what the Abbé Grégoire meant when he said (debating the issue of Jewish Emancipation in the French Revolutionary Assembly in the 1790's), "You have made their vices" by fettering them in ignominy; "now make their virtues" by granting them liberty and equality. Many, perhaps most, American Jews are of the first or second generation, so that some of them do manifest the kind of characteristics referred to, as do many Americans of recent Eastern European extraction. It takes a long time before such deeply ingrained attitudes disappear in a free society, for, as we are told in the Bible, it took forty years in the wilderness to purge away the stains and scars of the Egyptian bondage.

1. The Roman Period

THE OUTSTANDING CONTEMPORARY Christian historian of the Jews, James Parkes, begins one of his books with the following words, so apt they could hardly be improved upon:

The history of the Jews is the story of a people inextricably interwoven with that of a religion. Neither can be told apart from the other. It is obvious that there would be no story of Judaism if there were no Jews; but it is just as true that Jews would not have survived the long centuries of their total dispersion had there not been the cement of a religion moulded to their need either to transform or to tolerate the condition of their corporate and individual lives. . . . The history of the Jews is not the history of a "race"; for Jews were not of pure stock at the beginning of their story, and in their dispersion their borrowings have been physical as well as intellectual and spiritual.

Having insisted upon this all-important distinction and after a glance at the preceding centuries, we may begin our account of Jewish history in the first century A.D. (the era of the proto-schism, as it is sometimes called), when Jewish history and Christian history diverged and traced different paths of destiny.

The Persian and Hellenistic Period

This century was, perhaps, the grimmest up to that time in the long annals of Jewish history. True, in the years 597–586 B.C. the kingdom of Judah had been conquered by Babylon, the Temple of Jerusalem destroyed, and the principal leaders and influential citizens deported. But this period, known as the Babylonian Captivity, came to an end when Babylon was crushed in its turn by the vast Persian Empire, and the new conqueror Cyrus (558–529) permitted the Jews to return to their homeland in 538 and to rebuild the Temple.

For the next two centuries the Jews remained subjects of Persia, and though they paid heavy taxes and tribute to Cyrus in support of his wars against Athens and her allies, they nevertheless enjoyed religious freedom and considerable political autonomy. Occasionally the Persian ruler even appointed a Jewish leader as governor of the province (e.g., Nehemiah).

Such tranquility as the Jews enjoyed under Persian rule was not greatly disturbed by the annexation of Judea by Alexander the Great (356–323) in the course of his conquests. In fact, the same pattern of relations between the Persians and the Jewish community was to reappear as an archetype under the subsequent rule of Judea by other great empires, such as those of the Ptolemies and Seleucids, the Parthians, and the revived Persian state of the third to the seventh century A.D., as well as those of the Romans and Moslems. This meant that, with the sanction of the imperial government, to a remarkable degree Jews conducted their own affairs according to their own laws. Frequently, imperial governments enforced what the Jewish high priest (usually a favored member of the ruler's court) and his assistants commanded. Thus Judaism became an officially recognized and protected religion, and it is important to understand that the Jewish sense of community had its origin in this context. With its center in the synagogue, the community became a remarkably effective, stable, and enduring means of supervising, disciplining, instructing, and protecting its members.

Nevertheless, if Alexander was tolerant, he was also (as were his successors) an apostle of Hellenism, and he created a great society in which Greek civilization enjoyed pride of place. After his death, Palestine was ruled for a time by the Ptolemies of Egypt, who similarly interfered very little in Jewish life. But around 200 B.C., the Ptolemies suffered a number of defeats at the hands of the Seleucid rulers of Asia, with the result that Palestine passed under the latter's rule. Of all Alexander's successors, they were the most zealous hellenizers, a fact that directly affected the Jewish way of life. A hellenizing party among the Jews, which had already existed under the Ptolemies, was then so greatly strengthened that the existence of Judaism itself was threatened. The upshot of this factional struggle was that the Seleucid ruler Antiochus Epiphanes (175–163 B.C.) decided to extinguish Judaism once and for all by requiring complete submission to Seleucid rule and its Hellenistic civilization.

The Maccabean Revolt and the Hasmonean Period

But a man arose in Israel, Mattathias, who took to the hills with his five sons; there he organized a guerrilla resistance, summoning all who wished to maintain the Covenant of the Chosen People. Leadership fell to his son, Judas Maccabaeus (or Judah the Hammer), who inflicted a sharp defeat on Antiochus, expelled his troops from Jerusalem, and rededicated the Temple in 164 B.C. (This event is recalled annually in a kind of independence celebration known as the festival of Hanukkah.) As a consequence, the Seleucids had to concede peace, religious freedom, and eventually political independence to the Hebrews (128 B.C.). By then the Maccabees had become kings (the Hasmonean dynasty) and hereditary high priests. Thus the Jews had not only withstood the threat of Hellenism and hellenizers—the one people to do so successfully—but had regained political sovereignty as well.

The Hasmonean period was a turbulent one, characterized both by frequent assassinations and civil war, and by annexation and conquest which expanded the restored kingdom to boundaries little short of those existing during the time of David and Solomon. The decisive fact, however, was that the decrepit Seleucid power was gradually being replaced by that of Rome, a new and far more formidable foe.

Rome came to intervene in Jewish affairs in the classic manner. In 63 B.C. the Roman general Pompey was invited to give a decision in favor of one of the two claimants to the Hasmonean throne and, after much delay and uncertainty, responded by capturing Jerusalem, abolishing the monarchy, arresting one of the Hasmonean princes, and placing the other, Hyrcanus II, in a position of limited authority under the Roman governor of Syria.

The weak Hyrcanus was largely dominated by his scheming chief minister Antipater the Idumean. When the latter was assassinated, he was succeeded by his infamous son Herod who induced the Roman rulers (the Second Triumvirate) to make him king of Judea. And king he remained, thanks to Roman power, for forty-three years. In 37 B.C. he captured Jerusalem and for a while it seemed that the fate averted by the Maccabees would now overcome Judaism. A hellenizer but also a cruel and able tyrant, Herod seems never to have quite made up his mind about the Jews. On the one hand, he sought to conciliate the Pharisees, while massacring the Sadducees; on the other, he tried to win over the ordinary people by rebuilding the Temple in great splendor and magnificence, but at the same time antagonized them with the construction of pagan temples and cities. His last years were a reign of terror, punctuated by frequent rebellions. What angered the Jews was less his taxes and despotism than the threat that his hellenizing posed to their religion—a danger that only came to an end with his death in 4 B.C. Ten years later the emperor Augustus converted Judea into a Roman province outright, thus continuing the trend of diminishing Jewish autonomy that had set in with Pompey. This whittling-down process went on for another half century, during which corrupt and incompetent procurators—of whom Pontius Pilate was a notorious example—alternated with equally corrupt and incompetent descendants of Herod in misgoverning and abusing the province.

Crisis and Ferment

The period from the Maccabees' revolution through the fierce suppression by Rome of the Jewish revolts in A.D. 70 and 135 witnessed a great intellectual and theological ferment in Israel. Faced with recurrent crises arising from a triumphant Hellenism and the growing encroachments of Rome, Jews tended to fragment into profoundly antagonistic groups and divisions, more so than at any other period in their history. This evolution was, of course, in part related to the life and teachings of Jesus. Until the time of St. Paul, the growth of Christianity has the appearance to the historian of a reform movement within the fold of Judaism, rather than that of a new religion. However, since the story of Jesus is the most familiar one to Christians, we need but indicate here that from the Jewish viewpoint His earthly career was only one aspect of a profound crisis extending over three centuries, from 167 B.C. to A.D. 135.

The principal groups dividing Jews were the Pharisees, Sadducees, and Essenes, each of which sought to resolve the

great issues of the age in a particular fashion, or—to put it
another way—differed sharply in its interpretation of the
Bible and of Jewish tradition. The Essenes, who were
puritanical and ascetic, lived in rural areas, thus seeking to
avoid the taint of the world's wickedness and evil. The
famous Dead Sea Scrolls, it develops, belonged to the library of a Jewish monastic community that flourished before and during the lifetime of Jesus; it is not clear yet,
however, whether this Qumran community was identical
with the Essenes, a variant of Essenism, or a distinct sect of
its own. The Essene emphasis on the sharing of property,
bodily and spiritual purity, celibacy, mysticism, rural isolation, and even long periods of silence points up the fact
that Christian monasticism was a direct heir of Essenism.
The war with Rome of A.D. 66–73 was fatal to the
Essenes, whose ascetic ideal perished with them; a celibate
priesthood, for example, has never been a part of Judaism.

The Sadducees, also casualties of the war with Rome, felt
no necessity to flee the world. Comprising the priestly and
lay aristocracy, they were wealthy and conservative, and
their life centered around the Temple, which, with its ritual
worship, judicial courts, and schools, was a kind of Jewish
Acropolis. It was among the Sadducees, too, that Hellenism made the most headway. Their wealth, Hellenistic
proclivities, and conservative opposition to modification of
Jewish laws and institutions made them suspect in the eyes
of the common people, who favored the Pharisees.

The term *Pharisee*, in the Christian lexicon, is synonymous with hypocrisy and sanctimoniousness. It is a reputation that is quite undeserved, however, for the Pharisees
were democratic and liberal. Their attitude toward Jewish
law (*Torah*) and tradition was that they had to be adapted
to changing circumstances (within the framework of the
Oral Law). They also believed that such adaptation and
reinterpretation would meet all Jewish needs and require-

ments, and, in keeping with this position, they opposed Hellenism mightily. The Pharisees endured through all the difficulties with Rome, and it is from them that modern Judaism derives. Their central doctrine was that the Torah was the all-inclusive code of life—national and local, public and private, secular and religious. Their stress on exegesis in mastering the Torah and applying it indicates the importance they placed on intellect. As opposed to the Sadducees, it was knowledge of and insight into Torah rather than the performance of prescribed ritual ceremonies that mattered to them. Hence it was they who established academies for biblical studies; and, since Torah was a universal revelation and intelligence a quality to be found among rich and poor alike, the Pharisees opened their academies to everyone. It is principally owing to them that intellectual attainment came to have so high a place in the Jewish scale of values.

The Revolts against Rome

It is in the light of this proliferation of sects and flowering of religious ideas and messianic hopes that the Jewish revolts against Rome in 66–73 and 132–135 must be seen. The first revolt was also induced by Roman rule, which had become exceedingly corrupt and despotic. Tyrants like Caligula and Nero fancied themselves gods and demanded worship from their subjects, Jews included. This was the essence of paganism and idolatry, and therefore anathema to the Jews. In this connection it is significant that the insurgent party among the Jews called themselves Zealots; what they were zealous about was their religion, which seemed to them gravely threatened by Rome.

The revolt began in the last years of Nero's reign, when his despotism and idolatry became unbearable. It took Rome several years to suppress the revolt, partly because the Empire was caught up in a cycle of wars over the succession which was touched off by Nero's death. The year A.D. 69 was that of the four emperors—Galba, Otho, Vitellius, and Vespasian—who killed each other off in turn. Vespasian, who was the legate of Judea, renounced the command of the military operations against the Jews when he went off to pursue the imperial toga; his place at the head of the Roman armies was taken by his son Titus, who ultimately completed the bloody business.

We find a classic eyewitness account of this revolt in *The Jewish War* by Josephus, a Jew who was a commander of Jewish forces before deserting to the Roman camp. Captured by Vespasian, "the traitor of Jerusalem" (as he has often been called) was guilty of cowardice and duplicity. In any case, his purpose in writing the book was to demonstrate the rectitude of what the Romans had done. He also sought to justify himself, saying that not only had he done the right thing, but the only possible thing, and that he had remained, moreover, a loyal Jew. His obvious bias notwithstanding, Josephus' work is great history. He devotes nearly a third of it to Jewish history from the Maccabees to the outbreak of the revolt; it thus becomes a searing story of unrelieved horror and folly, of the crimes and treacherousness of the later Hasmonean and Herodian kings, of the Roman procurators, of even the most enlightened emperors, of the leaders of the insurgents, and of Josephus himself. It is a tale, too, of suicidal strife between rival groups and warring factions, of massacres of men, women, and children, of incredible heroism achieving nothing, and of the ruin that reached its climax in Titus' conquest and destruction of Jerusalem in 70. This victory of Titus, whom Josephus greatly admired, was commemorated by a panel in the Arch of Titus (still to be seen in Rome) which depicts Roman soldiers carrying from the Temple as spoils of war the famous seven-branched candelabra, the golden table, and various musical instruments.

The sequel to Titus' conquest was not religious persecution, for Titus thought he could attain his purpose of destroying Judaism by the simple destruction of the Temple, "since with the removal of its source [the Temple], the trunk [the Jews] will speedily wither." The Temple tax, paid by all Jews from time immemorial for the maintenance of the Temple, was appropriated by Rome in the form of the *fiscus Judaicus* to support pagan cults—a galling piece of idolatry to Jews. In addition, as in all her conquests, Rome enslaved many of the defeated.

The year 70 is the traditional starting point of the Diaspora, the dispersion of the Jews far and wide in the Roman world and beyond. Actually this dispersion had been going on since the time of Pompey (106–48 B.C.), who had captured many Jews and carried most of them off to the slave markets of Italy. Evidence of the great breadth of the dispersion can be found in the Jewish colony of the city of Rome (which was composed of Jews who had been brought there as slaves and subsequently purchased their freedom) and in the illustrious Jewish community of Cologne (which grew out of the transfer from Palestine to the Rhine Valley of a Roman legion that took with it many enslaved Jews). Finally, other Palestinian Jews simply emigrated on their own initiative for a whole variety of reasons. Among them was the fact that Palestine was the spoils of war and was ruled despotically. The temptation to leave, therefore, was strong, especially for Babylonia, which not only enjoyed independence and prosperity, but was beyond the Roman pale. Before long, every Roman city of any significance—even as far away as Britain—contained a Jewish community.

In spite of its crushing defeat, Jewish communities in Palestine and elsewhere managed to maintain their religious and cultural autonomy and, "in the retrospect of nineteen centuries," as the Jewish historian Gerson D. Cohen has put it, "Rome must candidly be acknowledged to have dealt with the Jews harshly but not viciously." If indeed the Roman emperors hoped that Jews and Judaism would disappear, they did not attempt to bring this about through massacres, expulsions, suppression, or proscriptions.

Despite Rome's restraint, the rub was that, for Jews, religious and cultural autonomy was indissolubly bound up with political sovereignty. For many centuries Judaism had been a state religion. Torah prescribed rules and laws for the conduct of state and public matters as fully as it did for private conduct, ritual ceremonies, etc. Consequently, it took a long time and much agony before the Jews could conceive of themselves as a non-political people or, to put it another way, to de-politicize Judaism. Accordingly, the Jews sought to revolt over and over again, despite Rome's undoubted tolerance and equally undoubted might. (It should be noted, in passing, that the revolt of 66–73 was not so desperate or rash as it is usually represented, since Jewish leaders felt that, with the growing restlessness against Nero's tyranny, their own rebellion would stimulate upheavals elsewhere in the Empire, with the result that Israel would ultimately regain its independence.)

It is considerations such as these which largely explain the second great revolt against the emperor Hadrian (A.D. 117–138) in 132–135. His predecessor Trajan (A.D. 98–117) had faced Jewish revolts, about which little is known except that he put them down in a bloody fashion. The principal casualty of these revolts was the Jewish community at Alexandria in Egypt. Its destruction marked the end of a great tradition, one which had produced the Septuagint Bible (the translation by Jews into Greek) and the great Jewish scholar Philo, who wrote in Greek and sought to harmonize Judaism and Hellenism. Alexandrian Judaism, with all its monuments to Hellenism (in the course of the period c. 260 B.C. to A.D. 100, a great many Jewish books besides the Bible were translated into

Greek there), went furthest in accommodating itself to Hellenism; but whatever possibilities lay in that direction were extinguished by Trajan's bloodbaths. This left Pharisaic Judaism, which frowned on Hellenism, more thoroughly in the ascendant than ever.

Hadrian began his reign by reversing Trajan's policies toward the Jews. He renounced Babylonia (conquered by Trajan), so that its Jewish population was once again free of Roman rule, and he may even have promised the Jews permission to rebuild the Temple. (What *is* certain is that Jews had the expectation that they would be free to rebuild the Temple, a purely religious action consistent with the religious and cultural autonomy they had within the Empire.) Instead, the temple Hadrian planned turned out to be a pagan one to Jupiter Capitolinus, to be built on the ancient site of the Jewish Temple. Coupled with this affront was Hadrian's prohibition of circumcision as well as other threats to the Jewish way of life. Nothing was more likely to goad the Jews into rebellion.

The leader of the second revolt was a man named Simon who, in keeping with the messianic expectations of the day, adopted the name Bar Kochba (Son of the Star). For a time, Simon made a real fight of it. The Romans were expelled from Jerusalem, for two years sacrifices were renewed on the Temple altar, and an independent state was created that went so far as to issue its own currency. Yet, even though it was a costly victory, and Hadrian could not make the traditional report to the Senate that "my legions and I are in good health," Rome ultimately won.

For the Jews the defeat was disastrous, worse in its result than Titus' war. Jerusalem, like a second Carthage, was utterly destroyed. Renamed Aelia Capitolina, it became little more than the site of a Roman military camp, where the temple to Jupiter was subsequently built. Jews were forbidden to teach or practice their religion, and were barred from so much as entering what was now a pagan town. In addition, many of the Jewish communities elsewhere in the province were destroyed, and to the half-million casualties of the war itself was added a heavy toll of martyrs, slaves, and deportees. If the dispersion in the preceding decades had been a trickle, it now became a torrent.

Had Hadrian lived much longer, he might well have succeeded in destroying Palestinian Jewry completely, but he died in 138. Under his successor, Antoninus Pius, the regime of martial law was revoked in favor of the more traditional policy of tolerance and autonomy—although for a long time Jews could not engage in missionary activity or visit the site of their Holy City. Judaism came to be officially recognized and protected by Roman law as a "licit religion." The last disabilities were removed altogether in A.D. 212 by the famous decree of Caracalla granting citizenship to all free men in the Empire. Generally speaking, from the time of Antoninus Pius Jews suffered no legal restrictions aside from the *fiscus Judaicus,* which continued to flow into imperial coffers for the benefit of pagan cults. And while there was possibly a certain prejudice against Jews, owing to their exclusiveness and foreignness, and to their unique privilege of exemption from participation in the imperial cult, they enjoyed nonetheless the same status as their neighbors.

2. The Age of the Talmud

THUS THE JEWS and Judaism survived the encounter with Rome. The Judaism that emerged from the two revolts was fundamentally different, however, from what had preceded them. For the destruction of the Temple, the loss of the Holy City, and the dispersal of the Palestinian Jews meant that the ancient priesthood (largely hereditary) and the ritual worship they had performed were entirely extinguished. Their place was taken by the rabbis in the capacity of scholars and masters of religious knowledge and wisdom (rabbi means "master" or "scholar"), of laymen rather than priests, of an aristocracy of talent rather than one of blood descent. Rabbinic or talmudic Judaism originated in the teachings of the Pharisees, who, as the opponents of the Saducean priesthood and aristocracy, had been gaining the ascendancy even before the Romans came on the scene. It is important to understand that rabbinic Judaism was essentially the result of a development intrinsic to Judaism, although its establishment as "normative Judaism" was undoubtedly hastened by the Romans' thoroughgoing dismemberment of the ancient social and religious pattern of the Jews and of Palestine. But if the Romans created a desolation, the rabbis carried out a reconstruction, one in which they were guided and inspired by Jewish traditions and modes, particularly in their pharisaic form.

Development of the Talmud

To skip over the rabbinic or talmudic period of Jewish history would be equivalent to giving an account of Christianity that ignored the patristic age. To grasp the place of the Talmud in Jewish history, it is necessary to remind ourselves that the central principle of Judaism had long been obedience to the will of God. Unlike Christianity, which came to place the greatest importance on correct belief and doctrinal purity, Judaism was fundamentally concerned with correct *conduct*. The law setting forth the code of conduct for Jews was the sacred Scripture, particularly the Mosaic Pentateuch, which Jews designate as Torah (teaching or instruction). The Torah, set down in a definitive text, was considered to be a God-given code governing the whole of life—from that of the nation to that of the private person—and thus included civil, ceremonial, ritual, and domestic law. This code was also complete, in the sense that every situation that occurred or would ever occur was governed by Torah, and that its every word and phrase had meaning and significance. The Jews thus became "the people of the book."

Since the code was complete, there could be no further additions through revelation. However, when Jewish society began to undergo profound changes, especially in the Hellenistic period, it became difficult to know which particular injunction in the Torah was to be followed and how it was to be applied in a given situation. Consequently, there began to appear, in about 200 B.C., a body of exegesis known as the *Midrash* (sermon), which can be taken to be the first body of talmudic lore. This work departed from a literal rendering of the Bible (which often did not seem to fit the context) in favor of allegorical interpretations and extensions of the biblical text.

The period from 200 B.C. to A.D. 200 saw a quite different development. This was the appearance of the

Mishnah (repetition), customs and usages which had been handed down from time immemorial by word of mouth, and which were supplementary to the Torah, or the Written Law. By A.D. 200 the Mishnah had been sorted out and codified by Rabbi Judah Hanasi, thus making further additions impossible.

A process similar to the one just described was repeated during the later Roman Empire, when exegesis and commentary became necessary in the application of the Mishnah. This new body of material—the most extensive portion of the Talmud—is known as *Gemara* (completion). The Gemara dates from the period after A.D. 200, by which time the term *Talmud* (instruction) came into existence and was used to identify the great body of the Mishnah and Gemara taken together. (There are, in fact, two Talmuds, the Palestinian—terminated by about 425—and the Babylonian—completed a century or so later. While there are these two distinct Talmuds, the differences between them are slight, since the point of departure in both instances is the same, the Torah and the Mishnah.)

As the Talmud gradually came to be conceived of as a single entity, new terms came into use to identify different aspects of it. Thus *Halachah* (law) designates those precepts and injunctions of the Talmud which are legally binding on Jews; it is sometimes called the "bread" of the Talmud. The "wine" is *Aggadah* (tale), a great body of literary materials—stories, legends, parables, proverbs, epigrams in prose and verse, etc.—which have a didactic or inspirational value. From about 700 onward, the task of rabbinic scholars became one of editing and commenting on the Talmud. Only from the twelfth century were attempts made to codify it, so as to establish Judaism as an integrated system of values and beliefs.

The Talmud—it cannot be overemphasized—is not a unified system of theology and law in which each part is consistent with every other part. Rather it is—if one had to define it in a sentence—a running commentary on the Bible's revelations. And, just as one can find several conceptions of God, human nature, love, justice, evil, retribution, etc., in the Bible, so too one finds greatly diverging views expressed in the Talmud. No necessity to harmonize or rationalize these differences was felt (at least not until the twelfth century) because scriptural revelation, being non-rational, is in fact above human reason. The rabbis— or, more accurately, the rabbinic schools of thought—differed greatly with one another, depending upon time and place. Moreover, there was no sacred priesthood or formal hierarchy, as in the Christian Church, to lay down the authoritative exposition of law and dogma (e.g., Gratian's authoritative codification of canon law and St. Thomas' *Summa*), binding upon all and sundry on pain of excommunication, incarceration, or burning at the stake. Accordingly, one rabbinic interpretation of Scripture or solution of an issue has no greater *official* authority than any other; instead, it is accepted or rejected according to the judgment of the individual Jew or of his local community.

Individual Scholars

Having traced the trends in Jewish legal and theological scholarship which culminated in the vast and enduring structure of the Talmud, we may now look at the long line of illustrious figures whose creation it is. The early anonymous scholars who, from 400 to 200 B.C., authored the Midrash are collectively known as the *Soferim*, usually translated as "scribes" but more accurately as "men of the book." Their successors were the Pharisees, who flourished until the Bar Kochba revolt and whose outstanding scholar was Hillel the Elder. Hillel came to Palestine from Babylonia in about 30 B.C.; his methods of exegesis and interpolation were basic to the development of the Talmud. For without rejecting anything from the past, he insisted that scholars in each succeeding generation were responsible for searching the Torah and Mishnah anew, guided by reason and discretion, in order to find new meanings and derive new legal precepts. Students of law will recognize in Hillel's approach an early, if not the earliest, concept of equity law. A famous example of a law he modified was the abolition of the *lex talionis* (an eye for an eye) in favor of monetary compensation.

Hillel was the sort of man around whom legends form. Born in poverty, he made his way in the academies by sheer determination and brilliance. A saintly and kindly person, he is best represented by his reply (suggestive of the Golden Rule) to a question addressed him on the nature of Judaism: "What is hateful to you never do to your fellowman. This is the entire Torah, all else is commentary. Go master it." His colleague, Shammai, was somewhat conservative in his reluctance to reinterpret and modify the law as liberally and democratically as Hillel had. Eventually, each came to head rival academies, a fact which gave rise to lively debates and did much to stimulate scholarly inquiry.

The next great scholar was Rabban Johanan ben Zakkai, the contemporary of Josephus and Philo. He was—to the degree that any single person can be so credited—the savior of Judaism in the wake of the destruction of A.D. 70. For it was he who saw that Judaism could be redeemed from the wreckage by its taking refuge in what has subsequently been called "a portable homeland." Tradition has it that he had himself smuggled out of besieged Jerusalem in a coffin and taken before Vespasian (or Titus), whom he petitioned to spare from destruction the coastal town of Jabneh (Jamnia) and to permit him to found an academy there. At Jabneh he and his colleagues gathered together all the texts of the law, exegeses, and commentaries of their predecessors (the core of the later Talmud) in order to prevent their being lost or forgotten in the maelstrom of ruin. This was a pious labor, looking to the day when the Temple would be rebuilt—in the near future, it was believed—and so special care was exercised in recording the ritual and ceremony of the Temple worship.

Without knowing it, however, Rabban Johanan was building for a future in which the Temple would be unnecessary to Judaism. He made in this connection a famous reply to a student who despaired of the future of the Jewish faith: "My son, do not weep. We have a means of atonement as effective as this [i.e., the Temple ritual and liturgy]. And what is it? It is deeds of loving kindness. As the prophet has said, 'I desire mercy and not sacrifice.' " Within a century, synagogues took the place of ritual sacrifice. (It should be noted at this point that, while such sacrifice has for well over a thousand years had no place in Judaism, nonetheless the greatest misconception among non-Jews is that blood sacrifice is still part of Judaic belief and practice.)

To the extent that Jews now had a capital city, it was Jabneh. Besides the academy, the *Sanhedrin* (Council and High Court) was moved there, probably at the instigation of Rabban Johanan, who was to preside over it during the last two years of his life. However, he did not elevate Jabneh to the traditional place that Jerusalem had occupied as the center of authority and direction (again because an imminent return to the Holy City was expected) ; instead he enjoined each local community to take upon itself the maintenance of the sacred teachings and the law. This proved to be a fillip to decentralization and made the synagogue the basic institution of Jewish life.

The trend of these times is indicated by the fact that Rabban Johanan, the undoubted leader of the Jewish people, was a scholar, not a high priest or a priest of the Temple. As the Temple gave way to the synagogues, so the leaders of the synagogues, the rabbis, displaced the priesthood. This was, moreover, a democratic transformation, since the priesthood had been open only to the hereditary aristocracy, whereas the rabbinate admitted anyone of the requisite intellectual ability and attainment. So pervasive was this change that the hero type of Judaism from that day on has been the scholar—he who "prays through study."

An invention of the Babylonian community, the synagogue can be traced back to the Captivity of the sixth century B.C., when, with the Temple destroyed and Palestine remote, the worship of God had somehow to be provided for. It probably arose as an institution when Babylonian Jews would go on the Sabbath to the house of some scholar to read the sacred books he had brought with him from Palestine, to hear his comments upon them, to receive instruction or guidance from him, to have him teach their children, etc. In time it came to serve as the communal assembly hall, clubhouse, local court, and charity center, maintaining such things as bath facilities and a cemetery. Thus the synagogue was not so much a church as it was a miniature polis; it was the hub of the local community's civic, intellectual and religious life. It is no exaggeration, then, to call the synagogue "the schoolhouse of the Jewish people" and to see in it and in the academies the twin institutional pillars of Judaism's survival after the Romans had destroyed the Second Temple in A. D. 70.

The two outstanding figures of the following generation were also scholars, Rabbis Gamaliel II and Akiba. Gamaliel—a descendant of Hillel—was Johanan's successor as head of the Jabneh Academy as well as leader of the Jewish community there. His position as leader was made formal by his designation as patriarch, an office which became hereditary in the "House of Hillel." The patriarchate and the Hillel claim to it were recognized by Rome by the second century; thereafter, until its abolition in 425, the patriarchs represented the Jewish community before the Roman government.

Gamaliel's career was a stormy one. For one thing, he was compelled by the scholars of the academy to retire from the presidency, since they felt their intellectual freedom was being infringed upon by his rather arbitrary and authoritarian manner. It was in Gamaliel's time, however, and partly under his influence, that the synagogue emerged in full measure, and that its simple service of prayer and hymns—largely unchanged to this day—took the place in Jewish religious life which was once reserved for the paschal ritual of sacrifice in the Temple.

With the advent of Rabbi Akiba ben Joseph we come to the great age of talmudic scholarship. His vast work of editing and commentary was highly imaginative and speculative; sometimes, however, he construed a passage in so fanciful or esoteric a way that his colleagues protested vigorously. Akiba and his school may be singled out for that consecration to knowledge which is so distinctive of Judaism. He and his disciples argued that it is ignorance that leads to sin, while knowledge brings fulfillment of the law. In this scale of values, study stood very high as one of the ways to the kingdom of Heaven. Since *to know* was an imperative, it is not surprising to find that academies flourished and that every synagogue became as much a school as a house of prayer.

Akiba was martyred by the Romans in the course of the butchery that followed upon the overthrow of Bar Kochba. He had hailed the latter as the longed-for Messiah, even though a colleague made a soberer assessment, upbraiding him with the remark that "grass will have sprouted from your cheek, but the Messiah will not yet have arrived."

The next great figure in this dynasty of scholars was the patriarch Rabbi Judah Hanasi, or the Prince (135–217). The greatest of the patriarchs, he was president of the

Sanhedrin and leader of the Jabneh Academy. Incorporating the insights of many of his predecessors, particularly Akiba, he successfully brought to a conclusion the compilation of what has remained the definitive Mishnah or Code of Oral Law—a collective effort that took some four hundred years to complete.

Jewish tradition has designated those scholars from Hillel to Judah who produced the Mishnah as *Tannaim* (teachers). The succession of scholars who authored the Gemara and rounded out the development of the Talmud have been set off by the designation *Amoraim* (interpreters) and carry us from about A.D. 220 to 500. Finally, there is the group of Babylonian scholars known as the *Saboraim* (the reflective ones), who take us down to the end of the sixth century and the eve of the Moslem conquest. It is not clear, however, precisely what they contributed, beyond putting the finishing touches to the Babylonian Talmud.

By the time of Judah Hanasi's death a tumultuous period had opened for the Roman world. Legion after legion rebelled and overthrew the emperor in favor of its own commander. But no sooner had the usurper donned the purple toga and installed himself in the imperial palace than another adventurer appeared on the scene to oppose him—and, not infrequently, to overthrow him. Such prolonged internal strife was the signal for Rome's enemies, east and west, to even old scores by marauding raids and annexations of her territories. Economic crises in the form of inflation, extortionate taxation, and prolonged depression soon beset the entire Roman world, and in the wake of continuous wars came famine and plague.

Palestine, which had never recovered from the earlier revolts, suffered grievously and many Jews emigrated to Babylon or, following the restoration of order by Diocletian, to Europe. In spite of such dislocations, Palestine still continued to produce outstanding rabbinic scholars and maintained its hegemony over Jews everywhere. In fact, the great work that had culminated in the completion of the Palestinian Talmud went on apace during this dark age under the guidance of the patriarchs. Among the scholars who made important contributions to it were the patriarchs Gamaliel III, Hillel II, Johanan ben Napha, who is said to have "laid the foundation of the Talmud," Simon ben Lakish, Haninah, Jannai, and Hoshaiah.

The End of the Patriarchate

By the beginning of the fifth century, however, the influence and prestige of the Palestinian community had declined acutely. The patriarchs were no longer the illustrious scholar-statesmen of former days, and in 425 the office itself was abolished by the emperor of a state that was already officially Christian. Jews and Judaism were now on the defensive. The academies fell on evil days, as few students came to their doors and the prevailing impoverishment of the community left them with no support. By the mid-fifth century these renowned institutions—where St. Jerome[1] in the previous century had learned Hebrew and biblical exegesis—were closed, and the center of Jewish life had shifted to Babylonia.

NOTE

[1] St. Jerome, as saint and scholar, has always been a most attractive figure to me; unlike most of the Fathers of the Church, he believed that "the Jews are divinely preserved for a purpose worthy of God."

3. Babylonia and Islam

THE BABYLONIAN JEWISH community dates from the destruction of the First Temple and the Captivity inflicted upon the Jews by King Nebuchadnezzar in 586 B.C. Though exiles, they were allowed to live in peace, enjoying religious liberty and communal autonomy of the kind we have already noted as being typical of the ancient imperial societies. When in the year 538 the Persian king gave them permission to return to their homeland, the majority remained in "the land between the rivers" where they had struck roots and become prosperous. Eventually Babylonia fell to the Seleucids, who in turn lost it in the middle of the third century B.C. to the Parthian state.

The Parthian Kings

The Parthian kings, whose kingdom had its center east of Babylon and extended as far as India, were remarkably tolerant. They were the most redoubtable enemies of Rome (witness their overwhelming defeat of Crassus) and perhaps for that reason felt it expedient to conciliate their Jewish subjects. The Parthians had no state religion, and in fact Jews were free to proselytize—which they actively did. Under the Parthian monarchs the Jewish community grew in numbers, prosperity, and eminence, and the degree of assimilation was extraordinary. Jews entered all professions, public offices, and trades, and since they were free to own land, many earned their living by agriculture. Local self-government (with the decisions of their own courts being sanctioned and enforced if necessary by the Parthian government) was an unquestioned prerogative of the Jewish community. Their political representative, the exilarch (prince of the exiles), enjoyed great prestige among the dignitaries at the royal court. This "state within a state," as it has been called, continued to look to Jerusalem, however; for it paid without interruption the traditional tax for the maintenance of the Temple, sent its ablest young scholars to be trained in the Palestinian academies, and deferred to the patriarchs in the settlement and interpretation of legal and theological questions. This notably beneficent state of affairs persisted for the most part until A.D. 226, when the Parthian monarchy was overthrown by the Sassanians, a Persian dynasty that established a great empire.

Sassanid Persia

This new state, which was to last until the Islamic conquest in the mid-seventh century, had as its official religion the ancient Persian faith of Zoroastrianism. The Sassanid kings, animated occasionally by a crusading zeal and egged on by the Magi priests, interfered with those Jewish practices that conflicted with Zoroastrian beliefs—e.g., burial of the dead, lighting candles on sacred days, etc. On the whole, however, the Jewish community flourished and continued to enjoy for two centuries and more the autonomy and tolerance they had experienced under the Parthians; the exilarch remained an important and even awesome personage in the royal entourage, while the academies experienced a golden age. (As institutions of higher learning, the academies were the counterpart of the synagogues which were centers of elementary education.)

The three outstanding academies were located at Nehardea, Pumpedita, and Sura, and date from the later Parthian and early Persian period. The city of Nehardea seems to have been founded by the Jews and to have had an entirely Jewish population. It prospered until it perished at the hands of invaders during a war between Persia and Palmyra (c. 260) —a casualty of war rather than the victim of an anti-Semitic massacre. Thereupon a new academy was established at Pumpedita, and still another at Mahuza.

The two Amoraim scholars who founded and breathed life into these famous academies were Rab and Samuel, both of whom flourished in the second quarter of the third century—the beginning of the Persian revival—and both of whom had been trained at academies in Palestine. Rab founded the academy at Sura, inaugurating there the Study Months (in March and again in September), which was a kind of venture in adult education. More than ten thousand students came to Sura to hear him expound on the Torah. Samuel's career at Nehardea was very similar, though in his day he was also famous as a physician and astronomer. Like Rab, he contributed to the liturgy of the synagogue service, initiated important changes in law, and laid the groundwork for the creation of the Babylonian Talmud. Above all, the two of them—with the help of their disciples—succeeded in raising the educational level of their community, with the result that the baton of intellectual leadership was passed from Palestine to Babylonia. Until the arrival of Judah the Prince's Mishnah (c. 220), Babylonian scholars had felt it necessary to appeal to Palestine for correct information and genuine tradition; now this authoritative work was ready at hand, enabling the Babylonian academies to become vital and independent centers of scholarship rather than mere shadows of those in Palestine.

The fifth and sixth centuries, sadly, saw a heightening of

religious zeal and intolerance in the Persian Empire. During this period Zoroastrianism was engaged in a ruthless struggle with the hated heresy of Manichaeanism, as well as in collecting and editing its sacred books, the Zend-Avesta —both of which activities were conducted under the zealous patronage of the monarchy and gave rise to a doctrinaire religiosity boding ill for the Jews. The heightened religious sensibility and dogmatism manifested themselves in the increasing subjection of Jews to persecution and massacre (such as that which wiped out the Jewish community of Isphahan c. 460). Furthermore, many Jewish practices were proscribed, e.g., keeping the Sabbath, burying the dead, proselytizing, and so on, while not infrequently Jewish children were forcibly converted to Zoroastrianism, academies were looted, and exilarchs and famous scholars were executed. Such, in short, is the melancholy story down to the last quarter of the sixth century, when a respite finally came. It was not owing to any royal change of heart, but rather to the strife and anarchy that came in the wake of army revolts, struggles among pretenders to the throne, and prolonged warfare with the Byzantine Empire.

It was under such threatening circumstances—remarkably similar to those confronting Palestinian Jewry in the fourth and early fifth centuries—that the Babylonian Talmud was completed (Rabina, its chief compiler, died in 499, at the height of the persecution). In both instances the desire to set down in permanent form the legal and intellectual heritage of Judaism must have been inspired by fears for the future. Men are frail reeds, but books endure.

The year 589 marked the beginning of a new era in the history of the Babylonian community. By then not only was the redaction of the Talmud complete, but that year saw the reopening of the academies and the emergence of a new office, the *Gaon* (Excellency). Originally the *Gaonim* had simply been heads of the academies and, as such, authorities in all religious and scholarly matters. In this role they had frequently quarreled with the exilarchs, until they gradually had overshadowed them—acquiring as a consequence a position tantamount to that held by the Palestinian patriarchate over the whole Diaspora before its abolition in 425. In filling this vacuum the Gaon's council constituted itself as a new Sanhedrin, and individual Gaonim brought such scholarly attainments and moral distinction to their office that, before long, they were being asked to give authoritative answers to questions for which there was no provision in the Talmud. These answers, or *Responsa*, ultimately built up to a great volume supplementary to the Talmud. The practice of appealing from far and wide to the Gaon as a kind of pope did much to preserve and strengthen Jewish identity as a single people and was also the means by which the Babylonian rather than the Palestinian Talmud became the standard work. However, though originating in the Persian period, the Gaonate was to reach the peak of its importance under the Islamic Empire, to which we shall now turn.

Islam

Viewed externally, the religion of Islam is a stepchild of Judaism and a cousin of Christianity. Its founder and prophet, Mohammed, was not a scholarly sage, but a child of the Arabian desert, with its primitive society and polytheism. Jewish trading communities, going back perhaps five centuries before his birth in about 570, were situated in Arabia, particularly in Medina, Mecca, and in the southern portion of the peninsula in Yemen (the biblical land of Saba) where, from about the third century, Christian communities also existed. Mohammed is believed to have sought out Jews in his native Mecca to learn about their monotheistic beliefs. He may well have learned enough Hebrew to read the Scriptures and enough Aramaic to familiarize himself with some of the writings current in the Jewish community. What is certain is that most of what he knew about Judaism and Christianity came to him orally— heard and overheard, as it were, in Mecca or on business trips he probably made to Yemen and possibly to Syria.

Mohammed incorporated into the Koran many of the figures and events of the Bible (there are also echoes of the Talmud in the laws he set down), and he seems initially to have addressed himself to the Jews of Mecca. In so doing, he conceived of himself as the last in the line of biblical Prophets, and of his teaching as the perfected form of Judaism and Christianity (which he did not separate), rather than as a new religion. A striking indication of this was his command to the faithful to turn five times daily in prayer toward Jerusalem; and only when rejected by the Jews of his hometown did he substitute Mecca, the pilgrimage center of his Bedouin kinsmen. At Medina, too, the seat of a much larger Jewish community, he was embittered by a rebuff. Once he became a power to reckon with, however, he took his revenge. On his initiative, the Medinese community was extinguished by expulsion, confiscation of property, and the massacre of six hundred men followed by the enslavement of their wives and children.

In the century following Mohammed's death in 632 Islam grew in importance and power as his successors conquered a vast empire extending to the Atlantic Ocean and the Spanish Pyrenees in the west, the Caucasus in the north, and India in the east. The Mediterranean thus became an Arab lake where for centuries, as an Islamic historian was much later to gloat, the Christians could not float a plank without Moslem permission. Practically all of the world's Jews were now subjects of a new empire, which included the old center of Jewish life in Palestine and the new one in Babylonia as well.

But the inauspicious beginning of Moslem-Jewish relations under Mohammed did not persist long after his death. Although the first caliphs were severe and persecutory and there was rigorous legislation against non-believers, this fell into abeyance; and Moslems soon came to have a certain regard for Jews, whom they viewed as non-idolaters. Furthermore, whereas Jews and Christians contested the claim to be "the children of Israel," no such quarrel divided Jews and Moslems, for the Moslems freely acknowledged considerable indebtedness to Judaism.

One of the consequences of Moslem tolerance was that Jews were free to migrate and took advantage of this by settling themselves throughout the length and breadth of the enormous Empire. Another was that they could pursue a livelihood in any way they chose, since none of the professions were barred to them, nor was any specific vocation thrust upon them. Interestingly, Babylonian Jews engaged to an unusual degree in commerce—owing, in part, to their being located at the heart of the Empire and the juncture of the ancient trade routes and to the fact that the network of Jewish communities lacing the Empire afforded them ready entry, credit, etc. But the basic reason was the sharp decline which occurred in Babylonian agriculture and the crafts dependent upon it when the irrigation system deteriorated, thus making it necessary for many Jews to turn to some other source of income.

The assimilation of the Jew within Islamic society was so great that Abraham S. Halkin, an outstanding Jewish authority on this period, speaks of "The Great Fusion." According to Professor Halkin, while autonomy permitted the continuation of the Jewish way of life and of the cultivation of traditional scholarship, the intellectual and cultural impact of centuries of Moslem domination was such as to result in "the creation of a new type of Jew." We have seen earlier that the Jews under Seleucid rule successfully resisted Hellenism, and that few of them ever bothered to learn Greek. By contrast, Arabic had become by the tenth century the vernacular of the Jewish communities; so much so, in fact, that the renowned philosopher Maimonides—whose case was far from atypical—wrote most of his works in Arabic rather than in Hebrew or Aramaic.

Jewish Scholarship

The Arabs were, like so many other conquerors, taken captive by the cultures of the peoples they vanquished, with the result that the cultural riches of Syria, Persia, India, and, above all, Greece were gathered together and translated into Arabic under the patronage of the caliphs. For four centuries the Islamic peoples held the intellectual leadership of the world—preserving, adding to, and transmitting to the Christian West the scientific and philosophical heritage of the ancient world. This golden age of Islam reached its apex in the reigns of Harun al-Raschid and al-Ma'mun (786–833), during which the whole corpus of Greek scientific and philosophical thought appeared in Arabic.

This epic achievement was one to which some Jewish scholars contributed. At the same time, a significant number of Jews became increasingly fascinated by this vast body of Arabic writings, and consequently became intellectual citizens of that wide world. For a very considerable time, this process of accommodation to foreign learning went on with no sense on their part that it was dangerous or distracting, with no recognition that it was simply the old Hellenism (though newly trapped out) which numerous injunctions in the Talmud warned against.

Ultimately, however, a reaction did set in in the form of the mysticism of Karaism and the Kabbalah, both of which we shall examine later. This reaction was above all against Aristotelian rationalism and logic, which increasingly appeared to be incompatible with the revelations of a divine plan and of a divine providence for the chosen people which were set forth in the Bible, the ultimate standard of truth. Aristotle's conception of the world as explicable in terms of abstract principles, the nature and workings of which can be grasped by the human mind; the sense conveyed in his writings that there are no bounds beyond which the mind cannot penetrate; and the voracious quest to know, to analyze, to probe, to dissect all things—this whole complex of attitudes and conceptions conflicted decidedly with the notion (characteristic of Jews, Moslems, and Christians at this time) that it was presumptuous as well as sinful to apply the standards of human reason to divine truth, the ways of God being mysterious beyond human comprehension. A succession of Jewish philosopher-theologians such as Saadia, Judah Halevi, and Maimonides wrestled over several centuries with the problem of the acquisition of truth by reason or by faith, through one's own faculties and judgment or by the authority of Scripture, before a reconciliation was ultimately effected between these two positions.

A parallel development is discernible within Islam, culminating in the works of Averroës, and within Latin Christianity, with St. Thomas Aquinas. However, in none of the instances cited was the resolution proffered accepted by all. Far from it, in fact, for each had his sharp critics; indeed, the debate went on—witness Spinoza—and still goes on today. Nonetheless, all three faiths alike had transcended irrevocably their own native theological and intellectual traditions. Philo was vindicated at last.

Saadia ben Joseph al-Fayuoni (882–942), who has been called "the father of Jewish philosophy," represents the first stage of the Jewish response to the challenge of Greek thought. As Gaon of the academy at Sura—at its zenith during his lifetime—he was the religious and cultural leader of the Jewish community. His translation of the Old Testament into Arabic was a sign of the times. On the other hand, he worked to strengthen Jewish tradition by his compilation of a Hebrew dictionary and by his Hebrew grammar. His most important philosophical work was *The Book of Beliefs and Opinions*, in which he asserted that the teachings and commandments of Judaism do not conflict with but are based upon and in harmony with reason and logic. Torah, he said, is "revealed reason," and Judaism is compatible with all truth, whatever its source. Saadia provided a logical proof for God's existence on the grounds that the creation of the world from nothing is impossible, while constantly reiterating that God's nature (beyond being one and unique) is unknowable and indefinable to the human mind. Saadia was a prolific philosopher and theologian, the author of numerous *Responsa*, the head of the academy of Sura, and a stalwart leader of the Jewish community, and with him the Gaonate reached its zenith. He is chiefly remembered, however, as the "Hammer of the Karaites," a heresy or schism of Judaism.

In Saadia's time, Judaism was doubly challenged: from without by the new learning, and from within by Karaism, which appeared at the time the more formidable danger. Karaism had its origin in the mid-eighth century, when Anan ben David was ignored by the rabbis in their choice of a new Gaon or exilarch. By way of revenge, he denounced the whole body of talmudic interpretive material built up by the rabbinate in the course of a thousand years. Karaism literally means "Scripturism" and reflects the founder's motto: "Search thoroughly through the scripture, and do not rely on my opinion" (or on the Talmud). The latter was regarded by Anan ben David as a mass of verbiage obscuring the real biblical teaching, and standing as a barrier to genuine religiosity.

This return to the pure texts of Scripture, with its concomitants of dismissal of historic tradition and rabbinic authority, has certain obvious parallels with Christian Protestantism. (One of the epithets flung at Protestant leaders, incidentally, was that they were Karaites.) Just as Luther would make every man his own priest, so the Karaites would make every man his own rabbi, capable of fashioning his own interpretations of Scripture and, as Anan proclaimed, "not relying on my opinion." Such a principle of individualism in religious matters inevitably gives rise to a proliferation of sects and divisions, and so it finally was in both movements. Yet, unlike Protestantism, the various strands of Karaism tended ultimately to coalesce into a single entity.

Saadia, who had a genius for invective and polemic, put the Karaites to flight by stealing what thunder they had (in that he himself was sympathetic to a fresh return to Scripture, *but* without bypassing the Talmud) and by combating vigorously their faulty reasoning and Sadducean literalism. Saadia's ultimate victory was an intellectual one, decided in the synagogues and academies rather than on the battlefield or in the chamber of an inquisition. Nonetheless, for the period of time it lasted (the tenth to eleventh centuries) Karaism had a wide and profound appeal and established itself in every area and at every social level of the Diaspora. In fact, it survives to the present, if only as a remnant. Its erstwhile influence was due, in part, to its resolution of the issue of rationalism versus faith, so critical at the time. The Karaites resolved it by ignoring rationalism and fastening narrowly on the Scriptures with a cry reminiscent of Luther's "Faith alone." Karaism also had appeal because it took on the character of a nativist movement for the preservation of Judaism against defilement by foreign influences. As though they were the new Maccabees, the Karaites proclaimed the sufficiency for Judaism of the sacred text, and they could equally claim to be obedient to the talmudic injunction to eschew Hellenism both by day and by night.

4. Islamic Spain

WITH JUDAH HALEVI (1086–1140) we come to Islamic Spain and the golden age of post-biblical Jewish history. Jews had already made their way to Spain in the Roman period; they became subjects of the Visigoths when that barbarian people conquered Spain in the fifth century. By the seventh century the Visigoths, who had become Christian in the interim, embarked on so harsh and vindictive a policy of proscriptions and massacres that when the Islamic invaders arrived in 711, the Jewish community welcomed them as liberators. Subsequently organized as the Caliphate of Cordova, Spain remained a self-contained Islamic state, rising to the zenith of its power and cultural glory under Abd-er-Rahman III in the middle decades of the tenth century. In all its achievements, Spanish Jews were to play a central role.

The Moors, as we should call them, granted the Jews internal autonomy and freedom. Every walk of life was open to them—military, political and diplomatic, scholarly, agricultural and commercial, industrial and financial—and in all of them they distinguished themselves.

A principal figure in much of this activity was Hasdai ibn Shaprut (died 970). Counselor, diplomat, and court physician to Abd-er-Rahman III, he was a generous patron of many fields of Jewish intellectual endeavor, e.g., Hebrew philology, translation of ancient texts, talmudic scholarship, and poetry. Another major figure was Samuel ibn Nagdela, who was prime minister to the king of Granada (one of many small states that emerged during the break-up of the caliphate in the early eleventh century), as well as a poet, talmudist, and literary patron. One of the beneficiaries of his patronage was the poet and philosopher Solomon ibn Gabirol (died c. 1058), whose treatise, known in Latin translation as *Fons Vitae*, exercised a profound influence on Christian thinkers such as Duns Scotus, all of whom assumed him to be a Christian. Gabirol's philosophic position was that of a mystic and Neoplatonist. His poems, deeply religious and mystical, eloquently express the Jewish sense of exile and longing for the homeland, though he also wrote a great many poems on secular subjects which are an example of the remarkable flowering of non-religious Hebrew literature that occurred during this period. (We may note parenthetically that, up to the tenth century, there was no secular Hebrew literature to speak of, and that its prodigious development thereafter—frequently inspired by Islamic models—is additional testimony to the unusual degree of Jewish assimilation to the host society.)

However, the special role reserved for the Jewish intellectual community of Spain was the translation and interpretation of the Aristotelian corpus of logic and science and its transmittal to Christian Europe. This work went on first in Moorish and then in Christian Spain, continuing down to the fourteenth century. Jewish scholars translated not only Aristotle, but Hippocrates on medicine, Ptolemy on astronomy, and Moslem commentaries on them (e.g., those of Averroës and Avicenna) from Arabic into Hebrew, adding to these works their own notes and commentaries. It should be added here that Maimonides' writings were made available to Christian scholars by these same indispensable cultural intermediaries, and that a similar process went on in southern Italy and Sicily. In both instances

Jewish scholars were the ideal channel of transmission, because of their intellectual footing in both Moslem and Christian society.

This brings us to Judah Halevi, rabbi, poet, philosopher. Born in Toledo, he was educated in science and logic, studied the Talmud intensively, and became a physician. But he threw it all over to become the greatest Jewish poet of the middle ages, "a flaming pillar of song" whose lyrics remind one of Petrarch. His search for human love became a quest for God, whom he found through mystical experience. With Halevi, we come full circle in the response to the philosophic rationalism which had more and more suffused Jewish thought since Saadia's time, and which reached a crescendo in the uncompromising rationalism of his younger contemporary, Moses Maimonides. In a manner reminiscent of Gabirol, Halevi comes down in favor of knowledge and truth arrived at by intuition, mystical union with God, and complete faith in biblical revelation. He cautions his readers against reliance on logic and reason; for him Aristotle, the culture hero of the day, was the enemy. And he is Maccabean in his warning to "let not the wisdom of the Greeks beguile thee, which hath no fruit, but only flowers." In a famous epic poem, he also hauntingly expressed the Jewish yearning for Temple and Homeland. For such writings, and for his pilgrimage to the Holy Land, where he died, Halevi is properly categorized as a Zionist.

During this period the Jewish community of Spain had once again begun to be the victim of persecutions. There had been ghastly moments in the eleventh century, e.g., in 1013 when the Jews of Cordova had been expelled, and in 1066 when those of Granada had been massacred. Similarly, during the early stages of the Christian reconquest, the heightened religious sensibility of the crusading warriors frequently led them to destroy synagogue along with mosque and to put Jewish prisoners to the sword as readily

as Moslems. Before long, however, Christian leaders saw
they had something to gain by conciliating so sizable a
minority, and they therefore granted to Jews the same
autonomy and freedom that they had enjoyed in the palm-
ier days of the caliphate. Thus it was essentially Moslem
intolerance that the Spanish Jews suffered in the twelfth
century and after.

What brought the long tradition of Moorish tolerance to
an end was the invasion from North Africa by the zealous
Almoravides, who, by way of reaction to Christian attacks,
were themselves filled with the crusading ardor. Hardly
were they established in Spain (1110) when they sought to
compel Jews to embrace Islam. In 1148 the fanatical Almohades supplanted the Almoravides, whereupon the practice of Judaism and Christianity was utterly prohibited, and
forced conversions became common as did martyrdom and
slavery. Many Jews sought refuge in the Christian kingdoms to the north, where they were welcomed and accepted.
It is hardly suprising, therefore, that the overthrow of the
Almohades and the decisive turning of the tide in favor of
the Christians in the battle of Las Navas de Tolosa in 1212
was hailed by Jews as a deliverance.

The end of the golden age of Moorish Spain is appropriately symbolized in the life of Moses Maimonides
(1135–1204), who was born and educated at Cordova.
The Almohadic persecution had caused his family to flee
while he was still in his early twenties, first to Fez, Morocco,
and then to Cairo, Egypt. It thus transpired that the
greatest Jewish thinker of the middle ages graces the history of Saladin's Egypt rather than that of Moorish
Spain.

Maimonides came to Cairo at the very end of the Fati-
mite dynasty which had ruled Egypt since 969. Claiming to
be the descendants of Mohammed's daughter Fatima and
therefore rightly caliphs, they conquered Egypt from the
Abbasids and founded Cairo as their capital. Though they

periodically carried out ferocious pogroms, the Fatimites did grant extensive autonomy to Jews and Christians, and were sympathetic patrons of scholarly enterprises similar to those we have seen elsewhere in the Islamic world. So it fell out that Cairo paralleled, if it did not equal, Cordova as a great cosmopolitan center with a large Jewish community that participated in the life of the host society as viziers, physicians, scholars, merchants, etc.

This state of affairs persisted in essence after Saladin displaced the Fatimites in 1171, and is typified by the fact that Maimonides became a famous physician to Saladin and his court. One of the surprising things about Maimonides is that, prodigious scholar and thinker though he was, he divided his time equally between the study and writing desk, on the one hand, and the active life of a physician and adviser to Saladin, as well as rabbi and intellectual leader of the Jewish community, on the other. Before long he was recognized as the most eminent scholar of the Diaspora, reaching a position somewhat akin to that of the Gaonim of a former day (the Gaonate, the academies, and the whole community in Babylonia had declined acutely by the middle of the preceding century). This being the case, it was to Maimonides that questions were put from far and wide, eliciting from him numerous and lengthy *Responsa*.

Maimonides wrote theoretical treatises on diseases and related medical topics; they are most remarkable, perhaps, for his conception of psychic factors as a cause of disease. He was also a great talmudic scholar and jurist, as evidenced by his authoritative codification in fourteen volumes of the legal portions of the Talmud, a work known as the *Mishneh Torah*.

But it was as a religious philosopher and exponent of rationalism that he most profoundly influenced Judaism, Islam, and Christianity. Maimonides believed deeply in the rationality of all law. Predecessors, like Saadia, had distinguished between rational laws which the mind could comprehend and willingly obey, and irrational laws which the mind was unable to comprehend but which nevertheless had to be accepted on faith as divine commands set forth in the Bible. Such distinctions Maimonides dismissed out of hand, for, with his Aristotelian frame of reference, he could not believe that God would enact irrational laws. Rather, it was only that the human mind was in some cases too limited and could not perceive their rationality.

It was to those Jews dismayed by the disparity between the biblical narrative and Greek modes of thought that Maimonides addressed his magnum opus, *The Guide to the Perplexed*. His faith in the rational powers of the human mind was such that he insisted, whenever the dictates of reason were certain of being true, that the seemingly inconsistent or contradictory statements of the Bible be explained in an allegorical rather than a literal way. Revelation, in other words, had to be accommodated to reason, not vice versa. For Maimonides a philosophical-scientific explanation of God and His attributes, of His teachings and injunctions to the Chosen People, as well as of the physical universe itself were all absolutely essential to Judaism; he even went so far as to make divine providence and solicitude for man dependent upon man's own philosophical knowledge and understanding.

Such views were in keeping with the ancient tradition of Judaism which exalted knowledge and intellect (an example of which we saw in Akiba) and did much to strengthen that tradition. They likewise inspired Jewish scholars and leaders to devote themselves to scientific and philosophical studies in addition to the study of the Bible and Talmud. But Maimonides carried his belief in the rationality of the human mind and in the rational basis of the Bible to such lengths that a fierce controversey was bound to erupt. Some Jews found his views so much more Aristotelian than Mosaic in their orientation that they burned his writings. An outstanding example of this extreme reaction occurred in Provence, where a group of Jews confided to the Inquisition that the *Guide* was dangerous and heretical for Jews and Christians alike, and the inquisitors obligingly condemned and then publicly burned the offending texts; this is the only example in history of Jews' being a party to book-burning.

Within Judaism this controversy raged throughout the thirteenth century, during which time there was an accelerating displacement to extreme positions, between which Maimonides' standpoint ultimately took on the appearance of a moderate middle ground. Thus, on the one hand, Maimonidean rationalists tended to become followers of Averroës, the Moslem philosopher whose Aristotelianism was so extreme that he proclaimed a radical separation between religious truth and philosophical-scientific truth, declaring that no reconciliation between them was possible. Such a viewpoint was anathema to Maimonides, for whom the mind was one and all truth consistent with itself; and when St. Thomas Aquinas set himself the task of combating the Christian Averroists and reconciling Christian dogma and Aristotelian science, he found in Maimonides— whom he refers to affectionately as Rabbi Moses of Egypt— plenty of anti-Averroës ammunition. On the other hand, the initial Christian reaction was, as we have seen, to burn Maimonides' books. The middle position triumphed, however, for one of the popes eventually commissioned a Latin translation of the *Guide* and, with the papal sanction, it soon became a central text for the Scholastic theologians, particularly for St. Thomas.

The Kabbalah and Jewish Mysticism

In the course of the thirteenth century Jewish thinkers tended to be increasingly deflected toward the mystical, intuitive, anti-rational conceptions that we have found in the work of Solomon ibn Gabirol and Judah Halevi. These views found characteristic expression in the medieval Jewish system of theosophy known as the *Kabbalah* (tradition). The Kabbalah claimed to be coeval with the Mosaic Torah, but that—unlike the latter—it was a revelation reserved not for the whole of Israel but only for a few initiates. Though some of it dated from as early as the eighth century, most of its materials are no older than the thirteenth. Mysticism, in the form of oral tradition and popular superstition, had grown up in the shadows of the Talmud, as scholars such as Gershom Scholem have shown, and from the thirteenth to the seventeenth century it usurped the place that philosophy had enjoyed within Judaism from Saadia to Maimonides. From the fifteenth century onward, it was equally influential within Christendom.

Kabbalah was essentially an esoteric system of biblical exegesis that exaggerated in the extreme the ancient Hebrew idea of the sacred Scripture as the Ark of the Covenant and holiest of holies, going to the length of assuming (regardless of context) that every word, letter, number, accent, etc., of the Bible had particular mystical significance. Kabbalah, which incorporated Neoplatonism and other pagan traditions of occult lore, degenerated at length into a system of symbols, magic, incantations, amulets, talismans, necromancy, miracle-making, foretelling the future, etc., and lent itself readily to belief in witchcraft, astrology, and alchemy.

Yet it is by no means all nonsense and hocus pocus. Many of the Kabbalists concerned themselves with the same problems that had exercised the philosophers—e.g., the nature of God, ethical good and evil, Creation, the exile of the Jews and their ultimate restoration to the Homeland; and their resolutions were often profound. The central text of the Kabbalah is the *Zohar*, an interpretation of the Pentateuch and the classical expression of Jewish mysticism. In treating the central issues, the Kabbalists had a much wider appeal than the recondite philosophers or even the rabbis steeped in the Talmud. Most notably, the Kabbalah stimulated hope in the arrival of the Messiah, a notion which was to have a tremendous appeal to European Jews of the thirteenth through the seventeenth century amidst all their trials and tribulations.

Beyond such considerations, the Kabbalah also has an important place in the history of science: for magic and mysticism have closer affinities with science than do the abstract principles and deductive methods of Maimonides. Kabbalists who invested numbers with magical properties helped to formulate the outlook necessary to scientific quantification, particularly when they proclaimed that a numerical or mathematical key lay at the bottom of nature's mysteries. Moreover, mysticism that recognized physical nature as part of God's divine creation stimulated experiment and observation that could evolve into the inductive method. All things of "the natural order are regarded as symbols of the supernatural order," and so the physical order becomes an object of study and an avenue by which to achieve mystical union with God.

Much the same kind of consideration applies to alchemists and astrologers. Indeed, the history of science from the fourteenth to the seventeenth century is filled with a great many figures, Jews and Christians, who combined kabbalistic magic with scientific learning and seem to have contributed far more to the scientific revolution of the seventeenth century than did the rationalist philosophers working on the basis of deductions from what Aristotle said.

5. Europe: The Latin Christian Middle Ages

Medieval Christian-Jewish Relations[1]

The historian of the Jewish middle ages finds himself caught up in a depressing story of man's inhumanity to man. Try as he will to emphasize the more positive aspects —Jewish achievements in scholarship, in commercial and financial endeavor, and moments of cordiality between Jews and Christians—they are decidedly uncharacteristic of the age, and he is confronted, rather, with a reign of terror. Though it leveled off and even eased now and then, the characteristic trend, nonetheless, was not a diminishing but a rising crescendo of fear and bloodshed which culminated in the hundred years inaugurated by the pontificate of Innocent III (1198–1216). This period, which a Catholic scholar, James J. Walsh, described in what was, until quite recently, a famous and influential book, *The Thirteenth, Greatest of Centuries* (1907) was actually among the worst of centuries for the Jewish community and was followed by wave upon wave of outrage in the fourteenth and fifteenth centuries. There was, then, no golden age or trail of glory for medieval Jewry in Christendom, as there indubitably was for it in Islamic society and Moorish Spain. True, there was eventually a trail of blood in Islam as there was in Christendom, but it is necessary to make a distinction.

Persecution was *not* characteristic or natural to Islam, coming as it did in a period of decadence and even then, only after a prolonged period of toleration; whereas, in Christendom, persecution was endemic from the very start and seems all too natural and characteristic. In fact, the following formula applies quite literally to Christian-Jewish relations in the medieval period: as the fortunes of Latin Christianity rose and flourished, automatically the lot of the Jews deteriorated and languished.

The Origins of Jewish Persecution

The fundamental basis of Christian animosity toward a people who equally revered the Old Testament is religious. Christian theologians and thinkers forgot or denied what was a central idea in St. Paul, namely, that both Christianity and Judaism were in some sense part of a single, ancient religious community; so much so that it came to appear as inconceivable that both peoples could be heir to the divine promises revealed in the Old Testament. In fact, Christians arrogated to themselves the doctrine of the Chosen People and—for the longest time—the very name "the children of Israel." (E.g., when in 1095 Pope Urban II, in his famous sermon at Clermont initiating the crusading era, referred to wresting the Holy Land from "the wicked race of Turks," he said it should be subject to Christian rule, because "that land which, as the Scripture says, floweth with milk and honey was given by God into possession of the children of Israel.") Not only did Christians consider themselves to be the people of Israel and deny the claim to Jews, they even espoused a kind of Christian Zionism. We may note that this latter notion underlay the establishment of Christian crusading states in the Holy Land, and was so rife that the greatest Jewish scholar of the age, Rashi, felt it necessary to combat and deny it, arguing that the Jews were the people of Israel and that the Holy Land belonged to them. Thus the crux of the matter was that Jews and Christians made what seemed to be irreconcilable claims to the ancient Hebrew heritage.

In the period from the Apostles to the fourth or fifth century, Christianity was busy defining itself, and felt an especial urgency about setting itself off from Judaism. The difficulty and the acrimony that this entailed are suggested by the fact that Christianity at that time had the appearance of a reform movement within Judaism rather than that of a new and distinct religion. To the Roman rulers the early Christians represented another Jewish sect. Moreover, since Judaism was recognized in Roman law as "a licit religion," it was necessary for the early Christians, if they were to practice their own ceremonies, to do so as Jews; otherwise they might find themselves falling afoul of the Roman authorities. Thus there was a kind of identity crisis, with some persons oscillating between Judaism and Christianity with very little sense of any difference between them.[2]

Theologians of the early patristic age were, therefore, strongly conscious of the need to separate Christians and Jews. Their efforts to do so were carried to drastic extremes, especially in the third century when the bonds between church and synagogue were sundered at last in a war of words. More and more insistence was made that Christians alone were heirs to the biblical promises, an inheritance which Jews had forfeited by their refusal to accept Jesus: furthermore, that His death had made them guilty of deicide; that as a people they were eternally hateful to God; that no punishment or degradation was too extreme for them; that they were given over to devil worship; that they were a plague with whom Christians should not consort; that they were pariahs for whom there could be no salvation, etc., etc. The most extreme form of

Christian anti-Jewish polemic appears in some of the sermons of St. John Chrysostom of the fourth century.

Christians did indeed acquire a conscious sense of their own uniqueness and difference from Judaism, but in the process of disidentification a whole pattern of vehement anti-Semitism—in attitude as well as in conduct—was invented and built into Christianity. And this pattern continues to bear its ugly fruit to this day.[3]

And so (as was suggested in the Introduction) it was at the urgent insistence of patristic theologians that a wrong theology of exclusiveness and irreconcilability was substituted for the right one, which insists upon the common patrimony of the two religions (Abraham being the fount), and the blending in that "good olive tree." And it is only with Vatican II that the Church has really begun to make up its mind where it stands with regard to Judaism, so that a Catholic theology of Judaism, up till now a "Cinderella," says Msgr. Oesterreicher, seems at last to be in the offing. To put it more accurately, if bluntly, the long-standing Christian theology of persecution and separation will be supplanted by one of concord and union. It will give due place to the uniqueness of Christianity, which has traditionally been asserted, but also to the patrimony it shares with Judaism; and it may turn out that Vatican II's celebrated phrase, "the people of God," will come to be defined as the people of the Church and the people of Judaism, both having a common destiny, although still divided on this earth by the "proto-schism" that dates from the earliest age of Christianity.

One thing more needs to be said to understand how the religion of the Prince of Peace became an endless source of terror to Jews. The anti-Jewish diatribes of the patristic theologians were part of a war of words, in which Jews replied in kind. But with the acceptance of Christianity by the emperors, beginning with Constantine the Great and culminating with Theodosius the Great, Christianity became the sole established religion of the Empire. Weapons that were formerly only words now became the sticks and stones of imperial and ecclesiastical legislation enforced by the state. Christianity had captured the state apparatus and utilized its coercive powers to win all the arguments, to reduce Jews to a pariah status, essentially without citizenship or rights. Under the necessity felt to separate Christianity from Judaism, Christian authorities sought to establish Sunday as the Christian day of rest and worship, a trend that was much strengthened by Constantine's edict forbidding judges to sit and townspeople to work on Sundays; although there was no interference with the Jewish Sabbath, "Sunday Laws" then and long afterward were often a hardship for Jews who had perforce two days of rest in an age when a living was hard to earn. The providential triumph of Christianity was invoked as proof of the validity of its claim to be sole heir to the divine promises. The Jew was deemed to be sinfully perverse in his flagrant adherence to Judaism (synonymous with error), and in his stubborn refusal to accept Christianity (synonymous with truth). As he walked the face of the earth, the Jew became the Eternal Doubter of the central Christian dogmas; he was, therefore, a stench in the nostril of God, who would look with favor on the eradication of error by book burning, forced conversion, massacre, mayhem, sacking, expulsion, etc. It may also have been, as Cecil Roth has said, that Jewish devotion to their religion and heroic acceptance of martyrdom gave rise in a subtle way to a strain of discomfort and unease in the Christian consciousness. But the ultimate result of any such misgivings was to strengthen the Christian antipathy for Jews.

I conclude, therefore, that the manifold violence inflicted on the Jews in the middle ages was not significantly economic (until later) or political or racial (since baptism spelled the immediate end of all Jewish disabilities), but was fundamentally religious in nature.

The change from classical antiquity is immediate in Constantine's time (312–337). His legislation reads like Christian polemic and defines Judaism not as "a licit religion" but as a "nefarious sect" and "sacrilegious assembly." Accordingly, his decrees direct that Jews cannot proselytize, cannot discourage those among them from apostatizing in favor of Christianity, cannot intermarry with Christians or even banquet with them. In the course of the fourth century death by burning, etc., is prescribed as the penalty for violation of these statutes and new prohibitions were added to the old. Jews at first could not own Christian slaves, then any slaves at all, nor engage in slave trading (slaves were the machines of the ancient world and to be without them was to be economically handicapped and excluded, except on the smallest scale, from agriculture and landholding). Jews were barred from military service and from honorable professions like medicine. New synagogues could not be built, old ones could not be repaired. Thus Christian invective was transposed into law and state policy.

An indication of how irreconcilable Jews and Christians were appears in their respective attitudes toward Constantine the Great and Julian the Apostate (361–363). These sobriquets were Christian dubbings, and in the Jewish view they were singularly inapt and should be reversed: Constantine as an "apostate" to the Roman traditions of tolerance and autonomy, and Julian as "great" because he resumed full toleration and autonomy for Jews, even promising them the right to rebuild the Temple.

All the anti-Jewish legislation of Constantine and the next century is restated in the Theodosian Code of 438. It was thus woven into the legal and constitutional framework of the later Roman Empire, and, since the Code became the basis for the codes of the Germanic kingdoms that replaced Roman rule in the West, e.g., the Franks in Gaul, it was likewise woven into the legal and constitutional fabric of medieval Europe. In fact, it was woven into the pattern of the medieval mind. It is true that Judaism was officially recognized and tolerated by the Theodosian and later codes. Judaism was in fact unique as a dissenting religion within Christendom. It may be that medieval Jews "never constituted a real problem," as the English historian Denys Hay claims, because in imperial, canon, and royal law they were officially tolerated and were liable to prosecution *only* if they proselytized, or if they accepted baptism and then renounced it (in which case they were considered heretics). But this dualism of condemning Jews to a pariah status on the one hand and safeguarding certain legal rights on the other *was* a "problem," because it was almost impossible to maintain. For it required the public authorities— royal or ecclesiastical—to walk the narrow path between preventing Jews from exceeding the meager rights they in ignominy held, and restraining Christians from infringing on those rights. In the Byzantine Empire, which theoretically at least was more persecutory than the Latin West, no such dualism prevailed: Justinian's famous *Corpus Juris Civilis* not only declared Jews ineligible for any public office (what occurred in the West without any specific legislation until later) but it interfered with their religious practices, such as prohibiting the celebration of Passover before Easter, the maintenance of academies, and the conducting of public discussion of biblical exegesis, etc.

In the West this dualism is best exemplified by Theodoric, the Ostrogothic king of Italy, from the time that he and his barbarian peoples conquered it in the 480's to his death in 526. The king protected the Jews, enforcing the stipulations of the Theodosian Code with regard to their status. When the Christian community of Ravenna sought to compel Jews of the city to receive baptism, both the king and the local bishop sought to prevent it. Nevertheless, the Jews were bodily flung into the waters of baptism, at the same time that their synagogues went up in flames. On the appeal of the Jews, Theodoric obliged the Christians to rebuild the synagogues and make other restitutions; in fact, he is reported to have said that, in matters of religion, the state has no right to compel a man to believe against his will—an ideal of tolerance that was not to see the light of day for a millennium. Theodoric's attitude may have owed something to his being an Arian Christian, an anti-Trinitarian heretic, which made the strict monotheism of Judaism attractive to him.

In general, the Arian kingdoms were remarkably tolerant of their Jewish subjects. E.g., Visigothic Spain, as long as it adhered to Arianism, permitted Jews considerable freedom in religious and civil matters. But at the end of the sixth century, the Visigoths simultaneously abjured Arianism for Latin Christianity and embarked upon a systematic persecution of Jews. A succession of ecclesiastical councils, meeting at Toledo with the king presiding, directed that Judaism be suppressed, that any practice of it be severely punished, that Jews be converted or exile themselves from the realm; what saved Judaism from extinction was the haphazardness and inefficiency in enforcing the code. But Jews suffered severely and not surprisingly welcomed the Islamic invaders of 711 as liberators from a hateful tyranny.

The heir to Theodoric's dualism was the papacy. Here, as in so many other respects, Pope Gregory the Great (590–604) was the chief one to inaugurate medieval papal tradition and practice. In his theological writings he castigates Jews in a flow of invective and vituperation familiar already in the earlier patristic writers, and as an ecclesiastic he was constantly on guard against what he called their "insolence" in exceeding legal right; yet, on the other hand, his epistles contain many injunctions to bishops warning them to treat Jews with kindliness and to refrain from forced conversions. This policy is summed up in his sentence quoted many times down the medieval centuries by his successors: "Just as license must not be granted to the Jews to presume to do in their synagogues more than the law permits them, so they should not suffer curtailment in that which has been conceded to them."

In this connection we may take note of a papal bull of 1120, which was a restatement of Gregory's position and an extension of it in the direction of leniency rather than rigor. Issued by Pope Calixtus II as *Constitutio pro Judaeis*, it was a kind of negative Magna Charta condemning forced baptism, assaults on Jews and their property, desecration of their synagogues and cemeteries, etc. Essentially the same document was reissued (under various titles) by subsequent popes at least fifteen times by 1450; and, on the whole, Gregory and his successors into the sixteenth century adhered to its dualist policy, difficult though it was to implement. In keeping with the distinction previously drawn in speaking of ancient Rome, we may say here that the medieval papacy also dealt harshly but not viciously with the Jews, so that the Jewish community of Rome is unique in Western Europe in its continuity from the ancient world. Elsewhere in Europe, Jewish communities were blotted out by massacre and expulsion, and were subsequently re-established; only that of Rome has an uninterrupted existence from the time of Cicero to the present day.

The Franks were the most successful barbaric invaders of the Western Roman Empire, in that they founded a kingdom that endured indefinitely and occupied a central place in medieval civilization—frequently as papal allies. In the time of Clovis (485–511), the Franks were converted from paganism to Latin Christianity. This did not mean that they immediately began to harry the Jews of Gaul. Clovis recognized them as having certain privileges in religion and commerce, though their status was distinctly an inferior one. Nevertheless, there is some suggestion of a more open society than elsewhere in the fact that Jews joined Clovis in

defending the town of Arles in Provence against Bur-
gundian attack. In the course of the sixth century Frankish kings became more deferential to their bishops, who
pressed for the enforcement of all the rigorous religious
and civil requirements we have seen in the Theodosian
Code, topping it off with forced conversion en masse or the
alternative of baptism or banishment. In his time, Pope
Gregory thundered at such episcopal and royal excesses,
and succeeded in restraining them. After his death, however, no sufficiently forceful hand could arrest the fanatical
hand of a king like Dagobert (629–639), who expelled all
Jews who would not accept baptism.

The seventh century was, in fact, a time of grave crisis
for Jews throughout the whole of the old Roman world.
For simultaneous with the rigors of Dagobert were those
inflicted on Jews by his neighbor, Burgundy, and (as previously mentioned), those of the Visigothic kings in Spain.
At the same time, the Italian Lombards, still another of the
barbarian peoples who had conquered the peninsula (as far
as Rome) and been converted to Christianity, threw down
to Jews the same gauntlet of baptism or banishment. Such
uniformity in treatment may well reflect the influence of
the Byzantine emperor, Heraclius (610–641). To a considerable degree the ancient Roman world was still a unity,
and it is probable that Heraclius, himself engaged in harry-
ing the Jews with the same alternatives of conversion or
expulsion, had commanded the Western kings (theoretically
still his subordinates) to follow suit.

Under Heraclius a great revival of Byzantine power took
place against the Sassanian Persians, in the course of which
Syria and Palestine were recaptured. Probably the reason
why he turned with such vehemence on the Jews was
that they had sided with Persia (understandably in the
light of the greater degree of autonomy, toleration, and
freedom they ordinarily enjoyed under Persian rule). Heraclius may well have been further embittered, in the last
decade of his reign, by defeat after defeat suffered at the

hands of the new Islamic conquerors irrupting out of the Arabian desert. In any case Palestine sank to its nadir during his reign, owing to endless wars fought over its eroded and barren territory and to his vengeful deportation and enslavement of so many of its remaining Jews.[4]

The Empire of the Khazars

The next four centuries of Jewish history are rather obscure though, on the whole, relatively happy ones. From about 700 until the Crusades, Jews were comparatively un-molested in their *Apartheid* status. If not many real rights were granted to them, such rights as they did possess were exercised without significant infringement and allowed Jews to preserve their own distinctive way of life. It was the age when the dualist papal policy prevailed most widely and most successfully. One of the most interesting aspects of the age was the Khazar Empire.

The middle ages saw the practically uninterrupted move-ment westward of primitive tribes from the arid plains east of the Aral Sea; they were ferocious nomadic horsemen who knifed their way into the settled communities of the West, carving out empires for themselves, and eventually were either assimilated to the conquered and converted to their faith (Islam, Latin or Greek Christianity) or were dis-placed by a new wave of marauders. Such were the Huns, Magyars, Turks, etc. Another group was the Khazars, a tribe which was probably mixed ethnically and appeared in the region north of the Caucasus about 570, when they were subject to Turkish overlordship. They broke up the state situated on the Volga of earlier nomads, the Bulgars, and proceeded to build a great empire of their own, run-ning from the Caucasus west to the Don River in the southern Ukraine and the region north of the Black Sea. By the early ninth century the Khazar domain extended as far as Kiev. Increasingly, they came into contact with the

Byzantine Empire, which alternately sought to conquer and convert them, and the Arabs south of the Caucasus, who approached them with the same alternating intentions. The Khazars, however, about 740, were converted to Judaism, which had been borne into this area by refugees from Constantinople. There is a theory that states it may also have owed its acceptance by the Khazars to Jews whose forebears, fifteen hundred years earlier, had been carried into exile from Israel (the ten lost tribes of the ancient northern kingdom) by the Assyrians. Probably most important was Judaism's penetration into the region across the Caucasus range from the Islamic Empire, that great bridge that carried Jews and Judaism as far as China. Among the Khazars, the Jewish regard for learning soon showed itself, for as a king boasted, one of his predecessors on the throne had "built synagogues and schools, and brought in Jewish scholars," probably from Constantinople and Baghdad. As the solitary example of a state whose official religion was Judaism, the Khazar Empire was precious to the Jews who knew of it (relatively few, though it was known to the Jewish community at the Moslem court of Cordova in distant Spain), because its existence contradicted the Christian sneer that Jews were without a country because they rejected Jesus. The Khazar Empire came into conflict in the course of the tenth century with the new Russian power that arose in the Dnieper Valley; it suffered a sharp setback in 969, losing its western lands. Although much reduced and weak, it lasted into the thirteenth century, when it disappears obscurely. Crimean Jews of today may descend in part from the Khazars.

Ashkenazic Jewry

But to return to Christendom. By the mid-eighth century the Frankish dynasty that had ruled since Clovis was overthrown by Pepin the Short, who was succeeded in 768 by his son, the celebrated Charlemagne. The new dynasty was powerful in its own right and did not depend on episcopal support nor defer to ecclesiastical wishes in regard to the status of the Jews. Charlemagne's policy could be guided, therefore, more by interests than by theological presuppositions. And in his enormous but economically primitive empire it was greatly to his interest to have a class of financial agents and merchants. He therefore went out of his way to encourage Jews by grants of autonomy and protection to initiate and maintain such functions, and it is owing to his policy that Jewish merchants made their way from the Islamic world into Europe to such a degree that *merchant* and *Jew* became virtually synonymous terms. We are indebted to one of these Jewish merchants, Abraham ben Jacob (or Ibrahim ibn Yakub), for the earliest detailed account of the first Slavic societies at the beginning of their history. Around the mid-tenth century Abraham, whether as merchant or ambassador, made his way to east-central Europe; he came from Spain and was probably in the service of the Caliph al-Hakam II at Cordova. He left the fullest description, written in Arabic and preserved by later Moslem writers, of the Slavic states of Poland, Bohemia (Czechoslovakia), and Wendia (between the Elbe and Oder rivers), as well as an account of the Balt peoples of Prussia. He noted that "the town of Prague is built of stone and lime and is the richest of towns in trade. There come to it Russians and Slavs from Cracow with merchandise, and from the lands of the Turks come Moslems, Jews, and Turks" with their many wares. Since Jewish economic endeavor is treated in a separate chapter, suffice it to say that many of the traders settled permanently in the empire, gathering together the fragments of the older, disrupted communities, and inaugurated a renaissance of Jewish life that carried down to the Crusades.

Charlemagne had interests other than economic ones that

led him to welcome Jewish immigration. He was the patron of biblical scholarship and of a revival of classical culture at his court, and Jews, as we have seen, could make important contributions as scholars and translators to such enterprises; they were especially sought out for their knowledge of Hebrew. He had the example of royal patronage of scholarship and of genuine religious tolerance in his contemporary Harun al-Raschid, the Abbasid caliph at Baghdad, with whom he exchanged gifts and maintained diplomatic liaison. A Rabbi Isaac served Charlemagne on a famous embassy, probably as an interpreter, to Baghdad. Tradition has it that he induced at least one Jewish scholar, Makhir, to abandon Baghdad for Aix-la-Chapelle. He also had a Jewish physician at his court, named Ferragut. He may also have been a patron of Jewish scholarship, establishing one Moses ben Kalonymus, an Italian rabbi, at Mainz; this may be the starting point of Jewish scholarship on the Rhine, where one of the great rabbinical families that produced numerous scholars in after centuries was Kalonymus. Jewish tradition focuses on Charlemagne as a great benefactor, but on the whole he merely exemplified the toleration and freedom bestowed on Jews by his dynasty from the early eighth century to 870, not long after which the empire broke up into fragments. The change in the position of the Jews since the seventh century is perhaps suggested by the conversion of Bodo, a chaplain at the imperial court, to Judaism about 840, although once it was known, he had, inevitably, to flee and made his way to Islamic Spain.

From the tenth century on, northern France and the Rhine Valley was the center of Jewish life within Christendom. The community grew in numbers, prosperity, and scholarship, so that by the mid-eleventh century, when Babylonia was declining in importance and eminence, the Jews of Christendom along with those of Moorish Spain were prepared to receive the mantle of leadership in the

Diaspora. It is from this time that there came into use the terms *Ashkenazim*—identifying German or, more broadly, transalpine Jewry—and *Sephardim*—referring to Iberian or, in the larger sense, Mediterranean Jewry. Reduced to shreds and tatters in the seventh century, greatly afforced by immigration in the eighth and ninth centuries, the Jewish community of Europe emerged in the tenth and eleventh centuries into vigorous life. In the wake of William the Conqueror they made their way into England— the westernmost point of the surge of immigration in the middle ages. By 1100 they were to be found in every town of any significance in Christendom. We may accordingly date the onset of the European age of Jewish history from about 1000, an age which was to last until the twentieth century.

The rise of the Rhine–northern France region to a position of intellectual importance in Jewish life is associated with a dynasty of outstanding rabbinical scholars. The great age began with Rabbi Gershom ben Judah (960– 1040), known as the "Light of the Exiles." Born at Metz, he spent his life at Mainz where he founded a famous talmudic academy. He introduced important modifications in the Mishnah which indicate an accommodation to changed social circumstances; e.g., he forbade polygamy (which had long died out in practice), required the wife's as well as the husband's consent for divorce, and in the name of privacy forbade opening letters addressed to someone else.

The greatest Jewish scholar of the Christian middle ages was Rabbi Solomon bar Isaac, known as Rashi (1040– 1105). Born and spending his life in Troyes (the capital of the county of Champagne in northern France), Rashi had been educated over a period of eight years in the talmudic academies of Worms and Gershom's at Mainz. He refers to his wayfaring life as a student "going from the academy of one scholar to that of another in search of interpretations of Torah." Having found what he sought, he returned at age twenty-five to Troyes and opened a talmudic academy of his own. By Rashi's day there was considerable danger that the Talmud would decline in importance and be forgotten by Ashkenazi Jews, because they found themselves in a society quite different and remote from that of the Talmud, and also because Aramaic (the principal language of the Talmud) was less and less understood. There was some danger too that such circumstances would undermine Jewish reliance on the Bible. Whatever such dangers might have been, they were averted by Rashi, whose commentaries on the Bible and Talmud made them once again thoroughly intelligible and relevant to Ashkenazi life. It was typical of Rashi that in the course of his exegesis he would define many terms in French, to insure their being understood by his readers, although the commentaries themselves were written in Hebrew. His style of exposition is, moreover, remarkable for its simplicity and lucidity. So successful was he in his purpose that continuity with the ancient Jewish past was assured, and most subsequent editions of the Bible and Talmud included as a matter of course Rashi's exegesis, which is still authoritative. His commentary on the Pentateuch was among the first Hebrew books to be printed (1475). Rashi's descendants together with students at his academy followed in his footsteps, their school being known as *Tosaphists* (adders), in that they rounded out and completed his work.

Rashi's birth in 1040 coincides with the deaths of the last outstanding Gaon and exilarch of Babylonia. His career and the school he founded symbolize the emergence of European Jewry and suggest that a great age of Jewish life and thought within Christendom was at hand, paralleling the golden age of Spain, had such efforts been sustained. There are some definite indications in Rashi's biography that Jews were being thoroughly assimilated to Christian society in every respect save religion, particularly in language, as we have seen with Rashi's frequent use of the vernacular. A hearty cordiality in social relations is suggested by Rashi's receipt of gifts from his Christian neighbors at Passover. There are in the chronicles of the eleventh century all sorts of touches like the adoption of synagogal melodies by Catholic priests, and of Jewish mothers singing Christian lullabies to their children. Whatever prospects there were of an irenic age of mutual esteem between Christians and Jews were abruptly terminated by the outbreak of crusading in 1095. In the last decade of his life Rashi and his people were buffeted about so severely that his death marks the transition to an age not of hope but of martyrdom.

The Crusades

The Crusades were an expression of the Cluniac reform movement that began with the founding of the Abbey of Cluny on the Rhone in Provence in 910 The distinguishing feature of the Cluniac movement was its exaltation of the spiritual, the clergy, and the Church over the temporal, the laity, and secular government. It had the effect of abolishing abuses first within the monasteries and then among the secular clergy, and ultimately it sought to disengage the Church entirely from the feudal morass of patronage and investiture. It went far to establish the clergy and episcopal hierarchy as a sacred priesthood, and the pope as the sovereign vicar of God who governed the Church and exercised by divine right a supervisory power over kings and emperors (whom he could depose). The Cluniac spirit gave rise to a heightened religious sensibility, one that found expression in a new and resplendent liturgy and particularly in the increasing number of pilgrim bands making the arduous journey to Jerusalem. (In the elev-

enth century there were 117 distinct expeditions as compared to only 16 in the tenth, 12 in the ninth, and 6 in the
eighth.) It was no coincidence that the first pope to
dream of what he called "the redemption of the Holy
Land" by "50,000 knights of Christ" was the greatest of the
reformers, Gregory VII. His proclamation that "the
Roman Church has never erred; nor will it err to all
eternity" points to the doctrine of infallibility, and to the
establishment of the court of the Inquisition (though it
does not come into existence until 150 years after
Gregory) .

The Latin Church thus came to be animated by a profoundly righteous and exalting religiosity that parallels a
somewhat similar transformation of Zoroastrianism under
Persian rule in the sixth century, as we have seen. In both
instances the new religious passion spelled disaster for the
Jewish communities, which had enjoyed a large measure of
tranquillity for three or four centuries previously. When
the Crusaders cried out "God exalt Christianity," it seemed
often to be a mandate to abase Judaism. When Pope
Urban II, the disciple of Gregory VII, addressed the Crusaders as "the children of Israel," his words may well have
carried for his excited listeners a reminder that the Jews
were children of the devil, Jesus' murderers, and God's
enemies. What point was there in redeeming the Holy
Land, asked popular preachers of Crusading like Peter the
Hermit and Walter the Penniless, if they left behind them
the worst offenders of all? Hence as great masses of humanity began to tumble together preparatory to setting out for
the Levant, they began to swoop down upon one Jewish
community after another, leaving a swath of ruin, robbery,
slaughter, and forcible conversions in Speyer, Worms, Mainz,
Cologne, and Trier in the Rhine and Moselle valleys, in
Lorraine and particularly in its capital of Metz, and
throughout northern France and especially in Rouen. In
almost every instance local officials—ecclesiastical and

feudal—sought to quell the rioters, with some success in a few places.

Thereafter, however, the inevitable accompaniment to every Crusade was a preliminary bloodbath. Bishop Otto of Freising, the kinsman and biographer of Frederick Barbarossa, reports the monk Ralph, "who was only moderately imbued with letters" and a preacher of the second Crusade, "heedlessly including in his preaching that the Jews whose homes were scattered throughout the cities and towns should be slain as foes of the Christian religion. The seed of this doctrine took such firm root and so grew in numerous cities of Gaul and Germany that a large number of Jews were killed in the stormy uprising." The same source mentions that St. Bernard of Clairvaux, the chief preacher of the Crusade, vainly sought to persuade Christians "to leave the Jews in peace . . . to leave them in God's hands."

Another motive for massacre undoubtedly was envy of the Jewish merchant class, an occupation increasingly coveted by Christians, and the opportunity to cancel debts owed to Jewish moneylenders. Moreover, the abysmal failure of later Crusades gave rise to the macabre notion among the masses that all would come to nothing until the Jewish cancer had been purged from the Christian fold. Thus the second Crusade of the 1140's rivaled in its horrors those of the first. The third Crusade in the 1190's saw the participation for the first time of England and the outbreak there of the anti-Jewish fury as well. Christian Spain spared its Jews such mistreatment, owing to the special circumstances of the Reconquest that made it expedient to conciliate so large, wealthy, learned, and influential a minority. Nor did Italian Jewry suffer from crusading fanaticism, since a more tolerant spirit continued to prevail there.

Anti-Jewish Legislation and Violence

The forces and trends we have been tracing reach a climax in the ordering of Jewish life formulated by the Third (1179) and Fourth (1215) Lateran Councils of the Church; they constitute the high-water mark of anti-Jewish legislation in the middle ages. In 1179 all the restrictions going back to Constantine were renewed and extended, so that, e.g., Christian households could not employ Jewish maids, nurses, or midwives, much less physicians; the Council laid the basis of the ghetto system by decreeing that Jews had to live apart from Christians. Both Councils condemned usury and sought to abolish its practice by both Jews and Christians, the significance of which appears in a later chapter. In 1215 legislation forbade Jews to appear in public on certain holy days of the Church calendar. No Jew was to hold public office or have authority over Christians, a measure intended to end the "court" or "privileged" Jews in the service of many kings and feudal lords. Above all, as of 1215, the Jew had to wear a distinctive dress—on his head a large hat, or over his heart a yellow or crimson circle, symbolic of the Dantesque circle of hell to which he or she was presumably condemned; the pariah status of Jews was thus shouted from the housetops and they became the obvious target for any mob, like the bandanna that inflames the bull. It was a far cry from Rashi's day.

The conciliar directives were not implemented immediately everywhere in Europe, largely because kings had their own aims in dealing with Jews. In the meantime a number of incidents and practices suggest the degradation to which the Jew was brought. "Blood accusation" and "ritual murder" appear frequently in the age of the Crusades, the earliest on record being that of William of Norwich in 1144.[5] Jews supposedly required the blood of a human victim, variously, to mock the Crucifixion, to make the bread for Passover, to thwart the Inquisition (at a later date) , or for some other form of superstitious magic. None of this had any basis in fact, for sacrifice was no part of Jewish ritual, and blood is considered abhorrent and an abomination by Jewish law.[6] But fact is a weak weapon against fanaticism and prejudice. A notably outrageous example of blood accusation was Simon of Trent's murder in the fifteenth century; he became the center of a local anti-Semitic cult that featured an insulting annual procession until the whole thing was suppressed by Vatican II, five hundred years later. Fact does ultimately prevail.[7]

"Host desecration" was another expression of popular fanaticism. With the proclamation of the dogma of Transubstantiation by the Fourth Lateran Council, the Host came to be regarded as specially potent, so that it was stolen (by Christians) and used by them for magical purposes; when so used, it was found to "bleed" (probably the result of a scarlet microbe that forms on stale bread in damp storage places) . Many Jews were accused and suffered death for supposedly having stolen and desecrated what to them could only have been an ordinary piece of unleavened bread that had neither special potency nor was the body of our Lord. But again logic is a weak weapon in defense against fanaticism and prejudice.

Fundamental to such conceptions of the Jew as a prime source of evil was the idea that he was the ally and instrument of Satan. Frequently the devil is represented as walking the earth in the guise of a Jew in order to tempt Christians. There is an odd conjunction here with the peasant, who is frequently villainized as having "a shifty look, one good foot and the other twisted" like the devil. Both the serf and the Jew performed indispensable economic functions for medieval society, for which they were neither loved nor appreciated; both were essentially rightless; both were frequently equated with animals and denied the status of human beings. A medieval manual for studying grammar gives expression to several of these notions: "What part of speech is peasant?" asked the master. "A noun," replied the scholar. "What sort of noun?" "Jewish." "Why?" "Because he is as silly and ugly as a Jew." "What gender?" "The asinine gender, for in all his deeds and works he is ever like unto an ass." In the case of the Jew it is more usually the predatory wolf to which he is likened, and in the stereotype of Shakespeare's Shylock and Charles Dickens' Fagin one may see how enduring such ascriptions have been.

The incidence of the black plague of the 1340's was another source of danger for Jews: they suffered noticeably less from it owing to the specification in their law of an elaborate code of cleanliness and hygiene, whereas Christians—as exemplified by St. Bernard of Clairvaux—thought cleanliness a form of pagan pride and diametrically opposed to godliness. The popular explanation was, however, that the Jews and lepers conspired to poison the water supplies (an accusation that had appeared several times in the preceding century), and the inevitable sequel was wholesale brutalities that annihilated numerous Jewish communities, especially in Germany. The whole nefarious business of blood accusation and Host desecration and a great many similar matters was condemned or restricted by many popes, steadfast as almost all of them were in the dualist policy, but their threats and restraints were to very little avail.

The Dominicans, as the Inquisitors par excellence, added many of their own inventions to the mounting arsenal of anti-Jewish weapons, and theirs had papal sanction. They had the right to censor Jewish books and burn them in public bonfires if they found heresy or blaspheming in them. We have seen how a group of anti-Maimonidean Jews in Provence spurred the Inquisition on with the result that the *Guide to the Perplexed* was burned; thereupon the Inquisitors looked into the Talmud and it was repeatedly burned in the course of the thirteenth century. Talmudic studies became a crime. The Inquisition's thoroughness is revealed in the statistic that one lone medieval copy of the Talmud survives, and indeed Jewish scholarship in Christendom was simply rooted up and destroyed. The friars also had the right to enter any synagogue, forcibly round up its members, and compel them to listen to a sermon—usually delivered by an apostate—that vilified Judaism, excoriated Jews, and suspended the Damoclean sword of forced baptism over their heads.

Public disputations, in that age when universities flourished, pitted spokesmen for the two faiths in unequal combat against each other, for the rabbi had to be cautious lest he be condemned for blasphemy. Arranged by the Inquisition and often held under royal patronage, such proceedings frequently were followed by a spate of book burning, as in Paris in 1240. There under the auspices of the royal saint and Crusader, St. Louis IX, such a disputation was held and followed by a holocaust of Hebrew books. St. Louis was the king of peace and justice, and sat often under the great oak at Vincennes to grant justice to all, great or humble, who petitioned him. I, who have a special reverence for him, find it particularly saddening that he should have the anti-Semitic fault of so many medieval saints. To Jewish historians he has the appearance of a hypocrite for his unfortunate observation that only learned clerics should dispute with the rabbis; "but a layman, when he hears the Christian law mis-said by a Jew, should not defend the Christian law, unless it be with his sword, and with that he should pierce the mis-sayer in the stomach, so far as the sword will enter." Having the highest sanction, such attitudes and proceedings could only reduce the Jew, wearing his pariah insignia, to a victim of endless attack and butchery; especially at the Easter season, when the Passion of the Crucifixion was not only recalled but re-enacted in the mystery plays and in the

Easter liturgy in the most excruciating spirit, were Jews made to suffer.

The National Monarchies

By the thirteenth century the national monarchies had emerged and the fate of Jews was more and more bound up with them. The monarchs of England, France, Spain, and the Holy Roman Empire claimed, each within his domain, to exercise the power of subjection over Jews that had once been the prerogative of Constantine and Charlemagne. The Jew was rightless and could do nothing except by royal permission in the form of a charter, such as began to be granted in the age of Charlemagne. In essence, Jews were the property of the king, who admitted or expelled and exploited or protected them as he saw fit; he could "tallage [tax] them at will."

ENGLAND

To England, Jews came at the behest of William the Conqueror, whom they served as financial agents. So, too, with his successors down to the end of the twelfth century, during which the kingdom—relatively untouched by the crusading fervor—was a haven from the bloodletting across the Channel. There were exceptions to this tranquillity, such as the blood accusations at Norwich in 1144, Gloucester in 1168, and Bury St. Edmunds in 1181. Nevertheless, it was only with Richard the Lion-Hearted (1189–1199) and the third Crusade that the pathological furies were unleashed in England. At his coronation, Jews bearing gifts for the king were set upon, and a riot erupted that consumed the Jewish quarter of London and did not die down until many of its inhabitants were murdered. Richard punished the troublemakers but could not restrain similar outbreaks and flareups throughout England, most notably in York. Many of the leaders were indebted to the Jews, and indeed from this time forward anti-Jewish passion in the island was about equally divided between hatred for them as the archcreditors when no one else had capital and as the archinfidels when everyone else believed.

Since Jewish economic history is presented separately, it will suffice to explain that the Jews were extremely profitable to the monarchy as a source of capital[8] and for their financial expertise. They provided the sinews of war and government, and accordingly were protected by the king. An example of such protection was the Exchequer of the Jews, which dated from about 1240. Since the rioters of 1189–1190 destroyed the records of their indebtedness to Jews and thus diminished the royal slice of the profits, Richard ordered that a public record be kept in the town archives of all such debts; there were twenty-six such archives and by 1240 they came under the jurisdiction of the Exchequer of the Jews, an organ of the central government. It provided legal assistance to Jews in collecting debts—none of which made for Jewish popularity—and received taxes and fees from them; it was, says Sir Walter Scott, "erected for the very purpose of despoiling and distressing them."

The Jewish community of England was remarkably developed under royal control. Kings did not press them to be converted, because, as one of them said, he would exchange a profitable agent for a mere subject. He appointed the chief rabbi and occasionally consulted with the community, particularly on matters of taxation, in the form of a "Jewish Parliament." By the time of King John, the crown faced a mounting financial crisis that led to those arbitrary exactions which brought him to Runnymede in 1215. On the way to Runnymede, as it were, the insurgent barons demolished the Jewry of London and, in articles 10 and 11 of Magna Charta greatly hampered the ability of

Jews to gain repayment of loans. Throughout the thirteenth century the English Jews were taxed and fleeced so mercilessly that they began to go bankrupt and could pay into the royal treasury in 1272 only about one-fifth what they had remitted a century earlier. They also began to lose out to foreign financial agents, such as the Lombards, and to a growing class of native financiers. By the accession of Edward I in 1272, they were so impoverished that their contribution to the king's income was, despite his extortionate methods, negligible and dispensable. He, in a remarkably statesmanlike way, sought to rectify the situation. In line with papal directive, he forbade Jews to engage in financial operations; instead they were to be allowed to enter commerce, crafts and even to lease (but not to own) land for agriculture. But this was too radical a break with tradition and prejudice. The scheme failed completely and Edward disposed of the whole problem by expelling the Jews in 1290 from England, where no Jewish community was to be seen until the sixteenth or seventeenth century. (Edward had expelled the Jews from his continental possession, Gascony, the preceding year, although it took a generation before this policy was effectively enforced. The king should not be idealized, although some modern historians have emphasized his piety as a Crusader, following a chronicler who credited Edward with acting toward the Jews "as behooves a Catholic prince"; for, as H. G. Richardson insists, the king's Christian conscience against usurious misbelievers in his realms "had been stirred by his financial necessities.")

FRANCE

The Jewish community of France was closely akin to that of England, but much larger and more important. The French kings were much more attuned to popular prejudice and ecclesiastical policies than their English counterparts. E.g., in contrast to England, French monarchs from 1182 on often sought to bar Jews from earning a livelihood by moneylending. That year saw their expulsion at the hands of Philip II Augustus, after he had cancelled debts owing to them and confiscated their properties. On his return from Crusade and in financial straits, he readmitted them and established the *Produit des Juifs* (1198) that corresponded to the English Exchequer of the Jews. Thereafter he fleeced these *servi camerae regis* (servants of the king's chamber) as did his successors, frequently remitting the interest debtors owed to Jews, sometimes even cancelling a quarter or third of the principal as well. His grandson, St. Louis IX, frequently did this. With him the prescriptions of the Fourth Lateran Council were rigorously enforced; he also sought personally to convert Jews. When he went on Crusade in the 1240's he ordered their expulsion, which was not carried out, however. Harassment was the order of the day over the remainder of the century, culminating with the bitter cup of expulsion in 1306 by St. Louis' grandson, Philip IV the Fair. He had no objection to usury, for after having borrowed from Jews up to the hilt, the king arrested them en masse: he cancelled his own indebtedness to them and transferred all other debts owing to Jews to himself and exacted every possible farthing when he collected; he then confiscated all their remaining property and expelled them from his prisons and the kingdom. His successors in the fourteenth century, confronted with the financial crises of the Hundred Years' War, recalled and expelled them again in moneymaking maneuvers. But this involved only a few financiers: admitted in 1315 and again in 1359, they were all thrust out again in 1394. Thereafter Jews are no significant part of French history until the Revolution of 1789.

Provence, as a semi-independent feudatory of the French crown, preserved its Jewish community with its vigorous intellectual life much longer, whereas in the north the great tradition of Rashi was the first victim of crusading. In an earlier chapter it was indicated how the tide of Spanish scholarship sped over the Pyrenees to animate intellectual centers in Provence and elsewhere, a development in which Jewish scholars played an important role on both sides of the mountains. In Provence, the Ibn Tibbon family was especially eminent over several generations for its scholar-translators, flourishing particularly in the twelfth century, the heyday of this work and the golden age of Provence with its great prosperity, troubadour literature, Romanesque architecture, and its urbane and tolerant princes and population. Unfortunately, the Albigensian heresy sprouted there and in Toulouse, which shared the cultural flowering, with the result that the popes beginning with Innocent III proclaimed a Crusade and unleashed the Inquisition against the two counties. Crusaders and Inquisitors frequently mistook Jews for heretics, causing many to suffer cruel deaths and depredations in the course of the attempt to ruin a civilization.

Nevertheless, Provence remained a center of joint Jewish and Christian scholarly activity in the transmittal of the classical heritage and Arabic learning to the West. Biblical and talmudic scholarship flourished also during the thirteenth century, especially in the time of David Kimhi, whose biblical exegesis was second only to Rashi's. Provence was important for European Jews and Christian scholars in the reception and criticism of Maimonides' writings. A scholar of the twelfth century, highly critical of Maimonides, was his contemporary Rabbi Abraham ben David. A more important figure was Rabbi Jacob ben Makir (died 1308), a talmudist, physician, and translator of several scientific and mathematical works from Arabic into Hebrew; what makes him a central figure was his translation of much of Maimonides' philosophical writings along with a favorable presentation of the sage's ideas to a circle of friends and students, Jewish and Christian, who followed his lead in the study of Maimonides, Aristotle, and Averroës. The tradition came to an end with Rabbi Levi ben Gershon, or Gersonides (1288–1344), who contributed to scientific and philosophical thought as an Aristotelian rationalist; he edited the works of Averroës, whose defender he was in preference to Maimonides. His fame as an astronomer caused the pope to commission a translation of his work on an early form of the navigational quadrant known as "Jacob's staff." By his time the militant spirit of the north had triumphed in southern France, with the exception of Avignon, the residence of the popes in the fourteenth century, who adhered there also to their long-standing dualist policy; thus Avignon, as a kind of island haven, was Gersonides' home, and he may have enjoyed extensive papal patronage.

GERMANY

Medieval Germany, in a judgment made by Cecil Roth before 1933, was the classic land of Jewish martyrdom. From the first Crusade on there is a rising tide of hatred and violence. During the period when the Holy Roman emperors ruled effectively—down to about 1250—there was some restraint. Thereafter the princely magnates and towns ruled themselves, and massacre and sacking, usually triggered by blood accusation or Host desecration charges, erupted frequently and for prolonged periods. Political authority was so fragmented in Germany that sometimes Jews had only to flee across a nearby frontier to escape, but increasingly flight only ignited a still bigger bonfire. In 1298 a Host desecration episode in a small town was so played upon by a demagogue named Rindfleisch that, before the storm subsided, it had swept over Bavaria and Austria, leaving 140 communities sacked and one hundred thousand Jews dead. In 1336–1338 a similarly devastating storm swept over the whole of northern and central Germany, carried out with impunity by a band of cutthroats wearing leather armbands as their insignia and calling themselves blatantly *Judenschläger* (slayers of Jews), because the authorities either could not or would not restrain them. In the 1340's came the ravages of the black plague, and, as we have seen, it too gave rise to a deluge of massacre, far worse in Germany than elsewhere. In subsequent decades, while bloodshed never died out, there came something of a lull which lasted to the end of the century. In the fifteenth century, however, the Church in Germany was on the defensive and fearful of the Hussite heresy in Bohemia; such circumstances had the predictable result of inflaming anew the hatred for Jews; all the ecclesiastical legislation that we have seen was stringently enforced, inflammatory sermons began to be preached, and inquisitorial ecclesiastics sought to ferret out one Jewish community after another. One of these hammers of the Jews was a Franciscan, the celebrated anti-Hussite preacher, St. John of Capistrano; he discovered profanation of the Host at Breslau and unleashed fearful vendettas against the Jews. Another was the German Cardinal Nicholas Cusanus (1404–1464), who was in so many respects a choice spirit and the most original systematic philosopher of the Renaissance; among other remarkable things in this astounding man was an ideal of religious liberty, but one from which Jews were excluded. He had that peculiar blindspot that we have seen in St. Louis, making both men righteous persecutors of the Jews. Thus the promising start of German-Jewish culture that we saw earlier in the Rhine Valley was cut short by the violence of the first Crusade and never allowed to recover. A perpetual state of terror and harassment is not conducive to scholarship; education falters in an environment where the academy and synagogue were the first targets in the repeated disruptions of the Jewish communities.

The explanation for such animosity against Jews is as much economic as religious: Germany was relatively backward economically, so that Jews fulfilled there only from the end of the thirteenth century on functions which they had rendered in England and France in the eleventh and twelfth centuries. Thus the phase of Jewish financial hegemony in Germany coincides with the period of the worst outrages that we have described. This situation explains also that while they were massacred in great numbers, they were neither exterminated nor expelled in toto. They were constantly being expelled from one German state or another, but were usually recalled because they remained the indispensable financial agents and sources of capital. Princes, bishops, and towns needed their services, and accordingly granted them minimal privileges and protection. In spite of catastrophes and the emigration of many to the colonial territories beyond the Elbe and to Poland, German-Jewish communities continued in many towns. Without interruption in Frankfurt and Worms, which somehow were immune to anti-Semitic explosions, or after restoration as in Hamburg, Jewish communities persisted; and down to the French Revolution they functioned as financiers and "court Jews" in the service of princes, and constituted the dynamic element in German economic life.

ITALY

Italy from 962 had been joined to Germany to form the Holy Roman Empire. Although certain cultural affinities between Germany and Italy continued long after, by 1250 the peninsula—broken up into numerous city-states in the north, the Papal States in the center, and the kingdom of Naples and Sicily in the south—went its own way. Very few Jews dwelled in the north until the fourteenth and fifteenth centuries, when many fled from Germany to the towns to become pawnshop brokers. Rome had, as we have seen, a Jewish community that went back to classical times. But it is in the southern kingdom that Jews added a glorious page to their history.

Southern Italy and Sicily had been conquered by 1100 by Norman adventurers who linked the island (conquered from the Moslems) to the mainland as far as Rome, and ruled the whole domain from Palermo as the kingdom of the Two Sicilies. The twelfth century was a golden age when the Norman kings ruled in harmony and tranquillity a population comprised of Latin and Greek Christians, Moslems, and Jews, groups that were frequently in mortal combat with each other elsewhere. As in Provence, rulers and people were tolerant and cosmopolitan. Under royal patronage, Salerno, Naples, and Palermo blossomed as intellectual centers until the mid-fourteenth century, and for a century and a half the kingdom was the intellectual crossroads of the world—north-south, east-west. It was a fertile source of translations from Greek (facilitated by the presence of a Greek-speaking minority) and Arabic (facilitated greatly by Jews).

When the Norman dynasty died out in 1189, the kingdom passed to the Hohenstaufen emperors of Germany, of whom the greatest was Frederick II (1194–1250), "the wonder of the world." Under his patronage the intellectual revival reached its apex. Himself brilliantly gifted and reared in Palermo, he was a product of the tolerant, skeptical, cosmopolitan environment of the south. The mighty antagonist of the papacy, he was no fanatical Crusader. As philosopher, jurist, poet, architect, scientist, mathematician, linguist, collector of ancient art, patron of sculpture, founder of the university of Naples, statesman, and soldier, he delineates the universal man of the Renaissance. His patronage of scholarship knew no bounds and led him to invite men of learning from far and wide to his court. Jews had a prominent place in this activity, especially, as in Provence and Spain, in preparing translations from Arabic into Hebrew and thus making them available to Christian scholars, who as a rule knew no Arabic. Frederick and his successors encouraged several Jewish scholars to learn Latin so as to enable them to complete the cycle of translation, and there is at least one example of a Jewish translator setting himself to master Greek in order to execute translations of Aristotle from the original.

One of the best known men at the imperial court was the scholar-physician Jacob Anatoli (1194–1256), a proponent of Maimonides and Averroës; he lectured at the university of Naples and may have had St. Thomas Aquinas among his students. His translation of Averroës from Arabic into Hebrew was the source of all the later Latin editions. Frederick himself was much interested in Maimonides' *Guide to the Perplexed* and commissioned a Latin translation of it, and he was also an intimate of Moses ben Solomon of Salerno, who wrote an elaborate commentary on it. Such figures as Anatoli and Moses were influential at the court and enjoyed personal communication with Frederick; his conversations with them were sometimes reflected in their writings, as when Anatoli reports that several of his allegorical interpretations of biblical passages had been suggested to him by the emperor. The principal interests at the court were scientific, so that a great corpus of medical, astronomical, and biological works was translated. Jews could and did study medicine at a famous school in Salerno, whereas they were barred from the universities of the north—the earliest record of a Jew taking a degree there (at Padua) occurs in 1409.

Under Frederick's son, King Manfred (died 1266), the great work went right on. A number of specific translations from Arabic and Hebrew into Latin that he commissioned are known, and he himself seems to have learned Hebrew. He was defeated and killed by St. Louis IX's younger brother, Charles of Anjou, who now became king of the Two Sicilies; and though he brought much of that intense religiosity that was so fatal to Jews in transalpine

Europe, he nevertheless continued the grand intellectual enterprise, taking into his service Jewish scholars whom he employed full time as professional translators. One of these was Farrachius, remembered for his translations of medical works. Sicily rebelled against King Charles' harsh government in 1282 and became a possession of Aragon, but on his death in 1285 the mainland passed to his descendants; they carried on his generous patronage of Jewish scholars until the mid-fourteenth century, when we have reference to one Kalonymus making important translations. Greek studies also continued there. The transition to the Renaissance, which centered in northern Italy and owed much to the cultural traditions that go back to the twelfth century in the south, is suggested by Petrarch's sojourn at the court of Naples in the 1330's.

SPAIN AND PORTUGAL

Spain was in the twelfth and thirteenth centuries the land of fascination and the great treasure house of the world's knowledge which increasingly lured Christian scholars. The secrets particularly of astronomy, mathematics, medicine, and philosophy were to be won there, and as we have seen, first under Moorish then under Christian auspices, Jewish scholars labored side by side with Christian and Moslem men of learning in translating, interpreting, and gathering in the great harvest. Toledo, under the patronage of its archbishop, was the principal center for translation from Arabic and classical sources.

The reign of King Alfonso X the Wise of Castile (1252–1284) represents the peak of Jewish intellectual life in Spain. The king himself was a writer as well as patron of learning. He is remembered chiefly for his *Tables* of planetary movements, compiled for him by two Jewish scholars, and a standard work of reference for astronomers until the seventeenth century. Jewish scholars were extensively engaged in the translation of scientific works into the vernacular Castilian, an important stage in the development of the Spanish language.

In Aragon the great scientific interest was geography and cartography, in which Jews were prominent, especially in making available for use the work of Arabic geographers. The Aragonese school of geography had its origin in the thirteenth century under royal patronage and flourished into the fifteenth; it is interesting to note that the school's greatest figure was a Jew of Majorca named Crescas. He was summoned to Portugal in 1419 by Prince Henry the Navigator to become the central figure in his famous school of navigation and astronomy, which played a key role in overseas exploration and discovery. For the medieval Jews, as for the Arabs, scientific knowledge was something highly prized, and their devotion to science and their rationalistic cast of mind was passed on to many of the Christian scholars and thinkers who came into contact with them in Spain.

The reference to King Alfonso the Wise brings to mind other things, unfortunately, than scholarly pursuits and the scientific temperament. For he issued a new law code, the *Siete Partidas*, which marks the onset in Castile of the enforcement of the anti-Jewish legislation of the Third and Fourth Lateran Councils; and even if the code was adhered to no more than intermittently, its existence was a sure sign that the tide of hostility was rising against Jews in Spain as it was throughout Christendom. If Spain is the most glorious, it is also the saddest chapter of medieval Jewish history.

The peak of Jewish felicity and freedom had come in the reign of Alfonso VI of Castile (1065–1109). He was a great figure of the Reconquest and it was to him that Toledo fell in 1085. Jews served in his armies and tradition reports that he did not offer battle on one occasion because it was the Sabbath. Whether out of tolerance or expediency or both, he granted full autonomy and civil equality to his Jewish subjects, despite the protests of Pope Gregory VII. Jews, with their command of Arabic, served him as diplomats as they did as physicians, financial experts, and ministers of state. Popular resentment and ecclesiastical objection sometimes led to explosions and turbulence, yet on the whole the Jewish community flourished throughout Spain in the twelfth century and after. Jews continued to serve in high offices of the royal governments; commercial enterprise was open to them; they enjoyed great fame as physicians and scholars; they were engaged in agriculture and handicrafts, particularly in making cloth and metalworking.

The battle of Las Navas de Tolosa, 1212, was the decisive turning point in the Reconquest: the Almohades were crushed and the Moorish domination of Spain permanently broken. For the next half century fighting was desultory and acquisition of territory small and piecemeal, until only the small state of Granada remained in Moorish hands. The Christian predominance was such after 1261 that it was no longer necessary to conciliate the Jewish minority, as it had been expedient to do over the two to three preceding centuries. The heightened religious sensibility that we have seen permeating the whole of Europe made it progressively more difficult for public authorities to control mob violence, particularly as it tended increasingly to be spurred on by demagogic fanatics. The *Siete Partidas* contained the seeds of the future. Nevertheless, Spain in the thirteenth century was the environment by far the most hospitable to Jewish life. Jews continued to be prominent as prime ministers, physicians, and in all the economic occupations; their intellectual life as expressed in scholarships and rabbinical studies flourished as never before; the autonomy of their settlements was hardly impaired.

It was in the fourteenth century that the violence that was so rife elsewhere in Europe began to spill over into Spain.

Massacres stimulated by the black plague erupted, if less ferociously than in Germany, in the 1340's; accusations of ritual murder and Host desecration became more frequent. In the course of the struggle over the Castilian throne between Peter the Cruel and Henry Trastamera, the Jews supported Peter, who lost, so that the triumphal entry of Henry into each town in turn was accompanied by a merciless sack of its Jewish quarter. That was in the 1350's; the fatal turn came in the Easter season of 1391.

A rabid archdeacon, Ferrand Martinez, confessor to the queen mother and a power at the court, preached such virulent sermons that the most baleful passions of his listeners were unleashed. He seems to have been preaching violence since 1378, but had been repeatedly checked by the king and the pope. The death of the king in 1390 removed that restraint, with the result that Ash Wednesday of 1391 saw the bloody sacking of the Jewish section of Seville, despite the efforts of the civil authorities to quell the berserk mob. An orgy of bloodletting and destruction spread like wildfire over the whole of Spain, presenting Jews—despite the civil power—with the cruel alternative of baptism or death. In many towns the whole community was exterminated, their quarter was everywhere left in ashes, and before the wave had spent itself as many as fifty thousand were dead.

But uniquely in Spain and probably a measure of their assimilation and loyalty to the host society, the great majority of Jews acceded to baptism in preference to death. The papacy had, as we have seen, opposed forced baptism, but no ecclesiastical authority ever denied the indelible efficacy of the sacrament once it had been bestowed, regardless of the motive of the giver or receiver. Baptism could not be renounced, and such converted Jews, or New Christians as they came to be known in Spain, became subject to the Inquisition. The two hundred thousand New Christians of 1391 were augmented in subsequent decades by later sword-point baptisms, such as followed the mayhem ensuing from the "fire-and-brimstone" preaching of the Dominican Vincent Ferrer in 1411. So it went, down through the fifteenth century.

The great majority of the New Christians, however, were so only in form; in everything but name they remained Jews and so, too, their children. These crypto-Jews or Marranos—as they were dubbed in Spanish, meaning "pig" —grew as a separate body but remained in surreptitious contact with their co-religionists, those who had managed to hide away and avoid the grim choice of apostasy or death. Such Jews could and did practice their religion openly, technically still enjoying the old freedom and autonomy, but were increasingly exposed to raging mobs and inflammatory preachers. As for the technically Christian Marranos, all doors had to open to them and they practically dominated Spanish life. They made their way in great numbers into the highest positions in the legal profession, the civil service, army, universities, and the Church— one of them became archbishop of Burgos. The government's financial administration was in their hands, and they made themselves felt in municipal government. The wealthier families intermarried with the proudest of the nobility, and before two or three generations there was hardly a noble family, not excluding the royal house of Aragon, that did not have its tincture of Jewish blood. This situation, we may note, gave rise in Spain by the end of the fifteenth century to a new form of anti-Semitism, that of race rather than the age-old one of religion; in the time of Ferdinand (his Marrano great-grandmother notwithstanding) and Isabella, Spanish nobles began to conceal their Jewish extraction and insist upon the "purity" of their blood.[9]

The potent allegiance of the Marranos to Judaism greatly disturbed someone of the perfervid piety and crusading temperament that imbued Queen Isabella. With the passage of time the Marrano problem worsened and the only solution conceivable in the circumstances of fifteenth-century Spain was to call in the Inquisition. Thus was established in 1478 by papal decree the Spanish Inquisition. It should be emphasized that it was *Spanish* in the sense that it was from the start an instrument of the state, operated by royal appointees, guided by state policy, and was frequently the subject of attacks by popes who sought to curb it, though in vain. On the other hand, it was ecclesiastics who had induced the crown to embark on the inquisitorial path and it was they, especially the Dominican Tomás de Torquemada, who propelled the bloody business from start to finish.

Torquemada is in the image of the Grand Inquisitor: he was Isabella's confessor, and had been the chief negotiator of the agreement of 1478 with Pope Sixtus IV. It was he who devised the harsh rules of procedure of the Inquisition and imparted to it its spirit of calm ruthlessness, glacial persistence, and slaughterhouse efficiency. The Marranos remained fair game for the Inquisition until the French Revolution, but they survived and their Judaism with them nevertheless; as the historian Cecil Roth has said, their adventure is "the most romantic episode in all history."

To Torquemada and the Spanish government it soon became evident that the Inquisition could make no headway against the judaizing of the Marranos so long as there were Jews in Spain who openly and legally professed Judaism. It was not enough to decimate them by massacre and forced conversion, or to reduce them to degradation and poverty by the steady erosion of their wonted freedom and autonomy. They still practiced their religion, and their example was not lost on the Marranos. The Inquisitors began to press for expulsion, and here again Torquemada's initiative was decisive. The royal decree of 1492 required Jews either to be baptized or be expelled from the realm within four months; it came on the heels of the fall of Granada and the completion of the Reconquest that same year. Both acts embody the crusading zeal.

The decree applied also to Spain's possessions, Sardinia and Sicily; on the Spanish conquest of Naples in 1510, it was carried out in southern Italy as well, and more vigorously in 1548. Navarre, a small kingdom in the Pyrenees, followed suit in 1498 and the remnants of the Jewish colony of Provence were banished in 1507, leaving papal Avignon as an exception to the rule. Portugal, where most of the Spanish exiles had fled after paying a head tax that was very lucrative to the Portuguese crown, carried out the same barbaric policy beginning in 1497; King Manuel was desirous of marrying a Spanish princess, but Isabella would entrust no daughter of hers to a realm still smirched by the presence of Jews. Manuel, thereupon more fanatical than his churchmen, set about executing what was tantamount to wholesale conversion by order of the king. His decree ordered all children four to fourteen to be baptized; seized they were and led away to the font by the king's men, who were so zealous that they carried off young persons up to age twenty or older. In some places it was assumed that everyone, young or old, was to be dragooned into baptism. The king's expectation that the parents would follow their children to the font rather than lose them altogether did not materialize; instead parents smothered their children and killed themselves in large numbers. The great majority of children, however, were distributed across the country to be reared in Christian surroundings and cut off forever from their parents. Meanwhile, some twenty thousand adults came together in Lisbon to embark on the ships that would carry them into exile, but they had to endure conversionist threats and sermons in surroundings little different from a concentration camp. Apart from his zealousness, the king was increasingly anxious that these very valuable subjects not be lost to the realm. And since a relatively small number of Jews were finally permitted to leave, it is inaccurate to speak of an expulsion; rather it was a General Conversion, as it is called in the Portuguese chronicles, in which the Jews were given no choice, but were simply bulldozed into conversion. Thus the royal policy had the ultimate effect of creating a class of Portuguese Marranos, comparable to those of Spain in their crypto-Judaism, except that they were even more steadfast.

The dismal fate of Iberian Jewry is appropriately symbolized in the career of Isaac Abarbanel (1437–1508). He was born in Portugal, practically the last corner of Western Europe to be caught up in the anti-Jewish frenzy. His father and grandfather had been well-to-do and influential; both had had the confidence of the monarch and had served the crown in high offices of state. To this position Abarbanel succeded, enjoying, as he said, "blessings, riches and honor under King Alfonso, a just and mighty king." But on the king's death, Abarbanel fell from power and had to flee for safety to Spain in 1483. Within a year he was summoned to the court of Ferdinand and Isabella to manage their finances, in straits owing to their costly war against Granada. He gained the confidence of the celebrated royal pair and became one of the most influential figures at court. Meanwhile, he was carrying on scholarly enterprises and writing a commentary on the Bible. As in Portugal, so now in Spain, his home became a center where Christians, Jews and Moslems met congenially together to discuss politics, philosophy, and religion. His own writings in those apocalyptic times show a mystical disposition; he was deeply imbued with Kabbalah doctrines and critical of the rationalist philosophers "who walk in darkness," although from this indictment he exempted Maimonides, of whose *Guide to the Perplexed* he wrote a paraphrase.

Abarbanel's influence over the monarchs was no match for that of Torquemada, against whom he pleaded to the king. "I supplicated him thus: Save, O King. Why do thus to thy servants? Lay on us every tribute and ransom, gold and silver, and everything that the children of Israel possess they shall willingly give to their fatherland. I sought out my friends, those who stand near the king and enjoy his confidence, and begged them to beseech and petition him to revoke the evil decree concerning our destruction and annihilation, but all in vain. I neither rested nor spared myself, yet the calamity was not averted." The implacable Torquemada was not to be gainsaid. Ashen and gaunt, he burst into the royal presence waving aloft a silver crucifix, and in a transport of passion shouted, "Behold the Crucified Whom the accursed Judas Iscariot sold for thirty pieces of silver. Your Majesties are about to sell Him for 30,000 ducats. Here He is, take Him and sell Him. I resign my post. No one shall impute this guilt to me. You, however, shall have to answer to your God." With that he threw the crucifix at the startled monarchs and disappeared; he had triumphed and the expulsion was carried out forthwith.

Abarbanel made his way to Naples, where he languished in penury for about a year. But again he was called to serve at the court of King Ferrante as counselor and financier; but again his public career was terminated, this time by King Charles VIII of France, who conquered southern Italy in 1495. Abarbanel moved on to Corfu, then a city of the Turkish Empire, where he completed important religious works such as the *Wells of Salvation*. His mystical bent grew stronger and he looked more and more to the Kabbalah as "the bearer of Truth" and to the messianic prophecies of the Bible to bring a measure of hope to himself and his fellow exiles; he went so far as to predict that the Messiah would come in 1503. His own messianic writings were extremely influential, reverberating over the next two centuries. His last years, saddened by the failure of the Messiah to appear, he spent in Venice, one of the few remaining havens in Europe.

It is impossible, then, to narrate medieval Jewish history as anything but a nightmare of horrors—injustice, massacre, expulsion, forcible conversion, contempt, hatred. In a word, it was a perpetual state of terror, one that was not alleviated but deepened with the passage of time. The few positive elements are minuscule in comparison to the overwhelming fact that Western Europe was devoid of professing Jews by 1500 except for a few huddling communities here and there. Thus the migration of the eighth to the tenth century and after, that had carried Jews as far west as England, had been arrested and flung back. Jews streamed eastward to seek refuge in Christian Poland and the Islamic Ottoman Turkish Empire, where, after a period of autonomy and prosperity, they again suffered persecution—upon the partition of Poland and the virtual demise of the "Sick Man of Europe" in the eighteenth century.

On the positive side of the historical ledger, we have emphasized the indispensable role of Jewish scholars as cultural intermediaries. To this may be added their development of representative or parliamentary institutions of self-government and possibly some important contributions to English law. Jews throughout the middle ages and into modern times were organized along communal lines in corporate bodies. In internal matters they were permitted to govern themselves according to talmudic law, and they adapted or extended that law to fit changing social circumstances. It came to be generally agreed that such adaptation, modification, or suspension through disuse of talmudic requirements had to occur in an official gathering of rabbis, entitled a "rabbinical synod" or "parliament." At such sessions, each rabbi represented either a single community with its synagogue or a cluster of them grouped into one entity. Meetings were frequent and their scope was wide— religious and social, as well as tax assessment by order of the king. Such new regulations as those of Gershom—not to open private mail, prohibiting polygamy, etc.—became binding as legislation passed by rabbinical parliaments. The Jewish Parliament is best known for England, but similar institutions existed for France, Germany, Spain, Italy, and a famous one of a later date for Poland—"The Council of the Four Lands." In keeping with the ancient pharisaic and rabbinic tradition, the talmudic law was elaborated and extended, and this process parallels very closely the method by which modification occurs under equity or case law. As was observed in an earlier section, the idea of equity is intrinsic to Jewish legal tradition from an early period.

Apart from the importance of representative self-government and equity law within the Jewish community, Jews may have had an important influence on English government and law, and thereby on the whole of the English-speaking world. The thirteenth was the formative century for the institution which later emerged as the English Parliament, and it may well be that the Jewish Parliaments served as significant examples of a deliberative representative body, and were imitated by a king such as Edward I when he fashioned his famous "Model Parliament." Much the same kind of consideration may apply to equity law in England. With regard to English common law, an essay by J. J. Rabinowitz makes what appear to be excessive claims for Jewish influence upon it: he concludes that the common law conception of the right of judgment creditors to seize the land of forfeiting debtors (a means to ensure repayment of loans), the recognizance, the general release, warranty of real property, the Anglo-American dower, the mortgage, posting bond, trial by jury, and the idea of the supremacy of law as set forth in the celebrated Article 39 of Magna Charta stem wholly or in part from Jewish sources. It is not possible, definitively, to affirm or deny his thesis. Yet it is most suggestive to recall that the Jews of England had among themselves a highly elaborate system of civil law, including a large number of legal instruments, forms, and devices that were far more developed and mature than anything known to English lawyers and jurists of the twelfth and thirteenth centuries, the formative age of the common law. Since Jews were engaged in commercial and financial transactions, they had to possess legal instruments and modes to secure repayment of loans, etc. Such conceptions and practices they brought with them to Europe as immigrants from societies where they were long in use and considerably developed. Again, in the period under consideration, Jews frequently held high financial and administrative posts in the royal government, and, given their strategic location, it is by no means farfetched to assert that Jewish influence was paramount in the creation of similar legal modes as part of the national law. In the common law conceptions of commercial and real property, we may see the Jew functioning again as the intermediary between Europe and much more advanced societies; it is much the same role as we have seen him play in the realm of culture. As to trial by jury and the supremacy of law, they have undoubted Jewish antecedents, but others were much more decisive for English legal and constitutional evolution.

But all these are mere footnotes to what was unquestionably the greatest achievement of medieval Jews: that they endured, that they endured as a people practicing their ancient religion. In so doing they were defying every normal expectation. What enabled them to survive was faith in themselves as the Chosen People, and optimistic faith in the expected Messiah, one that was sustained by the messianic prophecies of the Bible and the doctrines of the Kabbalah. In this Abarbanel was certainly symbolic, both in his hope-sustaining faith as well as in his being overly prone to expect the Messiah in 1503 (the Jews were the victims of many false Messiahs in the sixteenth and seventeenth centuries). What nurtured and sustained that faith, above all, was a remarkable system of education in the Bible and Talmud, one that extended to all from the cradle to the grave and centered in the synagogue—it is the familiar institutional framework that, we have seen repeatedly, was vitally important for Jewish survival.

NOTES

1 A remarkable parallel to medieval Christian-Jewish relations appears in the history of Ireland during the period it was under English domination. From the English conquest in the mid-twelfth century to the reign of Henry VIII the differences between the Irish and English were no more than those of conquered versus conqueror, while the gulf separating them was largely bridged by a common religion and by frequent intermarriage. This assimilation went on despite English legislation prohibiting intermarriage and the use of Gaelic. By 1450 assimilation of the English settlers and the weakness of the English crown were so advanced that England's hold on the country, from within and without, seemed about to be broken. But the renewal of the royal power that came, as of 1485, with the Tudor dynasty, and the religious revolution that Henry VIII sought to inflict on Ireland, constitute the decisive, indeed fatal, turn in Anglo-Irish relations. Efforts to ram Anglicanism down the Irish Catholic throat were frequent and brutal, even though they stopped short of sword-point conversions. Ireland rebelled and was conquered several times over; there were punitive campaigns and massacres carried out, e.g., by Oliver Cromwell and William III; the island became a colony whose Catholic landowners were progressively displaced by English immigrants.

Political in intent as English actions and policies tended to be, they were rooted in and sprang from religious issues. In the latter part of the seventeenth century, owing to the Catholic sympathies of the Stuart kings, there was a temporary relaxation of anti-Catholic laws, and a period of *de facto* toleration set in. However, from the Revolution of 1689 onward, the "Protestant ascendancy" in Ireland can be dated, and in the century that followed the Catholic population sank to the level of pariahs. Catholicism, like Judaism in the medieval period, was not outlawed; rather it was tolerated under a system of limitations and disabilities—i.e., there were no bishops (so that ordination of new priests was impossible and the priesthood was threatened with extinction), no schools, no seminaries, etc. Catholics were likewise barred from voting, from holding any public or political office, from the professions or any lucrative occupation, and from purchasing land (they could only lease it on hard terms and for short periods).

Though the Irish Catholic wore no infamous badge, his poverty and Gaelic speech were badge enough. Moreover, there is at least one direct parallel between Jewish and Catholic Emancipation (enacted by the English Parliament in 1829): just as Mendelssohn urged his co-religionists in Germany to learn German (as opposed to Yiddish) in order to strengthen their claim to civil equality, so, too, did Daniel O'Connell, the Irish Liberator, continue to preach about the necessity for his followers to learn English. Finally, one cannot but see in the recent disturbances in Londonderry and in Northern Ireland an echo of the old religious hatred and the bondage it entailed.

2 The mass as a form of public worship followed closely the pattern of services in the synagogue; early Christian music, particularly the Gregorian chant, was modeled on the hymns of the Temple worship at Jerusalem; Jewish Christians (who were numerous and important in the early Church) persisted in the ancient tradition of the Saturday Sabbath as a day of rest, and tended to establish it as the Christian day of worship also, although the day of worship for Christians—as sanctioned by the New Testament—normally was Sunday.

3 In this connection we may note that the principal source of anti-Jewish sentiments, such as those voiced by the above-cited St. John Chrysostom, was the New Testament. In it, disparaging reference is made in several instances to people whose name is translated as "the Jews." The term seems to designate the whole people, whether construed ethnically or religiously. But there is a linguistic confusion in the New Testament usage, for actually it does not always mean the entire people. In most instances the term *Judeans* (of which *Jews* is an abbreviation) is used in contradistinction to *Galileans, Samaritans, Idumeans,* and the residents of other Roman provinces of Palestine. E.g., Jesus fled from the Judeans to the Galileans, where they "received Him" (John 4:45). Furthermore, when St. Paul wants to identify the whole people, he says: "Hath God cast away His people? God forbid. For I also am an *Israelite*" (Romans 11:1). Since there were many Jews outside of Palestine, scattered in fact all over the Roman Empire, how conceivably can they be eternally blamed for events of which they had no knowledge?

Those who are blamed in the New Testament for the

Crucifixion are the Judeans, only a segment; to biblical exegetes it is a commonplace that ordinarily *the Jews* simply means Jesus' opponents and not the whole people. Further, we learn in John 11:45 that "many of the Jews . . . believed in Him." And even if we conclude (which I do not) that the famous verse of Matthew (27:25), "His blood be upon us, and on our children," is an eternal curse upon the Judeans, it is retracted by Jesus Himself when He says, "Forgive them, for they know not what they do." For this verse, so often invoked by anti-Semites, does not in fact pronounce any such curse. The Mishnah makes quite clear the distinction in Jewish law between a trial involving capital punishment and litigation over property. Perjury in property disputes could be compensated for by payment of a fine. However, in capital cases, as a matter of procedural law, witnesses, jurors, etc., were informed that the blood of the accused would be upon them and their descendants to all time if they gave false witness and caused him to be unjustly executed. Hence when the crowd before Pontius Pilate calls out this well-worn phrase of Jewish legal parlance, it is testimony not of their guilt, but of their innocence of deicide (since they never accepted that He was God).

To me the term *deicide* is particularly loathsome, not only because it is a false accusation, but because of the history the term has had. So that I fully agree with Bishop Stephen Leven of Texas, speaking to his fellow bishops at Vatican II, when he said this term is "an infamous blasphemy that was invented by Christians for the sole purpose of bringing shame and disgrace upon the Jews. For hundreds of years, and even in our own century, Christians have flung the word 'deicide' into the faces of Jews in order to justify all kinds of excesses, and even the murder of Jews. . . . We must remove this word from the language of Christians, so that it can never again be turned against the Jews." As already suggested, those Jews involved in the Crucifixion could not possibly be guilty of deicide, since they were unaware or unconvinced that He was God ("they know not what they do"). St. Peter and St. Paul also excuse the Jews on the grounds of their ignorance of His divinity (Acts 3:17; 13:27). A further indication that Jesus' divinity was far from obvious is the bafflement of Mary and Joseph at His conduct (Luke 2:49). And lastly, we should remind ourselves also that the fundamental teaching of the Church is that Jesus came providentially into the world to atone by His death for all mankind's sins.

One final word: the New Testament presupposes a continuity

between Israel and the Christian Church. Most of the New Testament authors were Jews addressing themselves to Jews, and even when writing to the Gentiles (e.g., Paul in Galatians) the Gentile Christians are seen as children of Abraham through their union with Jesus Christ (Gal. 3:27). Equally, the Jewishness of Jesus in His human manifestation must be insisted upon. His life, teaching and preaching, His messianism and vision of the kingdom of God, will be fundamentally misconceived if interpreted apart from His background in the synagogue and Temple and His life of worship and observance of the law (which He came to fulfill and not to abrogate). While highly critical of certain Pharisees, His own viewpoint had much in common with the best elements in Pharisaism.

4 Palestinian fortunes had declined continuously since the emperor Constantine's day. Jerusalem became a Christian city, symbolized perhaps by the pilgrimage made to it by Constantine's mother, St. Helena. Our sources do not give any consecutive account, but it is clear that the much diminished Palestinian community suffered incessantly (though with a greater or lesser intensity) from forced conversions, riots, massacres, destruction of synagogues, and violent polemics. There was also some decrease in the Jewish community due to the attraction of a triumphant Christianity and to the social pressures generated in a situation where adherence to Judaism closed off all honorable careers whereas baptism opened almost all doors.

The tidal wave of persecution returned several times in the course of the seventh century, with the result that Jewish communities were so badly reduced and scattered that they might have expired altogether. This was fortunately averted by the new conditions which prevailed in the eighth century, when Jewish immigrants from Babylonia (then in its great age) inaugurated a major revival.

5 Blood accusation predates Christianity, for there were such accusations under pagan Greek governments—e.g., Alexandria.

6 For example, part of the Jewish dietary laws (*Kashrut* or Kosher) forbids the eating of meat from which the blood has not been drained. In fact, for a Jew the consumption of blood is equivalent to an act of barbarism and cannibalism.

7 The Anglican cathedral of Lincoln, England, affords another striking example of truth eventually vindicated—after seven hundred years. In 1255, when the cathedral was Catholic, a little boy named Hugh was supposedly "martyred by the Jews" to acquire his blood for ritual purposes; in 1955 the old tablet commemorating Hugh and excoriating the Jews was replaced by

a new one that reads: "Trumped-up stories of 'ritual murders' of Christian boys by Jewish communities were common throughout Europe during the Middle Ages, and even much later. These fictions cost many innocent Jews their lives. Lincoln had its own legend, and the alleged victim was buried in the cathedral. A shrine was erected above and the boy was referred to as 'little St. Hugh.' . . . Such stories do not redound to the credit of Christendom and so we pray—'Remember not Lord our offenses, nor the offenses of our forefathers.' " This action was taken before Vatican II.

8 Not only by loans, fees, mulcting, etc., but also, on the death of the Jewish financier, with or without heirs, by escheat; i.e., the debts payable to a Jewish financier became, on his decease, payable to the crown. Thus when Aaron of Lincoln, the wealthiest Anglo-Jewish moneylender of the age, died in 1186, debts owed to him reverted to the king, who set up a special exchequer (*scaccarium Aaronis*) that took twenty years to collect all the monies. Aaron was in part the model for "Isaac the Jew" in Sir Walter Scott's sympathetic and essentially accurate rendering of Jewish life in twelfth-century England in *Ivanhoe*.

9 Such attitudes gave rise to an astoundingly jaundiced conception of Spanish history and culture, which had to exhibit "purity" also. Indeed it is only relatively recently that Spanish scholars, such as Professor Américo Castro, have begun to recognize the magnitude and profound significance of the Jewish-Marranic (and also the Moorish) contribution to almost every aspect of Spanish life, throughout the middle ages and until well after the Reconquest had ended.

6. The Early Modern Period

THE RENAISSANCE was one of the most seminal ages in world history. Its greatest triumphs came in the realms of art and scholarship. Extending from 1350 to 1550, the age has been characterized by its greatest historian, Jacob Burckhardt, as urban, commercial, and lay rather than ecclesiastical and feudal. True, it was clearly a Christian, not a pagan era. Nevertheless, its humanist ideal of classical civilization as a model for imitation in many aspects of the life of that day made it a significant rival of Christian civilization. For, with the Renaissance, there came an end to the almost complete cultural and intellectual allegiance to the Church and to the Faith of even the most powerful and original minds, an allegiance that had lasted for a millennium and more.

One of the central ideas of the Renaissance was a concept of natural religion (Nicholas Cusanus, for example, sought a concord of all faiths, claiming that there was "one religion with many manifestations"). In other words, Jew, Moslem, and Christian all worship the same God, the differences among them being only in expression and form. Thus the characteristic spirit of the Renaissance was tolerance of differences, coupled to a curiosity about all things.

Such an outlook could not but improve the status of the

Jew and give rise to a more appreciative attitude toward Judaism. The popes took the lead in this by ignoring or softening ecclesiastical legislation with regard to Jews. Not infrequently, Jews were dispensed from wearing the pariah insignia and, the age-old prohibition notwithstanding, a galaxy of eminent Jewish physicians began to serve popes, ecclesiastics, princes, nobles, and townsmen.

But this is only part of the story. For one of the most striking characteristics of the Renaissance was the degree to which the Jews attained an optimum synthesis of their ancient way of life with the culture of the host environment. Thus, in addition to achieving fame as physicians, Jews participated in all the manifold activities of this era. They wrote and produced dramas, compiled scientific and philological treatises, composed music, and played an important role in scholarly publishing and printing, etc. Characteristically, these same individuals were also active as rabbis, biblical and talmudic scholars, and religious Hebrew poets. Ghetto walls did not go down, it is true, but they did not prevent the Jew from remaining faithful to his religion and at the same time engaging in the pursuits of the Renaissance man, scholar, and artist. In short, although it was more limited in time and space, the symbiotic relationship of Jews to the Renaissance surpassed the one achieved previously with Islam.

Italy

It should be pointed out, however, that the Renaissance into which Jews entered so freely and so creatively was confined essentially to northern and central Italy (its home and citadel), and fell within the time span stretching from the end of the fourteenth to the mid-sixteenth century. In France and in England there were, of course, no Jews to participate in the Renaissance, while in the Iberian peninsula anything but the Renaissance spirit of toleration pre-vailed. Germany, too, remained a land of persecution, whereas Poland—the principal home of European Jewry—was relatively untouched by the Renaissance movement.

Jewish communities in the Po Valley and Tuscany dated from a relatively late period. One of the principal centers was Ferrara, ruled by the Este dukes, who invited Jewish refugees from Germany, Spain, Portugal, and southern Italy to settle there as financial agents. Ferrara was surpassed, however, by Mantua. There, under the Gonzaga dukes, Jews were first invited in about 1460 to function as pawn-brokers and, as elsewhere, became the nucleus of the com-munity. They were soon followed by traders, metalsmiths, and many others. If Jewish writers referred to Mantua as "the joyous city," it was because Jewish participation in the life of the court, in Hebrew and humanist scholarship, as well as in music, dance, and theatrical productions reached its peak there—particularly in the early sixteenth century when the bluestocking duchess of Ferrara, Isabella d'Este, presided over its court. It was in Mantua, also, that the first of several Italian Jews was ennobled, and that a proj-ect was undertaken in the 1560's to establish a Jewish university, one that would combine the traditional talmudic approach of the academies with the humanistic scholarship of the Renaissance. (Though the project had ducal ap-proval and was launched, it ultimately became a casualty of the Counter-Reformation.)

Both Mantua and Ferrara were centers of Italian drama and the former, in particular, drew freely upon the talents of Jewish actors and producers. Much the same applied to music and dancing, for, in keeping with the classical tradi-tion, they were taken to be basic to a true education and, therefore, there were numerous Jewish teachers and practi-tioners of these arts at the Mantuan court. Certainly this was true of opera, a Renaissance creation, and a field in which Jews contributed significantly (e.g., the epoch-making productions at Mantua of Monteverdi's *Orfeo* and *Arianna* in the early seventeenth century). Finally, it was in Mantua, too, that the first Jewish impresario appears, Leone de'Somni Portaleone. Portaleone, who had learned the dramatic arts in an amateur company of Jewish players which gave performances of religious dramas (Purim plays), subsequently entered the service of the duke as playwright and director. In this role he presented his own works in the ducal palace with a remarkable company of Jewish actors and singers, and became an honored member of the court and a noted figure of his age.

Several themes of the Renaissance—the eminence of Mantua's Jews, the assimilation of Jews into the Renaissance environment, the mutual regard and reciprocal influence of Christian and Jewish thinkers—are well illustrated by the career of the Jewish historical scholar, Azariah dei Rossi (1514–1578), author of *Meor Eynayim*, or *Enlightenment of the Eyes*. A citizen of Mantua, he was the first Jewish thinker since Philo in the first century to go beyond the bounds of the Jewish cultural tradition and to use non-Jewish sources (the accounts of the classical historians, among others) in the interpretation of Jewish ones. His book, which was published in Mantua in 1573, breathes the spirit of free inquiry and, to a considerable degree, accepts a secularist interpretation of certain events. He disposed, for example, of a lot of myths—such as the death of the emperor Titus owing to a gnat entering his brain on the way from Jerusalem to Rome—by applying the humanistic historical canons of verification and textual evaluation. This was too much for many of the Jewish leaders of his day, who, contrary to Rossi's Renaissance spirit of innovation, embodied something of the Counter-Reformation's spirit of censorship. The work was generally condemned by the rabbinate and had very little impact on Jewish thought; it marks at once the high point and the end of Jewish participation in the Renaissance. On the other hand it quickly became a basic work to Christian students of Jewish history. (Rossi's new approach to Jewish studies was vindicated at last in the nineteenth century, when a school of German Jewish scholars, led by Leopold Zunz, republished the *Meor Eynayim* and began where Rossi had left off; their conceptions—and with them Rossi's—dominate the study of Jewish history to this day.)

In Florence, where the Medici adhered to an ideal of toleration, Jews were to be found after 1434. The Medici were typical of Renaissance princes in the lengths to which they went to establish a Jewish community of pawnbrokers and small loan bankers—a popular policy calculated to conciliate the poorer citizens.

Among the oldest communities were those at Pisa and Siena, while one of the most attractive centers was at Urbino in the court of the Montefeltro dukes, who were among the most enlightened patrons of art and literature. The ducal library, including a great many Hebrew manuscripts, became the core of the Vatican collection when the duchy was annexed by the papacy in the sixteenth century.

The Jewish community at Rome dated from antiquity, but other large communities were to be found in the Papal States at Ancona and Bologna. Once the Great Schism was healed by the Council of Constance, the papacy put itself at the head of the humanist movement and, under the Medici popes Leo X (1513–1521) and Clement VII (1523–1534), the patronage of Jewish scholars and the encouragement of Christian Hebraists reached its height.

Venice was famous for its Jewish colony, dating from about 1500 and lasting until the eighteenth century, as an island of tolerance. Though it is true that the term *ghetto*[1] is of Venetian provenance (it refers to the decree of 1516 which concentrated Jews in the area of the new foundry, or *geto nuovo*), nevertheless, the ghetto walls of that city were less of a barrier than any others to assimilation. Similarly, in the harsh period of reaction under the Counter-Reformation papacy, traditional Venetian anti-clericalism was strong enough to preserve an exceptional climate of freedom in which Jews and Christians could intermingle. Venice also remained the great center for the publication of Hebrew books, while Padua (which it controlled) was the site of the greatest Renaissance university, in which Jews were to be found not only as students, but also as professors.

Development of the Hebrew Renaissance

In an important sense the Renaissance flowering was the fruition of the scholarly enterprises which occurred in southern Italy and Sicily, Provence, and Spain. The first phase, reaching its zenith in the twelfth century, was a Latin Renaissance whose characteristic endeavor was the translation of classical and other manuscripts from Arabic and Hebrew into Latin—a process in which Jewish scholars and translators functioned as indispensable cultural intermediaries. The second was the Greek (or Hellenic) Renaissance, in which Christian scholars were no longer content with translations, but went back to the Greek originals. Since very few Jews had any knowledge of Greek, they played only a small role in this phase, and only a few Jewish scholars appear now and again on the scene.

There is a further explanation of this phenomenon that should be noted. Whereas Christians had gone to school with Jewish masters in the Latin Renaissance, in the Greek sequel the reverse was true. The reason for this is that in the earlier period a Jew who sought a scholar's education went to synagogal schools and academies, which were far superior to Christian institutions. By the fourteenth century, however, this was no longer true and Jews increasingly began to seek entrance to Christian universities (the earliest record of a Jew taking his doctorate is at Padua in 1409). Thus, while having had a decisive role in educating Christian society up to his own level, the Jewish scholar came now to play a more passive one during the Greek Renaissance.

Side by side with the Greek was a Hebrew Renaissance. In the humanists' view there were three "sacred" languages —Latin, Greek, and Hebrew. It is true that the study of Hebrew—the language as well as its great corpus of writings —was pursued as an adjunct to biblical studies, especially north of the Alps. But in Italy the interests of the humanists were not confined to exegesis and theology. Instead, they began to study Hebrew literature and history for their own sake, and Jewish studies soon became a branch of the humanistic curriculum and the "new learning." Indeed, it was the Renaissance humanists who propounded the concept that our Western civilization is fundamentally a fusion of the Hebraic and Hellenic heritages.

Jewish teachers of Hebrew now emerged as a professional class. For example, Elias Levita (1468–1549) was the outstanding teacher of Hebrew of his day. Aside from writing poetry—*de rigueur* for the Renaissance scholar—he compiled a reference guide for the Talmud. So great was his reputation, in fact, that Francis I of France invited him to hold the chair of Hebrew studies at the University of Paris, but he refused this remarkable offer on the grounds that his co-religionists continued to be excluded from France. Yet, although Jewish savants such as Levita contributed to the Hebrew Renaissance as teachers of Hebrew and as authors of grammars, learned prolegomena, and commentaries, the movement was essentially the achievement of Christian scholars. One such figure was the German Cardinal Nicholas Cusanus (1401–1464), who moved in humanist circles in Rome, had a smattering of Hebrew, and was familiar with the Kabbalah, which he compounded with Platonic mysticism to form a theory of religious toleration.

Another was the Florentine humanist Gianozzo Manetti (1396–1459), who learned both Hebrew and Greek from servants he kept in his house, and became secretary to Pope Nicholas V, who commissioned his translation of the Psalms. Otherwise, the chief use Manetti made of his Hebrew learning was to write a tract against the Jews (reversing Cusanus, who was tolerant in theory but not in practice).

But the outstanding figure of the Hebrew Renaissance was the celebrated Count Giovanni Pico della Mirandola (1463–1494). As a student in Padua, he had heard the lectures of the gifted Jewish scholar Elijah del Medigo, who was an exponent of Aristotle and Averroës. They became fast friends, with Pico commissioning Elijah to do an extensive series of translations of Aristotle and Averroës into Latin. When Pico went to Florence, he had his ex-teacher join him there to translate a whole library of philosophical works, particularly those of a Platonic and Neoplatonic nature.

While in Florence, Pico was a member of the celebrated Platonic Academy, presided over by Lorenzo the Magnificent, and including the famous translator of Plato's whole corpus of writings, Marsilius Ficino. Many discourses went on there among a circle of participants that included the famous Jewish poet and mystical writer, Judah Abarbanel (1460–1530), usually cited as Leone Ebreo, and author of a profoundly influential work of philosophy, the Platonic *Dialogues of Love*. Probably the best expression of the intellectual and aesthetic spirit of the Florentine Academy, the *Dialogues* have as a main theme the idea of "Platonic love"—the phrase was coined by Ficino. The work went through many editions and translations, and influenced a host of contemporary and later thinkers, Christian and Jewish, among whom Spinoza—with his doctrine of "the intellectual love of God"—was the greatest. What a melting pot the Academy was!

Pico and his colleagues brought to the Academy a rich bouquet of profound scholarship and recondite lore drawn from Plato, Plotinus, Hermes Trismegismus, numerous Arabic writers, the Scholastics, and, above all, the Kabbalah. It all finds expression in Pico's nine hundred theses, with its famous preface "On the Dignity of Man," particularly in such theses as: "There is no science that can more firmly convince us of the divinity of Christ than magic and Kabbalah," or "In the Kabbalah I find what I find in Paul; in the Kabbalah I hear the voice of Plato—that strong bulwark of the Christian faith. There is, in short, no subject of controversy between Church and Synagogue but finds the support for our Christian side in these books." Pico was also familiar with Maimonides, the Midrash, and the Talmud, made several translations from Hebrew and Aramaic, and, more than anyone else, was responsible for making Hebraic learning an indispensable part of the humanist's equipment and of the humanistic curriculum.

The Reformation

In 1490 Pico had a conversation with the German humanist Johannes Reuchlin (1455–1522), imbuing him with an enthusiasm for Hebraic studies. This meeting was of cardinal importance, for in Reuchlin's subsequent career we may see the profound significance the Hebrew Renaissance was to have for the Protestant Reformation. Reuchlin not only proceeded to master Hebrew under the tutelage of the rabbi and physician Obadiah Sforno (recommended to him in that age of easy social intercourse by Cardinal Grimani) and publish a pioneer Hebrew grammar and dictionary, but he immersed himself in the Kabbalah and Talmud. His *De Verbo Mirifico* is a dialogue among a Jewish scholar, a Christian savant, and a Greek philosopher in which the first of the three gets the best of the argument.

Reuchlin also dedicated himself to biblical exegesis as inspired by the Kabbalah, but he rendered scriptural passages so extravagantly that he fell into endless controversy with Johannes Pfefferkorn, a converted Jew of Cologne. The ultimate result was that Pfefferkorn, who wanted to fan anew all the fires of persecution by banning the practice of interest-taking, forced conversions, and the consigning to the flames of all Jewish books except the Bible, brought charges of heresy against the humanist and sought to hail him before a court of the Inquisition. Reuchlin ably defended himself and the cause of Hebraic studies in what soon became a classic battle of the books. Practically all the humanists rallied to his support, and he published their pledges in his *Letters of Eminent Men.* (A clever gambit of Reuchlin's friends was the publication of *Letters of Obscure Men,* a work which purported to be the letters of Reuchlin's antagonists, but which actually was a satire of his clerical opponents' intellectual inadequacies, foul motives, and evil lives.) In the midst of these proceedings Reuchlin, undaunted, published his *De Arte Kabbalistica,* dedicating it to Pope Leo X; it is a dialogue that brings a Jew, Moslem, and Greek together, and whose conclusion is that the Kabbalah is the oldest revelation proffered to man.

Reuchlin sought to have his case, the *cause célèbre* of the time, adjudicated in his bishop's court rather than in the Inquisition's, and to make his final appeal to the papal curia at Rome. With this in mind he wrote a long and famous letter to Pope Leo X's Jewish physician, Bonnes de Lattes, pleading for his assistance. There is no better symbol of the toleration and acceptance of Jews during the Renaissance than the fact that a Christian scholar, writing in Hebrew, should request a Jewish savant to intercede in his behalf with the supreme head of Christendom. Reuchlin was ultimately reprieved, but not before the sense of outrage at ecclesiastical abuses had greatly deepened in Germany. Above all, he was the Pico of the north and imparted a strong impulse to Hebraic studies. We may note that his younger contemporary Erasmus thought that "a fair knowledge of Latin, Greek, and Hebrew is of course the first thing," although he himself never mastered Hebrew; he was, however, the spiritual father of the Collegium Trilingue of Louvain, where provision was made for the humanist study of the three "sacred" languages. By such works, as Garrett Mattingly put it, "Erasmus laid the egg that Luther hatched."

One of Reuchlin's students was his nephew, Philipp Melanchthon, who in turn was the chief lieutenant of Martin Luther. With Luther we are brought foursquare with the Reformation. Luther had a knowledge of Hebrew, but his debt to Jewish scholarship was more profound than that fact implies. For he was greatly influenced in his biblical exegesis (and so, too, the whole course of his movement) by the medieval Christian scholar Nicholas of Lyra (1279–1340), a man of whom a limerick had it that "If Lyra had not piped, Luther had not danced." Lyra was almost unique among medieval Christian scholars in that he knew Hebrew, had studied the Talmud, and in his own exegesis of the Bible stressed the literal meaning and followed Rashi so closely, translating him word by word, that he was called "Rashi's ape."

Luther himself was initially attracted to the Jews and, like Mohammed, expected to convert them wholesale. In fact, he castigated "popes, bishops, sophists, and monks" as "coarse blockheads" who did "nothing but curse Jews and seize their wealth," as well as advising and begging "everybody to deal kindly with the Jews" and "to allow them to compete with us in earning a living." But, twenty years later, disappointed in his expectations, he turned on them with a savage fury (again much like Mohammed). "What shall we Christians do with this damned, rejected race?" he then asked. The answer: burn their synagogues, homes, and books; forbid their rabbis to teach; not allow them to travel; compel them to renounce banking and finance and earn their living "by the sweat of their noses"; but, really to resolve the matter, let them be expelled as "France, Spain [and] Bohemia" had done. Moreover, this diatribe was couched in the most vituperative language, and stands unique in the corpus of anti-Semitic writings until one comes to the Nazis.

For some time there was a danger that the German princes would follow Luther's injunction. (The Lutheran princes of Saxony and Brandenburg did, in fact, expel their Jews.) One reason that a general expulsion did not materialize was that Josel of Rosheim, a Jewish leader of Alsace, was successful in intervening with the princes as well as Emperor Charles V, who granted a charter renewing many Jewish privileges. Nonetheless, Luther left his mark, in that the Lutheran states adopted and strenuously enforced a whole battery of Catholic legislation confining Jews to ghettos, requiring the wearing of the yellow badge, etc.

Other Reformation leaders besides Luther who were schooled in Hebrew include John Calvin, a profound and exacting Hebraist (a fact that is especially noticeable in his voluminous Old Testament exegeses), and Ulrich Zwingli, an outstanding classicist and student of the religious and philosophical speculations of Pico.

With the seventeenth-century Buxtorf family—a dynasty of professors of Bible and Talmud, of Hebrew, Aramaic, and Chaldaic, over three or four generations at the University of Basle—we come to the formal establishment in the universities of rabbinic and talmudic studies as an academic discipline. This is the high tide of the Hebrew Renaissance.

The Counter-Reformation

We can see, then, in both the Renaissance and Reformation a recognition—at least in part—of Western Christian civilization's Judaic patrimony. At the same time, both movements opened vistas of toleration and perhaps even emancipation. Yet neither the Renaissance nor the Reformation was without the stain of persecution, and in many ways Protestantism actually appears to have been an unmitigated disaster for Jews—as we have seen in Germany. Moreover, the Reformation gave rise to the Counter-Reformation, which meant that the Church, challenged as never before, went on the defensive and became extremely distrustful and intolerant. Beginning in the mid-sixteenth century, Jewish books, by papal command, began again to be severely censored and the Talmud repeatedly went up in flames—just as though Reuchlin had never lived. The popes revived the old anti-Jewish legislation and enforced it to the hilt; the infamous badge reappeared; Jews in the Papal States were expelled from all the various towns and herded together in the ghetto at Rome (at one point a pope was on the verge of extinguishing even that ancient community); there was a recrudescence of forced conversions, blood accusations, Host desecrations, and massacres, etc. By 1600 this renewed vindictiveness had made its way into every corner of Italy and with the exception only of Venice—but that a notable one—an iron curtain was rung down, closing out the Renaissance. In the bloody and prolonged slugfests that followed between Catholic and Protestant powers, toleration became a luxury which neither side could allow itself, with the result that Jews for a time fared equally badly in all camps.

In spite of all this, however, recognition such as Luther's that Judaism has "a strong Scriptural basis" and that "Christianity is nonsense without Biblical support" ultimately made possible a more tolerant disposition, once the immediate stress of danger and fear had passed. Thus, the seventeenth-century Calvinists of Holland as well as the Puritans of England were avid readers of the Old Testament, named their children after its heroes, and guided their lives by its precepts; and it was these Bible-reading cultures that first granted refuge and then full toleration to all Jews to practice their religion and to enjoy many civil rights. And among these Jews were, most notably, the Marranos.

The Marranos

The history of the Marranos constitutes a veritable diaspora within the Diaspora. Expelled or having fled from the Iberian peninsula, they made their way, as we have seen, to Islamic societies in Morocco or Egypt, to the Turkish Empire, to Italy, England, France, the Lowlands, Germany, and the New World. In the Ottoman Turkish Empire (a purely military-agricultural society) they encountered the warmest welcome, where, owing to their talents, they flourished as "court Jews," civil servants, lawyers, physicians, diplomats, and entered all the economic occupations. With its thirty thousand Jews, Salonika became a new "Mecca" for them, and so, too, Smyrna and Constantinople. Freedom of worship and extensive self-government were undoubtedly theirs, despite occasional outbursts of fanaticism; for, so important were they to the functioning and well-being of the Empire, that so long as the Empire endured, they enjoyed genuine rights. Only in the eighteenth century, when the Turkish state became "the Sick Man of Europe," did persecution raise its ugly head again and cause Jews to flee in great numbers.

Palestine under the Turkish Empire

Palestine was a province of the Turkish Empire, and so happy were the relations between the Jews and the sultans that the centuries-old process of emigration and depopulation was reversed, and the sixteenth century saw a considerable increase in the number of Jews residing in their ancient homeland. As an example of what we may call practical Zionism, Joseph Nasi (nephew of famed Gracia Nasi), who was a Marrano banker, fled from the Portuguese "iron furnace" and obtained the sultan's permission to rebuild from its ruins the ancient city of Tiberias as a Jewish city-state. Joseph eventually rose to so high a position under the Turkish sultan that he virtually became the ruler of the Empire. He was made duke of Naxos and used his great influence and wealth to assist his people, as he had already done in the Tiberias project.

A mystical rather than practical Zionism centered at Safed in Galilee. Another of the Jewish colonies that grew up in the sixteenth century, it is remembered for its messianic leader, Isaac Luria, "the Lion of the Kabbalah" (1534–1572). Luria lived the life of a hermit, concentrating on messianism, mystical experience, asceticism, repentance, and ethical good. Inspired by the Kabbalah, his complex doctrines had a great appeal to his many followers —most of whom were Marranos—since it offered them a respite from their torments with its promise of an imminent coming of the Messiah. Safed was famous in this time also as the home of Joseph Karo, whose family was expelled from Spain in 1492. A follower of Luria, he is remembered for his codification of talmudic law, the *Shulhan Aruch*, a work that is still relied upon as an authoritative guide.

Italy

A mark of the degree of Jewish assimilation and semi-emancipation during this noontide period of the Renaissance is to find that, in Italy, Zionism commanded very little interest. Thus, for example, when asked to aid a concrete Zionist project, an influential Italian banker, Ishmael da Rieti, replied, "I have no desire for Jerusalem; I have no desire or affection except for my city of Siena." On the other hand, the vast majority of Jews, particularly the Marranos, suffered enormously, and for them Kabbalah and Zionism had a profound appeal.

Renaissance Italy had an obvious attraction for the Marranos, and they settled there in great numbers. The benevolent policy of the Este dukes soon made Ferrara a principal Marrano center, and Marranos contributed greatly to its cultural flowering. In 1581, however, papal pressure compelled the duke to accede to the punitive ecclesiastical policies of the Counter-Reformation. Accordingly, there were arrests and burnings at the stake until the community was finally broken up. Survivors from Ferrara and elsewhere in Italy made their way to Venice, the one haven during the storms of the Counter-Reformation. True, until the mid-sixteenth century, Venice had officially pursued an anti-Jewish policy of its own, expelling its Marranos in the 1490's and again in 1550. Thereafter, though, the Venetian Senate recognized that there might be solid benefits in terms of trade and finance if Marranos were admitted, and so decided to open wide its doors to them. The city of the lagoons adhered without interruption to its tolerant (and profitable) policy, and by the seventeenth century its ghetto had become a byword for economic well-being and cultural attainments. Venice long remained the capital of the Marrano dispersion and was perhaps the first settlement where they could openly return to their religion. The friar and anti-papalist historian of the Council of Trent, Paolo Sarpi, typified the Venetian attitude when he asserted that the Marranos were not Christians, because forced conversion was invalid, and, therefore, Inquisitorial proceedings could not be instituted against them if they reverted to Judaism—no matter how many generations had passed since their forbears' forcible baptism.

The grand dukes of Tuscany—the Medici rulers of Florence and its extensive territories—did not take long to note the profits that Venetian acceptance of the Marranos brought to the state treasury, and one of them decided to gain the same advantages by converting Pisa and Leghorn into free ports and inviting Jews, particularly Marranos, to settle there. Charters promising self-government and immunity to "Inquisition, Visitation, Denunciation or Accusation" were issued by him, which his successors adhered to faithfully. The result was that both towns grew enormously. From a fishing village of a few souls Leghorn, for example, became an important industrial, commercial, and financial center, while its religious and intellectual life flourished remarkably for the next two centuries. No ghetto was established there for its seven thousand Jews (nor, for that matter, at Pisa), so that when Napoleon's armies swooped into Italy, it was the one town where they found no walls and gates to smash down.

France

In France, Marrano settlements were to be found at Bayonne, Rouen, and Bordeaux where, as early as 1474 and throughout the sixteenth century, royal charters granted "foreign merchants" extensive commercial and civil rights. Since the laws of expulsion still stood in France, such charters were given to Marranos as Christians, and not as Jews. On the other hand, there was no Inquisition to haunt them, so that, while they necessarily continued external conformity, the Marranos could revert more and more openly to their ancient beliefs and rituals. There were places, of course, where anti-Jewish murmurings and occasional outbursts of fanaticism occurred. Rouen's community, for example, was a casualty of one such outbreak and was destroyed. Those Jews who managed to survive fled either to the Lowlands or to Hamburg.

Apart from their economic activity and the dividends that accrued as a result to the national treasury, the Marranos also leavened French cultural and intellectual life. Mention may be made here of the fact that the immortal Montaigne had a Marrano mother, and that included among the many famous Marrano physicians was Jean-Baptiste de Silva, rector of the University of Paris' medical school and physician to Louis XV.

Germany

One of the great ports in northern Europe, the Free Imperial City of Hamburg, which looms so large in Sombart's theories on the origins of capitalism, followed no official policy of encouraging Marranos (who were ostensibly Catholics) ; however, it did recognize their value to its economic life and, therefore, if only passively, tolerated their presence. By 1575 the Marrano group was sizable and significant in the city's commerce, and during the next half century introduced colonial trade in cotton, spices, and tobacco, as well as being prominent in the founding of the great Bank of Hamburg. Simultaneously, they began to throw off their Christian disguise and to espouse Judaism more openly. In 1612 Hamburg's Senate, petitioned to expel the Jews, decided instead to permit them to reside there. Additional concessions continued to be granted, and in 1650 freedom of worship, public and private, was achieved. Hamburg's Jewish community flourished there-

after as no other in Germany, setting an example of enlightened treatment of Jews for certain German princes of
a later day.

The Netherlands

The Marrano community in the Netherlands dates from
the early sixteenth century. (In 1512 the Mendes family,
Portuguese Marrano bankers, established at Antwerp what
soon became their main office.) For the Spanish Marranos
in particular, the Netherlands was a natural place to seek
refuge, since it was ruled by the Spanish Habsburgs, the
Inquisition was not established there, and commercial opportunities were great—Antwerp being the greatest European port outside the Mediterranean. In 1537, just as the
Portuguese Inquisition was getting into high gear, the emperor Charles V granted a charter permitting New Christians to settle in Antwerp and enjoy full rights. Boatloads
of Marranos made their way from Spain and Portugal and,
within a decade, the port had become a great Marrano
center. But with this development, there also came persecution and threats of expulsion. In 1549 and again in
1550, even though the Christian merchant leaders of the
city resisted his intention, Charles V issued an edict requiring all Marranos of less than five years' residence to de-
part. One consequence was that the entire Mendes family,
who had used their great resources to assist Marranos to flee
from Iberia and had converted the Lowlands into a great
escape route, suddenly fled to Turkey.[2] This was the limit
of the Marranos' difficulties, although their situation remained uneasy and perilous.

It is no surprise, then, that with the Dutch Revolt of
1567 the Marranos found themselves hearty supporters of
the insurgents who were trying to gain independence from
Spain. Antwerp was sacked and it declined rapidly there-

after as a commercial center, but eventually the Northern Provinces emerged as Holland, becoming independent *de facto* by 1600. (The Southern Provinces, which included Antwerp, were retained by Spain but passed to Austria a century later.)

The seventeenth century was the great age of Holland. A Calvinist society, it was animated by great zeal, and built up an extensive mercantile and colonial empire in two generations. Amsterdam ousted Antwerp as the Venice of the North and the Dutch went from triumph to triumph. To this achievement (as is indicated in the chapter on economic history), the Marranos contributed significantly.

Inevitably it came to the attention of the authorities in Amsterdam that there were "Papists" in their Calvinist midst, and this led to the arrest of a large group of Marranos while they were privately conducting a solemn Jewish ceremony. Their leader made an appeal, in Latin, stating that the Inquisition harried them more ferociously than it did Calvinists and that the presence of the Marranos could be a great asset to the economic life of the city. This argument won the day and the Marrano settlement was duly authorized. The first Jewish congregation was inaugurated and synagogues began to be built. A splendid one, which still stands, was constructed in Amsterdam in 1675, a fitting symbol of the happiness, toleration, and prosperity which Marranos had enjoyed there since 1615 when, following a recommendation of the celebrated jurist and classical scholar, Hugo Grotius, the Dutch government formally granted asylum and freedom of religion to Jewish settlers.

Intellectual life also flourished in "the Dutch Jerusalem," particularly in the person of its most famous son and one of the greatest philosophers of all time, Benedict Spinoza (1632–1677). Spinoza was well educated in Latin, the Greek classics, and Descartian science as well as in the Bible, Talmud, and earlier Jewish philosophers (especially

Maimonides, who seems to have left him more "perplexed" than "guided"). However, owing to his rigorously rationalist biblical exegesis, he was eventually excommunicated by the synagogal leaders of the community, who seemed to fear that any scandal in their midst would bring the Dutch authorities down on their heads. Whether or not it was that they were unwilling to take any risks, or that a touch of the Inquisition got into them, a famous painting by Hirzenberg clearly shows that they were appalled by the young man's iconoclasm and heterodoxies.

A lovable human being in his personal relations, Spinoza lived a secluded life, earning a living as a lens grinder. Excommunicated though he was, his outlook, nevertheless, remained essentially Jewish, as in his belief that religion requires charity and ethical conduct far more than it does strict adherence to doctrine. At the same time, his influence on science has been profound and his reputation as a philosopher has steadily grown. As for his co-religionists' fears, they never materialized. What limitations remained were comparatively minor, such as prohibition of marriage with Christians, or attacks on the Calvinist Reformed Church. Indeed, the community flourished to such a degree that, by 1700, Amsterdam boasted four thousand Jewish families, renowned for their piety, energy, learning, and prosperity. So matters went until the fatal 1940's.

England

Marranos made their way to England in the early sixteenth century, where they were to be found as representatives of the great Marrano banking firm of Mendes at Antwerp. This bank became the principal agent of Henry VIII in making foreign loans, and at least once he intervened with Spain in behalf of a more tolerant treatment of Marranos. Elizabeth I was equally permissive and many, if small, crypto-Jewish communities were to be found in England by the time of the Armada. Thereafter, these settlements languished and died out, owing largely to the fears set off by the trial and execution of Roderigo Lopez. A leader of the English Marranos and physician to Elizabeth, he fell afoul of the Earl of Essex, who had him brought to trial on charge of plotting to poison the Queen. (The subsequent uproar found echo in Shakespeare's *Merchant of Venice.*)

Yet, half a century later, it is already possible to speak of English philo-Semitism. English Puritanism generated an Old-Testament-reading culture to such a degree that some Englishmen were accused of "judaizing," while others went to Amsterdam in significant numbers to enter the Jewish community there as proselytes. According to prophecy, some Puritan sects expected the second advent of Jesus once Jews were scattered over the entire world: on the supposition that the American Indians were descendants of the Ten Lost Tribes, they concluded that England alone was devoid of Jews and were, therefore, anxious to invite them. Though these religious motives certainly inspired Oliver Cromwell, who took the initiative with regard to the Marranos, he was equally animated by imperial and economic motives. Cromwell has been called "the first Englishman to think imperially," and in the commercial and colonial rivalry with Holland, he was quick to see the advantage to England of Marrano energy, expertise, and capital.

Hence when Rabbi Menasseh ben Israel (1604–1657), the leader of Dutch Jewry, an illustrious scholar and teacher of Spinoza, came to England in 1655 to petition the Lord Protector for the readmission of Jews, he was well received. But Cromwell could not induce his followers to accede to his wishes; so, after much theological and mercantile objection had been voiced, he simply and informally invited Jews to come and settle, to practice

Judaism freely, and to be assured of his protection. Since nothing was put in writing and no laws were passed, Menasseh went home dejected, thinking he had failed. Yet this illogical English compromise worked out for the best; for, when the monarchy was restored and everything Cromwell had done was undone by Charles II, there was nothing formal to undo with regard to the Jews. Moreover, as an impecunious prince in exile, the new king had been assisted by Amsterdam Marranos. The result was that, when he was petitioned to expel them, he granted them instead a charter of protection in 1664, and another in 1673, guaranteeing freedom of worship. After the Revolution of 1688–1689, the Dutch William III became king and was quick to confirm and extend Jewish privileges and to place a few Marranos in his service as "court Jews."

Thus London took its place beside Venice, Amsterdam, Hamburg, and Leghorn as a Marrano center; if anything, the status of Marranos in England was better than anywhere else. Disabilities were few and unimportant, and even the unequal taxation that made them so profitable a source of income in other countries was practically unknown. The English attitude toward Jews is summarized by Cromwell's contemporary, the political philosopher Thomas Hobbes, who was no Puritan or even religious: "If the human being were truly humane, there would be no Jewish problem." In short, the presence of Jews in England remained unquestioned, their rights tended to be enhanced rather than impaired, and their acceptance and assimilation went so far as to confer social equality upon them and to pave the way for their political emancipation in the nineteenth century.

From the above review, it can be seen that the Marrano dispersion in Europe was vast. Scandinavian kings sought to induce them, with some success, to settle in their domains as commercial and financial agents. Similarly, a handful of them were to be found in Vienna, in Russia, and even as far off as India. Of special interest was their settlement in Ireland, where evidence of their presence is manifest in such modern-day Irish names as Cohan (Cohen) and Dunleavy (Levy), although not every Dunleavy is of Marrano origin, since the name can also be traced back to twelfth-century Ireland.

The New World

Marranos were the first Jews to make their way to the New World. Whether Columbus was or was not of Jewish extraction cannot be established, though the tenor of historical scholarship would indicate that he was not. At any rate, Marranos as financiers contributed greatly to his expedition, as well as encouragers of his plans (since they were still in high places in the government and at the court), as authoritative sources of astronomical, navigational, and geographical information, and even as crewmen. Marranos were quick to see in the American colonies a possible place of refuge from the Inquisition, and they emigrated in great numbers from both Spain and Portugal. Unfortunately, though, the Inquisition was not long in pursuing them there, and in 1520 we find a Marrano, Hernando Alonso, who accompanied Cortez on his expedition in 1519, among the first victims in the New World to be burned at the stake.

Though Spanish policy sought to prevent Marranos from going overseas, the prohibition was not very effectively enforced and occasionally the ban was lifted altogether. Portugal followed an opposite policy, encouraging Marrano emigration, while making deportation a characteristic sentence of the Inquisition for those not condemned to the stake. By the end of the sixteenth century great numbers of Marranos were to be found in Portuguese Brazil, Spanish Mexico, Peru, and a few in the Philippines. They played important roles in the commerce of both empires and were engaged, it was noted by a contemporary, in the export-import of everything "from brocade to sackcloth, and from diamonds to cumin seeds." But, in reverting wholesale to their ancient beliefs and practices, they brought the Inquisition down upon themselves. In 1571 Philip II established a new arm of the Inquisition in Mexico City, where Marranos were especially numerous, and somewhat later still another tentacle appeared in Peru. As a result, by 1650, Marranism was practically expunged from the Spanish colonies.

No separate branch of the Inquisition was established in Brazil. Nonetheless, Marranos were harassed there by the bishop, who was armed with inquisitional powers, and were frequently arrested, fined huge sums, sent back to Portugal for trial, etc. It is not surprising, therefore, that in the early seventeenth century, when the Dutch tried to conquer Brazil, Marranos in that country as well as in Holland were eager supporters of the Dutch scheme. Dutch efforts made some headway, and each time a town capitulated, the victorious Dutch commander offered protection and religious liberty to all who accepted Dutch rule.

The most interesting case is the city of Recife, or Pernambuco, taken by the Dutch in 1630. In 1642 a large party of Marranos arrived there from Amsterdam, led by Rabbi Menasseh's colleague, Isaac Aboab de Fonseca (1605–1693), traditionally honored as the first rabbi in America. Menasseh himself desired to visit the flourishing community, but a Portuguese resurgence shattered such hopes.

In 1654 Pernambuco had to be evacuated, as did all the Dutch conquests in Brazil before long. Some of the fugitives made their way to Surinam (Dutch Guiana), where their descendants are still to be found. Another contingent of about two dozen made their way to New York, then New Amsterdam. (Its testy governor Peter Stuyvesant ordered them to leave, but was overruled in the name of justice by the governor of the Dutch West India Company.) Most of this contingent remained in the town, but a small number moved on to Newport, Rhode Island, and founded a distinct community there in about 1658—the first such in English colonial territory.

Throughout the eighteenth century small groups of Marranos continued to arrive from Holland and England. A new community appeared in Savannah within a year of the founding of Georgia (1732), but Newport remained the most flourishing congregation. In 1763 a synagogue was built there which is still standing, still in use, and a famed monument of colonial architecture. In any case, 1654 remains memorable as the year in which a Jewish community first appeared in territory that subsequently became part of the United States. We should add that, both in the English and Dutch domains, the normal state of affairs was from the start full religious liberty.

Spain and Portugal

Back in the Iberian "iron furnace," Marranos continued to fare badly. In Spain, where the Inquisition had been hounding them since 1478, crypto-Jews were all but extirpated in the course of the sixteenth century. In Portugal, where the Inquisition dated only from the 1530's, the Marranos seem to have been of greater pluck and fortitude, and so survived in greater numbers. In both countries anti-Jewish feeling became distinctly racial, and there were growing demands—as in a petition of the bishops to the Portuguese crown—that the "New Christians" wear distinctive garb or insignia and be confined to ghettos just as their unconverted forebears had been. Reflecting the growing racial conception of the issue, the distinction between "Old" and "New" Christians was preserved into the eighteenth century. Jewish blood became all the "evidence" the Inquisition needed. Many incendiary pamphlets and tracts assailed Marranos (the latest of which came in 1924!), and there was increasing pressure that they, too, be expelled.

The Inquisition continued actively in pursuit of the Marranos until the age of the democratic revolutions. Portugal's great minister, Pombal, brought his country out of the middle ages, first by thoroughly subordinating the Inquisition to the crown and then, in 1773, by abolishing all distinctions between "New" and "Old" Christians; he also suppressed the claim of noble families to "purity" of blood. As for Spain, the Inquisition was extinguished by Napoleon's invading armies, only to be restored upon his downfall and not definitely abolished until 1834. Both nations had been in the doldrums for a century or two by then, and their decline undoubtedly stemmed in a very large measure from the expulsions of the 1490's and the subsequent actions taken by the Inquisition. By depriving themselves of tens of thousands of persons who constituted as a group much of the dynamic element in the national economic life, both countries brought upon themselves commercial upheavals and credit crises which made either economic growth or stability impossible.

Though by the Napoleonic era it was generally assumed that crypto-Judaism had died out, according to George Borrow, an English missionary of the 1830's, three and a half centuries of relentless effort had failed of its object. Borrow reported that a Marrano—one Abarbanel—had confided to him that he had great wealth "in gold and silver, and stones of price: for I have inherited all the hoards of my forefathers. The greater part is buried underground: indeed I have never examined the tenth part of it. I have coins of silver and gold older than the time of Ferdinand the Accursed and Jezebel [Isabella]; I have also large sums employed in usury. We keep ourselves close, however, and pretend to be poor, miserably so; but, on certain occasions, at our festivals, when our gates are barred and our savage dogs are let loose in the court, we eat our food off services such as the Queen of Spain cannot boast of, and wash our feet in ewers of silver, fashioned and wrought before the Americas were discovered, though our garments are at all times coarse, and our food for the most part of the plainest description." To a question about molestation by public authorities, Abarbanel replied, "People of course suspect me to be what I am; but as I conform outwardly in most respects to their ways, they do not interfere with me. True it is that sometimes, when I enter the church to hear mass, they glare at me over the left shoulder, as much as to say—'What do you do here?' And sometimes they cross themselves as I pass by; but as they go no further, I do not trouble myself on that account." Abarbanel added that the Marranos had no kind of formal organization or leadership, although "there are certain holy families who enjoy much consideration: my own is one of these —the chiefest I may say."

But little attention was paid either to Borrow or to other similar revelations, for it was assumed that the policy of toleration had at last proved fatal to Marranism. So that there was considerable astonishment when, as late as World War I, large communities of Marranos were discovered in the secluded districts of northern Portugal and Spain practicing faithfully a secret religion which, though much altered and shrunken, was still recognizable as Judaism. Oblivious of any form of Judaism but their own and having lost touch with the Hebrew language, the Marranos were only with difficulty convinced that other Jews were, in fact, their co-religionists. At the same time, unaware that the Inquisition was long since dead, they still lived in fear of its possible machinations. Such a combination of fidelity and endurance are unique in the annals of human history.

Poland

Such are the dimensions of the Marrano epic. The one area in Europe that they did not penetrate to any significant degree was Poland, which in the early modern era was numerically the center of the Jewish Diaspora. The tide of Jewish immigrants had first begun to flow into Poland from Germany as a consequence of the violence and persecution that accompanied the Crusades. Owing to Polish economic needs, they soon were being actively welcomed, particularly after the devastation and depopulation wrought by the Mongol invasion of eastern Europe in the 1240's. Thus, in 1264, King Boleslav the Brave issued a charter of liberties and protection to attract Jewish settlement, a policy adhered to consistently by his successors down to the end of the seventeenth century. At the height of Jewish entry into Poland, King Casimir IV the Great issued a second great charter in 1354, confirming and extending Boleslav's.

Poland entered into dynastic union with Lithuania in 1386, and in the two centuries after 1450 it was the largest state of Europe, running from the Baltic to the Black Sea and including most of Ukraine. Polish rulers found themselves in much the same position as Charlemagne's dynasty, viz., they ruled a vast domain that was economically primitive. Ukraine and Lithuania were especially in need of economic development and, accordingly, they were now opened up to Jewish settlement under the auspices of the Polish crown.

Together with German settlers, who were invited for the same economic purpose, Jews created and built up, almost *ex nihilo*, Greater Poland's commercial, industrial, and financial structure. To agriculture also they imparted a new efficiency, often becoming the estate managers and financial agents of the Polish nobility. In the course of this long period of economic growth, many new towns and villages sprang up with an entirely Jewish population. Since the new communities—as provided in the royal charters—were virtually self-governing city-states, Jews were able to preserve in full vigor their own institutions and mores, their own culture and language (Yiddish); these conditions proved to be a decisive barrier to Jewish integration with the Polish community at large.

In the sixteenth century the intolerant spirit of the Counter-Reformation made its way into Poland, but it had little impact on Jewish-Polish relations. Overridingly this was because Jewish economic activity remained indispensable to the crown and the nobility. Moreover, the prolonged balance of power that existed between Calvinist Reformers and Catholics made for a situation in which there was considerable tolerance and conciliation of Jews (somewhat along the same lines as that period in Spain when it was about equally divided between Christendom and Islam). Thus sixteenth-century Poland saw, not the ferocious repression and the disabilities of Jews that characterized Christendom elsewhere, but rather the high point in Jewish autonomy and parliamentary self-goverment throughout the whole history of the Diaspora.

The royal charters permitted Jews to preserve to the full their own way of life and to govern themselves according to the Torah and Talmud. One measure of this autonomy was that Jewish learning and scholarship were very quickly organized. Every Jewish town of any pretension boasted its own academy and distinguished scholars, and Polish Jews characteristically prided themselves on the number of their young men who devoted themselves "to prayer by study." Here, as always, the hero type was the scholar and not the merchant. Thus the well-to-do merchant would maneuver to fashion a match for his daughter with some promising young scholar—poverty-stricken though he may have been—rather than with the scion of some commercial magnate.

Insulated from the host society as Jewish life in Poland was, study and scholarship tended to be narrowly concentrated on the Talmud and purely Jewish subject matter. This situation gave rise to a kind of learning that was increasingly divorced from the life of the people, given over as it frequently was to intellectual games like *pilpul*—the clever yet arid and sterile resolution of seeming paradoxes in the Talmud. Thus, while Jewish education functioned within the context of the communal life, it tended to become divorced from that life, and a reaction to this state of affairs was inevitable, as we shall see.

One fascinating expression of Jewish communal life in Poland was the Council of the Four Lands, which paralleled the "Jewish Parliament" that we have seen in England in that it collected taxes and remitted them to the royal treasury. The Polish king designated the sum he expected to be raised, and the Jewish leaders apportioned it among the various towns and villages, assessing each family a particular amount. By 1551, when a royal decree officially recognized and sanctioned its functions and powers, the Council was regulating the Jewish community's economic and fiscal affairs, representing it at the royal court and in the Polish parliament of nobles and ecclesiastics, directing religious observances, organizing and supervising a hierarchy of courts in which it functioned as a supreme judiciary, etc. In short, there was no aspect of Jewish life—religious, cultural, educational, social, economic—which it did not guide. Each Jewish community sent an official as its representative to the Council, and to these lay and religious leaders were added six outstanding rabbinical scholars. (A similar body for Lithuania, an offshoot of the Council of the Four Lands, dated from 1623.)

The Council thus constituted a state within the state. Unfortunately, however, it was not the only state within the Polish kingdom. The nobility, the ecclesiastical hierarchy, and the German merchant towns all enjoyed great rights and prerogatives at the expense of the monarchy. In spite of this, from about 1450 to the Thirty Years' War that ended in 1648, the constitutional monarchy of Poland stood up well against numerous threats from outside its borders. By 1467 the threat of the German "Drive to the East" had petered out, Russia was divided and weak, and the Ottoman Turks were far enough away so that Polish society could afford the luxury of parliamentary procedure and consent rather than royal decision and dispatch, of communal prerogative rather than communal obligation. But with the rise of Russia after 1612 and of Prussia after 1640, Poland found itself constitutionally handicapped in its efforts to fend off these strong and aggressive powers and to counter the divisive forces of its ethnically and religiously disparate society. Its inability to withstand these pressures ultimately proved fatal, and in the latter part of the eighteenth century it was partitioned out of existence.

The first act in the tragedy of Poland's dissolution was the Cossack rebellion of 1648–1651. The Ukrainian Cossacks were Greek Orthodox Christians who, discontent with submission to "heretical" Roman Catholic Polish rule and to its financial and administrative agents, the "unbelieving" Jews, were increasingly attracted to the rising Russian state and its people (their co-religionists). Led by Bogdan Chmielnicki, they rebelled with unchecked fury, inflicting a series of massacres throughout Poland that, for duration, brutishness, and the number of victims claimed (over two hundred thousand Jews were slaughtered within the space of two years), surpassed anything in the long history of Jewish suffering up to that time. After rivers of Polish as well as Jewish blood had flown—the era is known as "The Deluge" in Polish history—the crown finally began to make headway in suppressing the rebels. But it was too late, for, at this point, Russia and Sweden (a great power in the seventeenth century) intervened and Poland had to surrender most of Ukraine to Russia. Worse still, Poland thereafter became the battleground for Russia, Sweden, Prussia, and Austria.

Since the Polish crown could not control the states within the state, it could no longer enforce the protection and privileges granted to Jews by royal charter. For Jews, therefore, the sequel to Cossack massacre was persecution at the hands of churchmen, who made or acquiesced in endless charges of ritual murder and Host profanation—despite strenuous papal objections. Another aspect of the general situation was the emergence of a native middle class which clamored for an end to Jewish commercial and financial activity and, indeed, for the expulsion of the Jewish populace. Finally, a prolonged economic depression settled upon Poland which, compounding other disabilities, made it impossible for the Jewish community to meet its tax obligations. In 1764 the Council of the Four Lands was abolished by the Polish parliament, so as to enable the government to extract larger direct taxes. Communal self-government continued in many respects, but the life of Polish Jewry had been shattered.

The sad point to which Jewish life had deteriorated is depicted vividly in the autobiography of Solomon Maimon (1754–1800), who recalls how the Polish nobleman Prince Radziwill, seemingly demented, had one day driven "with the whole pomp of his court to a synagogue, and, without anyone to this day knowing the reason, committed the greatest havoc, smashed windows and stoves, broke all the vessels, threw on the ground the copies of the Holy Scriptures kept in the ark, etc. A learned pious Jew, who was present, ventured to lift one of these copies from the ground, and had the honor of being struck down by a musket-ball triggered by His Serene Highness' own hand. From here the train went to a second synagogue, where the same conduct was repeated, and from there they proceeded to the Jewish cemetery, where the buildings were demolished, and the monuments cast into the fire." (Since the prince was a law unto himself, obviously no recourse was ever possible.)

Beginning in 1648, a vast tide of refugees from Poland swept westward, particularly into the German states. It continued throughout the eighteenth century and the extinction of Poland in the Partitions of 1772, 1793, and 1795 among Russia, Prussia, and Austria; indeed, it persisted into the twentieth century, swelling or diminishing according to the degree of economic depression and violence, but never ceasing. This redistribution westward was the most significant event in Jewish history since the medieval expulsions from western European states.

Once again the freedom, prosperity, and intellectual sophistication of a golden age had given way to persecution, poverty, and degradation. Viewed against this background, it is not surprising to find Jews ardently expecting the coming of the Messiah and seizing desperately on almost any self-styled one that came along.[3] This hope is reflected in the words of the English ambassador at Constantinople who reported in the mid-seventeenth century that "all the cities of Turkey, where the Jews inhabited, were full of the expectation of the Messiah; no trade or course of gain was followed. Everyone imagined that daily provisions, riches, honors, and government were to descend upon him by some unknown and miraculous manner," and was sure that "the restoration of their kingdom was at hand."

The most famous of the so-called false messiahs was Sabbatai Zevi, a subject of the Turkish Empire, who proclaimed himself as the messiah in 1648, in his native Smyrna, and declared 1666 as the onset of the millennium. In that year, he sought to take over Constantinople, but was imprisoned instead by the sultan and saved his life only by apostatizing to Islam. Nevertheless, Jews throughout the Diaspora could not bring themselves to renounce him, but "flocked in great numbers to the castle where he was imprisoned, not only from the neighboring parts, but also from Poland, Germany, Leghorn, Venice, Amsterdam, and other places." Neither his apostasy nor his death in 1672 dispelled Jewish faith in him. In fact, a cult grew up that lasted into the present age, and learned rabbis (particularly in Poland) argued heatedly over his authenticity.

A distinctly Polish offshoot of Sabbateanism were the Frankists, founded by Jacob Frank (1726–1791), another self-proclaimed messiah. Frankism was a quasi-Christian Kabbalist sect from which Frank himself ultimately apostatized to Christianity.

Even more distinctive of the Polish milieu of that day was the life and teaching of Israel ben Eliezer (1700–1760), better known as the Baal Shem Tov, or Master of the Good Name. The Besht (as his title is abbreviated) was a charismatic figure and his followers looked to him and his personal teachings (he left practically no writings) for inspiration. He was the founder of Hasidism which, with its anti-intellectual tinge, was comparable to the contemporary Pietism or Wesleyanism; he emphasized personal union with God through prayer, emotional conviction, and gladness of heart. He loved nature rather than books, gained fame as a faith healer of the sick, and expressed his teachings in a revivalistic mode. His idea of mystical joy echoes Luria and messianism, but is of a simpler kind—namely, that one impulse from a vernal wood will teach us more of moral good than all the sages can. All of this had a far wider appeal to his Polish brethren—degraded by persecution and grinding poverty as they increasingly were—than the subtle but arid intellectualism of *pilpul*. Some of his aura ultimately fell to his disciples, who were known as *Zaddikim* (the righteous ones) and were regarded in awe as priestly mediators between God and man.

Hasidism, being outside the main stream of normative Judaism, gave rise to much controversy. The leading vindicator of talmudic Judaism and a trenchant critic of Hasidism was the formidable scholar Elijah of Vilna

(1720–1797), on whom the ancient title of Gaon was popularly conferred. (He became known as the Vilna Gaon, Vilna being the "Lithuanian Jerusalem" in his day.) His native Lithuania, we should note, had been far less affected by the upheavals that had devastated Poland, and it was, therefore, less susceptible to mysticism and emotionalism. For the Vilna Gaon, desertion of study in favor of warbling one's joyous woodland notes was heresy. He never left his studies for more than a few hours, and ordered his whole life—including that of his family—according to that consuming passion. A rationalist rather than a mystic, he ranged far beyond the limits of Jewish learning, mastering many secular disciplines, such as mathematics, astronomy, physics, philosophy, and music. In vigorously countering the influence of the Besht, he did much to restore talmudic learning and normative Judaism in the Polish domains, ruled in his lifetime by Russia and Prussia. He, too, gained a place in popular tradition, for a Jew who adheres to the strongly rationalist position will frequently be dubbed a "Litvak," i.e., a Lithuanian, a disciple of the Vilna Gaon.

NOTES

[1] We should remember that *ghetto* has its origin in the Jewish past and was no mere synonym for *slum*, as it has become for us. The idea of a ghetto derives from the efforts of the Lateran Councils of 1179 and 1215 to segregate Jews from Christians, part of which was a decree that Jews live in isolation. Subsequently, royal and municipal governments established compulsory ghettos by law; they were walled and had gates that closed each evening at curfew, by which time Jews had to be inside or suffer various penalties; outside the ghetto, Jews had to wear the yellow badge. Ghettos were typically small and overcrowded, making them prone to epidemics and disastrous fires. It is true that ghetto seclusion strengthened Jewish communal

life and that Jews had ordinarily lived nearby each other long before laws compelled them to do so; such considerations hardly justify the ghetto system, especially if one recalls how visible a target the ghetto was to Crusaders or rioters. The walls kept the Jew *in*, they did not keep his enemy *out*, and in fact the high casualty rate of attacks on ghettos suggests that the circumambient walls did more to trap than protect the fleeing victim. The last ghetto in western Europe, that of Rome, was abolished only in 1870, when Italian unification was completed; thereafter, Jews in many European cities continued to live in a particular sector, which was loosely designated as a ghetto.

2 A kind of underground railway developed, reminiscent of that in behalf of Negro slaves in the days of the Old South before the American Civil War: it featured guides, stowing away, forged papers, information and assistance centers, etc. From 1580 to 1640, Spain and Portugal were united under the Habsburg dynasty at Madrid, with the result that more Portuguese Marranos fled, frequently via Spain, to the Lowlands, although more and more travel restrictions and obstacles were put in their way.

3 Even at the height of Jewish felicity in the Italian Renaissance, one David Reubeni came forth as the messiah and was widely accepted by his co-religionists; he even managed to enlist the sympathetic interest of the pope, a scion of the Medici family, Clement VII. Within a generation, Isaac Luria, spoken of earlier, appeared at Safed and, thereafter, the doctrine grew rapidly and culminated with Sabbatai.

7. The Enlightenment

THE EIGHTEENTH CENTURY is the age of the Enlightenment, a cultural and intellectual movement that in significant ways revived the ideas and tendencies of the Renaissance. From the perspective of Jewish history, the ultimate significance of the Enlightenment was its fruition in Emancipation. For the *philosophes*, "the party of humanity," as for the ancient Stoics, man as man enjoyed natural and inalienable rights. "Are Christian and Jew rather more Christian and Jew than Man?" asked one spokesman of the age. Thus differences of race and religion were taken to be mere accidents, and the aim was for all men to unite in worship of the goddess of reason.

Such ideas did, in fact, open the way to Emancipation—political, legal, and eventually social—but the inertia of age-old prejudice could not be overcome by the mere force of ideas. It took the flood tide of revolution in 1789 to effect Emancipation and, although much was undone in the period of reaction and restoration after 1815, the decisive breach had been made.

The conduct and policies of governments had, from the sixteenth century on, been increasingly dictated by secular and mercantilistic rather than religious and ecclesiastical considerations. Kings like Frederick the Great of Prussia thought in terms of the economic strength of their state: if

Jews, for example, could contribute to that strengthening, they were glad to afford toleration and protection to them. This, together with royal indifference in matters of religion —Frederick said he would build mosques for Moslems if they would come to settle—did provide in the eighteenth century a basis for the toleration of Jews. Particularly was this true of Germany, where it was the classic age of the "court Jew." The origins of Emancipation, then, are to be found in the secular and mercantilistic conception of the state and society as well as in the ideology of the Enlightenment, while the actual instrument for cutting through the Gordian knot of ancient prejudice and antipathy was the French Revolution of 1789.

The policies of Frederick the Great of Prussia and Emperor Joseph II of Austria illustrate the impact of the Enlightenment on the status of Jews. In 1671 Jews had been recalled to Brandenburg, a possession of Prussia, by the Great Elector Frederick William I. This mercantilist and Calvinist prince (he had lived as a young man in Holland during the heyday of the Marranos) was "moved particularly by the desire to further business in general" to admitting fifty Jewish families into his territory. Conditional to their entry was the payment of an annual sum as "protection money"—an echo of the *fiscus Judaicus*—and a similar sum for permission to marry; in addition, they could not build a synagogue, though they could practice Judaism freely in their homes and could purchase their own cemetery.

In 1750 one of the Elector's descendants, the mercantilist and agnostic Frederick the Great, issued a charter for the Jews of his domain, one which came to be generally applied in most of the German states of that day. Four categories were spelled out: "general-privileged," essentially "court Jews" who had full economic and residential rights; "regular-protected," Jews who had limited economic and residential rights but could pass them on to their eldest sons;

"special-protected," Jews who had the same rights as the previous group but could *not* pass them on; and "the merely tolerated," Jews who had no rights to speak of and who were bound to the ghetto. Frederick opened up those enterprises to Jews that he judged were beneficial to the state economy (particularly the manufacture of silk), but closed off others in which they would compete with the native population. Thus they were "enjoined not to brew beer!" and were also forbidden to enter the crafts.

Jewish bankers—considered "general-privileged"—directed royal financial affairs and Frederick welcomed their investments in the country's industries. Yet, at bottom, the king disliked Jews and sought both to prevent "the surreptitious entry of unlicensed Jews," and any natural increase among them through marriage ("the fixed number of Jewish families at present is not to be exceeded except by our royal command"). Furthermore, he severely restricted their rights of self-government ("the rabbi and the elders have no right of real jurisdiction") and though "for the present" he permitted them many functions, his charter contained provision for their ready absorption into the national legal and administrative structure. In defense of Frederick it should perhaps be said that he was the supreme autocrat, a ruler who meticulously ordered the lives of all his subjects, not only Jews; and that, with his friend Voltaire, he embodied the opposition to revealed religion so basic to the Enlightenment. While this opposition expressed itself fundamentally as an attack on Christianity, Judaism also came under assault, and in some instances this gave rise to a contempt for Jews.

Indeed, Voltaire's ill feeling for Jews runs like a vein of iron through the enormous bulk of his writings. His article on *les Juifs* in his *Philosophical Dictionary* is a crude tirade, in the course of which he refers to them as "an ignorant and barbarous people," and could bring himself to be no kinder than to conclude, "still we ought not to burn them." A most suggestive recent book by Rabbi Arthur Hertzberg, *The French Enlightenment and the Jews*, further emphasizes this aspect of the Enlightenment: "An analysis of everything Voltaire wrote about the Jews throughout his life establishes the proposition that he is the major link in Western intellectual history between the anti-Semitism of classic paganism and the modern age"; and "Modern, secular anti-Semitism was fashioned not as a reaction to the Enlightenment and the Revolution, but within the Enlightenment and Revolution themselves."

All this notwithstanding, it is my judgment that the anti-Semitism of Voltaire and others of the era was a vestigial prejudice, that it did not have roots in the thought of the Enlightenment, and that many of the *philosophes* were anti-Semitic *despite* the tolerant ideology they adhered to (just as we in America have been long in practicing inequality despite our Constitution's provision of equality to all). The Enlightenment, it therefore seems to me, cannot be interpreted as the indispensable link between classic prejudices and medieval, Christian-inspired anti-Semitism, on the one hand, and the secularized, racial, genocidal anti-Semitism of the modern age, on the other. In short, blemishes, not malignant cancerous growths, disfigure the Enlightenment's attitude toward the Jews. What is well taken in Rabbi Hertzberg's book, however, is that Christianity, whether Catholic or Protestant, does not stand alone as the root origin of modern anti-Semitism.

The more positive side of the Enlightenment is exemplified by Frederick's contemporary, the Habsburg Emperor Joseph II. In 1745 his mother, the devout Catholic Empress Maria Theresa, had expelled the Jews from Bohemia, whose capital of Prague contained one of the oldest and largest Jewish communities in Europe, on the grounds that the Jews of Alsace were "disloyal." It was the sign of a new era that her action led to the registering of numerous diplomatic protests, particularly by England and Holland,

and that within a year the edict was rescinded and the Jewish community re-established. Her son, who declared that he loved "all humanity without exception," inaugurated his reign by abolishing the protection tax and the infamous badge. He followed this in 1781 by issuing a famous Toleration Patent, which granted Jews full religious liberty, greatly broadened their rights in choosing an occupation and a place of residence, and opened the public schools and universities to them. They were permitted to own property in full legal right, build schools and engage their own schoolmasters, enter all the professions and be eligible for all civil and military offices. The Patent should not be overemphasized, however, since it had only limited success in affecting long-standing attitudes, and because Joseph II's successors ignored its provisions. The one item of the Patent that did have an immediate and permanent effect was the requirement that every Jewish family adopt a fixed surname. Christian names were forbidden, and sometimes if a Jew was not quick to choose one himself, an absurd name was imposed on him by the registrar. Most took names derived either from their profession or place of residence, or else from flowers, animals, and minerals. It is for this reason that many Germanic Jewish names include the form *stein* (stone) or *berg* (mountain). Yet, despite such limitations, Joseph II's policies mark the sharpest contrast with Frederick's, and were certainly a milestone in the treatment of Jews in Catholic Europe: to Joseph they were human beings; to Frederick, objects of gain.

The period in Germany from 1648 to the Revolution of 1789 was the great age of the "court Jew." Practically all of the numerous German courts, whether Protestant or Catholic, had their "Jewish factors." "Court Jews" were especially important in the reconstruction of the state and the economy in the wake of the ruin resulting from the religious and dynastic wars. The best known was Joseph Süss Oppenheimer (1698–1737), or *Jüd Süss* as he was called, who was in the service of the duke of Württemberg as finance minister and factotum extraordinary. Aside from his supreme competence in state finance, he was rich, handsome, learned, and a brilliant conversationalist; as a consequence, he was much sought after by fashionable persons and courtiers, and his splendid house became a grand salon. Oppenheimer's death on the gallows after an outrageous trial is all too typical of the fate of the "court Jews": on the duke's death he was done in by the nobles, at whose expense—economically and politically—he had built up the state apparatus.

Moses Mendelssohn

Three strands of Judaism, though not mutually exclusive, are discernible in the eighteenth century. The first two have already been mentioned: Normative Judaism with its emphasis on the Talmud, as represented by the Vilna Gaon (although he went beyond the pale of strictly Jewish scholarship in his studies of secular subjects); and Hasidism, a revolt of the untutored heart against rabbinic authority, which emphasized good deeds and simple joyous piety, as represented by the Baal Shem Tov (although he never went so far as to attack talmudic learning). The third strand, *Haskalah*, or Enlightenment, a form of *Aggiornamento*, centered in Germany and is best represented by Moses Mendelssohn (1729–1786), a kind of latter-day Azariah dei Rossi. An important figure in both the European Enlightenment and the Haskalah, Mendelssohn was born in Dessau, Anhalt, and later went to Berlin, the capital of Prussia and the center of the Jewish Enlightenment. His knocking at the entrance to the city has been characterized as symbolic of the Jewish community's knocking at the gate of the modern world. In any event, it marked the beginning of the next phase of Jewish history.

Mendelssohn tried to build a bridge between Christianity and Judaism, by means of which Christians could come to a genuine knowledge and sympathetic understanding of Judaism and Jews, and over which Jews could make their way to a mastery of the physical and social sciences of the day. If Jews were to enter into the European heritage, they needed, in Mendelssohn's view, the linguistic key of German; therefore, he never tired of emphasizing the necessity to learn German in place of Yiddish, as he himself had done with great difficulty owing to strong rabbinical opposition. His translation of the Bible into a magnificent German was an epochal event in bringing German Jews to abandon Yiddish as their native language.

Lifting himself by his own bootstraps, Mendelssohn had overcome the twin disabilities of the ghetto—poverty and intellectual backwardness—and, as a result, had gained entry into polite society. The bridge he envisioned was to be a social as well as a cultural one, and his life is most significant for its having offered to his brethren the aspiration of social equality through the example of his own attainment of it. He became, remarkably, a "culture hero," and was warmly admired by the outstanding philosopher of the age, Immanuel Kant, and beloved by the greatest German literary figure of his generation, the dramatist and critic Gottfried Lessing.

Both Kant and Mendelssohn were admirers of the eccentric philosopher Solomon Maimon, whose fascinating autobiography has been referred to earlier. Maimon hailed from Lithuania, but went to Berlin in his twenties. A perceptive critic of Kant, he was a rationalist in the tradition of Maimonides, whose name he took to indicate this discipleship. His waywardness and extravagance frequently exasperated his protector Mendelssohn, who feared he might misrepresent Jews and Judaism to the general public. As for Lessing, through his dramas he brought the Jew upon the European stage for the first time as a human and noble personage, rather than as the traditional Shylock, villain, or fool. His well-known *Nathan the Wise* was, in fact, a portrait of Mendelssohn and a powerful plea for religious liberty.

Mendelssohn's passport to the world outside the ghetto was not great wealth as had typically been the case with the "court Jews"—although he eventually acquired a comfortable living as a partner in a silk factory, one of the industries promoted by Frederick. Nor was his passport baptism, as it tended to be in the next generation, for he remained a staunchly devout Jew whose most notable work was an apologia for Judaism, *Jerusalem*. Rather, it was his charm, social grace, literary style, and intellectual power (though he was physically unprepossessing) that gave him entry to German society and philosophical circles and made him the prime example of the *Salonjude* or salon Jew.

In his presentation of Judaism, Mendelssohn interpreted it as a thoroughly rational religion, having no mystical cobwebs or kabbalistic lore. As such, it could well stand the critical assessments that the *philosophes* might subject it to. Like his favorite, Maimonides, in *The Guide to the Perplexed*, he emphasized that there were no mysteries which men had to accept on blind faith; for Judaism as a system of ethics rather than of doctrines was consistent with freedom of thought. "Among all the laws and commandments of Moses, there is none saying 'Thou shalt believe' or 'Thou shalt not believe.' They all say 'Thou shalt do' or 'Thou shalt not do.' " Thus, his life was laid in two scenes: one, as a loyal Jew who not only practiced his religion but did much to accommodate it to the prevailing rationalism and, two, as a productive participant in the intellectual life of the European Enlightenment. This required a difficult kind of balancing act, for as he voyaged on strange seas of thought his co-religionists looked askance at him; as he retained his Jewish moorings his Christian or *philosophe* friends raised a skeptical eyebrow.

Such tensions began to manifest themselves divisively within European Jewry as the eighteenth century drew to a close, and the general tendency—as illustrated by Mendelssohn's own children—was to go one way or the other. Some remained Jews, some became Christians, and still others free thinkers.

8. The Jewish Role in the Economic Development of the Western World

THE ROLE OF THE Jews in the medieval and modern economic life of the Western world has been the subject of much inquiry, controversy, error, and prejudice. It should be noted at the outset that in the ancient empires of Persia, Rome, Islam, and even in the severely persecutory Byzantine Empire, there were no special occupations from which Jews were either excluded or to which they were confined, and that they had in general considerable autonomy. Only in Western Christendom (beginning in the fourth century when the Jew lost his citizenship) did occupational segregation become the order of the day. In fact, the common stereotype of the Jew as having some special attribute or genius for business basically stems from this segregation. In historical studies this viewpoint has frequently taken the form of asserting that Western capitalism owes its origin and early development to Jews or—in its more extreme form—that the spirit and practice of capitalism reflect or are synonymous with the spirit and practice of Judaism.

The most famous expression of this view appears in *The Jews and Modern Capitalism*, published in 1911 by the German economic historian Werner Sombart (1863–1941). What understandably damns him in the eyes of Jewish scholars was his adherence to Adolf Hitler, but he should nonetheless not be dismissed as just another Jew-baiter.

He sought to refine, by carrying it one step further back, the well-known analysis by Max Weber in *The Protestant Ethic and the Spirit of Capitalism*, 1904–1905; for Sombart the "ethic" derived from the Old Testament, and so was not Protestant nor Puritan, but Semitic. His work is scholarly economic history, not polemic or invective. Accordingly, I shall consider his Nazi allegiance a form of aberration and shall meet his interpretation of Jewish economic life on its own ground of economic history. For the book does possess undoubted merits as well as perverse errors, and it is a pleasure to note that a recent reissue of it had the blessing of one eminent Jewish economic historian and an introduction provided by another.

The Jews and Commerce

From Constantine in the fourth century to Charlemagne in the eighth, the Jew became essentially a person without rights in a society where the badge of citizenship was Christian baptism. A Charlemagne, for example, could fleece Jews of their wealth and property, expel them, execute them, etc., without any necessity to have recourse to judicial proceedings. Some emperors, too, collected the *fiscus Judaicus*, claiming it as their right since they were the successors of Vespasian and the ancient emperors, and interpreting the tax as payment for protection. With the fragmentation of authority among feudal magnates, many of them, along with kings, ecclesiastics, and municipal governments, claimed and exercised the same arbitrary power over Jews, though they stopped short of insisting upon the *fiscus Judaicus*.

Such rightlessness meant that the Jew could do nothing without permission granted to him in the form of a charter (for which he had to pay heavily). The earliest of such charters, which dates from 840, was bestowed by the emperor Louis, the son of Charlemagne. Thereafter and in keeping with the fragmentation of authority, numerous charters were granted to Jews by kings, barons, popes, bishops, abbots, towns, etc.

But these charters kept all the honorable sources of livelihood closed to the Jew. Obviously he could not enter the greatest of medieval callings, that of the priest or monk. He could not become a knight or member of the ruling feudal class, since this required Christian oaths. Similarly, imperial edicts specifically excluded him from a military career (which he had not infrequently entered before Constantine's time), and he was likewise barred from holding land or engaging in agriculture, since this involved as a precondition military service as a knight.

Given this general situation, the Jew perforce had to seek a source of livelihood elsewhere, and trade was the obvious choice. It cannot be overemphasized that the profession of merchant commanded little respect or prestige in Christian Europe until perhaps the twelfth century. The New Testament view prevailed which made it difficult and unlikely for the merchant or rich man to make his way to Heaven— he was the camel that had first to pass through the needle's eye. An ascetic, other-worldly orientation predominated, and poverty as exemplified by the Apostles was both the vow of the monk and a high social ideal. The merchant with his peddler's pack might be indispensable for the supply of salt and iron plowshares, or similar items not produced on the largely self-sufficient manorial estates; but he was frowned upon and distrusted as a vagabond, if not as a robber. Certainly no Christian soul was supposed to taint himself with such worldly trafficking. And so it was left open to the Jews, who, having no Christian rivals, had no trouble purchasing charters for the right to trade. The anti-commercial bias and the economic backwardness of Europe conspired to open the field to Jews, and so prominent were they in the foreign and intra-European trade

that in the age of Charlemagne and down to the eleventh
century *Jew* and *merchant* were virtually synonymous terms
(although the actual volume of goods—luxury items and
such—was the merest trickle) .

Now it becomes clear that the Jew was thrust into commerce by circumstances quite beyond his making, not because he was racially inclined to it or because his religion
turned him into a money grubber.[1] It is important to
understand that the early middle ages were economically
primitive and that a theologically inspired viewpoint prevailed making merchants and merchandise suspect and un-
worthy of Christian endeavor; whereas the Jew came from
and maintained contact with a society where urban life,
trade, manufacturing, luxury goods, were commonplace,
and were accepted as a matter of course—not by Jews alone
but the whole society. It was as merchants that many Jews
came, frequently by royal invitation, to Europe from the
Byzantine and Islamic world and beyond in the sixth to the
eighth or early ninth century. There is frequent reference
to "Syrians" as itinerant merchants, most of whom were
Jews; one item of their trade was slaves (about which
neither the Jewish, Christian, nor Islamic religion was
much exercised at this stage) , who were purchased among
the Slavic peoples or in the Byzantine Empire and sold in
Spain and throughout the Islamic world. There was one
group of Jewish cloth merchants in the ninth century
whose operations extended from China to Christian and
Moslem Europe.

The position of Judaism with regard to commercial
and financial activity for profit is that it accepts it as
necessary, neither encouraging nor discouraging it, but
moralizing and regulating it, just as it sought to moralize
and regulate every aspect of Jewish life in a way obedient
to God's will. There was, moreover, no other-worldly or
anti-worldly ethic in Judaism that would have condemned
trade, for Essenism—with its puritanical fear of the taint of

this world, its asceticism, and its ideal of poverty—had long since died out in the first century. If one searches through the Talmud, it is clear that the rabbis understood much about such matters as currency, loans and their regulation and control by legal instruments, and banking practices generally; that they also had a keen mathematical sense; and that they not infrequently earned a living by trade or finance. Such facts have been taken as proof of Judaism's spur to capitalistic activity. But any such notion is more than offset by a host of warnings in the Bible and Talmud against the acquisition of wealth for its own sake, e.g., "The world rests on three things: on law, on worship, and on bestowal of kindness," or "The knowledge of law is not to be found among merchants and traders." The Prophets, too, are full of devastating attacks on those who prefer riches to righteousness and wisdom; so, too, are the Proverbs. Intrinsic to Judaism is a far stronger sense of social justice than of capitalistic enterprise. This can be seen, e.g., in the long-standing tradition that called for wealth and land to be periodically and equally redivided during what was called the Jubilee Year. Moreover, the hero type in Judaism has always been the scholar, whereas the merchant is frequently regarded with contempt for his general ignorance. "We do not delight in merchandise," says Josephus. The "ethic" that the Jewish business man carried with him to Europe was, therefore, not one of a religiously inspired acquisitiveness.

The Jews and Finance

In Christian Europe during the course of the tenth through the twelfth century, commerce became progressively tolerable, respectable, and even honorable, so that eventually the canon lawyers softened or withdrew their former strictures and prohibitions on mercantile activity.

Trade—both local and foreign—became attractive to Christians. At an accelerating rate after 1000, Jews began to be displaced from commerce by Christians, in part by sheer force and violence such as accompanied the first Crusade. Jewish retirement from the field also stemmed from their inability to compete with Christian merchants organized into guilds; these were Christian fraternal institutions from which Jews were automatically barred, and which frequently enjoyed the advantage of official support and patronage in towns like Venice or Milan.

Such circumstances led the Jew away from trade and, perforce, into banking and finance, where he was a pioneer and had no Christian rivals. As in trade earlier, so now in loans and credit operations, the European Jew enjoyed membership in a society that extended to China, one in which the floating of loans, moderate interest-taking, etc., were widely known, practiced, and under no ban of suspicion. It is not that the Jew invented credit—he may well have, but it cannot be established—but that, within the community and the international contacts it brought him, he had access to credit, what Christian Europe so notably lacked. Here his religious teaching, contrary to some Sombart-inspired notions, presented at least one grave obstacle, namely, the famous passage of Deuteronomy that is so central to Christian as well as Jewish economic thought. It reads, "Unto a foreigner thou mayest lend upon usury; but unto thy brother thou shalt not lend upon usury," by which one's co-religionists were taken to be one's brethren. In time an adaptation to changed circumstances—in the manner of the Hillel school—permitted the Jewish moneylender to receive interest from a fellow Jew. But what was more decisive—as we cannot overemphasize here and throughout —was the impact on Jewish economic activity of actions taken by Christian authorities. The Third (1179) and Fourth (1215) Lateran Councils of the Church, acting to implement the Deuteronomic injunction, forbade Christians to receive interest ("usury") and thereby opened the way for Jews. Such various developments explain why, between about 1000 and 1300, Jews were almost the sole bankers and financiers in many countries, especially north of the Alps. By 1250 *moneylender* and *Jew* were practically interchangeable terms, in much the same way that *merchant* and *Jew* had been in the Carolingian age.

By the end of the thirteenth century a further parallel to what we saw earlier in trade occurs. As banking and credit manipulation came to be seen by the end of the thirteenth century as necessary, profitable, and therefore at the least tolerable to the Christian conscience, canonical prohibitions against them were relaxed—in practice if not in theory. One of the greatest banking institutions of the thirteenth century was the Templars, originally a militant order of crusading warrior-monks, so far had the canonical restrictions been forgotten. By then Jews were being displaced by northern Italian and southern French financiers. Here, too, Jewish withdrawal from the field was frequently effected by riot and massacre, inspired and guided to a large degree by debtors who were quick to utilize the reservoir of ill will against Jews as an excuse for cancelling the debts they owed them. For much the same reason, Jews were expelled from England (1290) and France (1306) by the kings, who, after borrowing to the hilt, cancelled their own debts to Jewish moneylenders, made all other debts owing to Jews payable to the crown, confiscated most of the remaining Jewish property, and sent the whole community off in a woebegone procession. In France the expedient was used of expulsion, recall, and expulsion again as a profitable device.

Jewish difficulties in finance were also attributable to their growing inability to compete with Christian bankers who had the advantage of large, centralized, and efficient organization in addition to the backing and patronage of their governments, popes, kings, etc. This left Jewish mo-

neylenders, in those countries where they continued to reside or were readmitted, with little more than small-scale
local operations of the pawnshop variety.

The Jews and the Spread of Capitalism

One of the more erroneous notions, still sometimes held,
is that Jews were important in the formation of capitalist
enterprise in the Italian cities that later became centers of
the Renaissance flowering—Florence, Venice, Milan, Genoa,
Pisa, etc. Until the fourteenth century Jews lived principally in Rome and the south, and thus could not have
played the role ascribed to them. In fact, when Jews
finally did move north (e.g., to Florence in 1437 at the
invitation of the Medici), their major occupation was not
high finance but the conducting of pawnshops for the
poor. It was all right for the Florentines to pursue their
foreign banking operations but, within the city itself, such
practices touched the quick of usury, that bogey of the
town fathers, and so were left to Jews. The small-potatoes
pawnshop operations at a late date were the only economic
role of Jews in these supposed citadels of capitalism.

The more economically advanced a country became, the
fewer Jewish financiers were to be found in it. Thus
expulsion in the later middle ages, economically considered,
has some of the features that expropriation and nationalization in favor of native interests have in our own time—a
kind of coming of age of the national economy. When
Jews ceased to be important in English and French finance,
they became the pioneers of commercial development in
the economically backward countries of Europe—eastern
Germany, Poland, Bohemia (Czechoslovakia), Hungary,
etc. This cycle was to be repeated over and over down to
the nineteenth century when Rumania was brought to the
economic "take-off stage," as it is now called, by the Jewish

community who were recent settlers there. At some point the economic activity of the Jews, indispensable as pioneers in initiating trade, banking, industry, etc., ceased to be indispensable—with the result that the Jewish financier became *persona non grata*, and his envious Christian rivals, having learned much of his economic methods, utilized prejudice and stereotype to fashion him into the hateful "Shylock" and so displace him.

We may see in this pattern a parallel with the realm of scholarship: Jewish scholars and translators were indispensable intermediaries in transmitting the classical heritage and stimulating Christian intellectual activity down to the eve of the Renaissance. Just so were the Jews, as economic intermediaries, transmitting to a Europe as backward economically as it was intellectually the economic techniques of an advanced society. As initiators of economic activity— not only priming, but creating the economic pump—the Jews' importance was of the first order; thereafter it shrank to minimal proportions. Their contribution is summed up precisely in Professor Baron's metaphor referring to them as "economic catalysts."

Some of the generalizations adduced above are clarified and substantiated in a recent study by R. W. Emery, *The Jews of Perpignan in the Thirteenth Century.* (Perpignan, a small town in southwest France, had a Jewish community of about four hundred which was among the largest and most prosperous in thirteenth-century Christendom.) Based on the surviving records and documents of the notaries of Perpignan, Emery's book, though a highly specialized monograph, is extremely interesting as a case study by means of which some of the traditional notions and shibboleths regarding Jewish economic activity can be tested.

To start with, Emery finds no justification for the belief that the Jews played a leading role in the development of new economic institutions or methods, nor that their religion generated a set of intellectual conceptions and moral attitudes that made them natural capitalists or the founders of capitalism, as Sombart claimed. The Jews of Perpignan were preponderantly moneylenders, not because their religion induced in them a capacity for profit calculation, but because most other sources of livelihood were closed to them. Emery confirms the displacement of Jews from commerce, for the thirteenth-century Perpignese Jews were not significantly involved in trade, foreign or local. The one reference in the notarial records to the slave trade, for which the medieval Jew was supposedly notorious, is to a Christian slaver. The two staples of the city's economy, cloth production and agriculture, were practically devoid of Jews. Among the other crafts only the smiths included some Jews, but in no way very noticeably; for Jews were automatically excluded from craft guilds, as from those of the merchants. As for agriculture, Emery confirms the view that Jews did not and could not own real estate, with the exception of small lots and houses in towns, and, rarest of exceptions, such holdings as the vineyards of the scholar Rashi. Moreover, if for the Christian land was the most secure investment, for the Jew of the middle ages it was the least so, since it was the most obvious form of property and he could not take it with him in the event of expulsion. He was safer in keeping his wealth in as liquid a form as possible so as to conceal or remove it as necessity dictated. Such practices, of course, constituted a fillip to capitalistic enterprise, but if initially important it became a mere rivulet in the stream of Christian capital investment flowing by the thirteenth century. Moreover, it was a practice forced on Jews from outside and owed nothing to their religious teachings.

Emery also deals with the question of moneylending and usury. Although restricted by the Church to taking "interest" (roughly equivalent to the "just price") but not "usury" (considered excessive), Jews frequently received royal support for "usurious" activity. Kings, as we have seen, were recognized in law as having sole jurisdiction over Jews as royal chattels, and they came to look upon Jewish economic activities as necessary and profitable to the crown. (In twelfth-century England, for example, the Jews—though less than one percent of the population—contributed 10 percent to the royal income.) And since no such transactions could be conducted without a royal charter, costly alike to purchase and to renew, kings in effect were the Jews' silent partners. As such they often came into conflict with ecclesiastical courts trying to enforce the canonical ban on usury, and sought to enforce in the royal courts their own decrees licensing Jews to collect interest at higher rates than the Councils of 1179 and 1215 allowed.

We may see in Emery's work how these rates, varying though they did according to time and place, were generally high. Frequently they were set at a maximum of 12 to 20 percent, but royal decrees generally permitted much higher rates. Thus 40 to 50 percent was not unusual, and 80 to 100 percent far from rare. This does not mean, however, that the Jewish moneylender was a "Shylock," for his Christian competitor was equally or still more exacting of the pound of flesh. (In this connection it is instructive to note that the poor of Paris protested to the king on these grounds when he expelled the Jews from the country in 1306.) It demonstrates rather that the risk of non-repayment was great, that the taxes and fees which Jews had constantly to pay into the royal coffers to preserve their privileges were high (expenses, incidentally, to which Christian financiers were much less subject), and that capital was extremely scarce. The Shylock myth, made immortal by Shakespeare's *Merchant of Venice*, is thus to a considerable degree of royal manufacture—especially if we remember that kings commonly required Jewish moneylenders to pay large "fines" in order to exceed the legal rate, which was prohibitively low. To Emery, the villain Shylock, depicted by Shakespeare as grasping, full of deceptions, preying on the poor, the weak, and the unprotected, is no more than a "conventional stereotype," of whom there is no trace in the actual sources of medieval life.[2] Finally, we may note here that Emery singles out Sombart only to say that his data from Perpignan in no way bear out, but contradict, the German scholar's divagations on the character of medieval Jewish economic life.

The Court Jew

Royal dependence on Jewish wealth gave rise to elaborate legislation for the regulation and protection of the Jewish community. Thus, in England, a body known as the "Jewish Parliament" was set up to deal with taxation, the settlement of disputes within the community, the choice or confirmation of rabbis, etc. Beyond protecting so as to exploit his golden goose, what Cecil Roth calls "the royal milch-cow," the king frequently conferred on Jews such posts as the ministry of finance. A Jew brought to such offices not only great financial expertise and resources but an unequivocal loyalty to the king, often the one rampart between him and the courtier wolves, who were envious of his position and anxious to bring him down. This is the phenomenon of the "court Jew" or "privileged Jew." Here, as first with Jewish commercial and then with Jewish financial activities, there is a displacement in time and place from the more advanced to the less advanced societies, as the Jewish minister of the treasury, master of the mint, agent for provisioning the army, etc., gave way to Christians who had learned from them the necessary techniques.

Little is known of the "court Jew" in England and France down to the expulsions; in Spain he was important (as Isaac Abarbanel's career indicates) down to 1492. But,

from the fifteenth to the eighteenth century, he was prominent at the German courts (of which there were hundreds)
and in eastern Europe. It was they, especially after 1648,
who directed the mints and controlled the currency,
financed and provisioned the army, managed the investment of the prince's wealth, and procured for him such
luxury items as jewelry, tapestries, silk cloth, and works of
art. Sometimes royal confidence in and dependence upon a
Jewish minister was such that he could intercede with his
master to relieve some of the disabilities of his ghetto-
bound co-religionists, to prevent their expulsion by this
princeling or that town, and to gain for them greater
security and prosperity—and German Jews did on the
whole gain both greater security and prosperity, and even a
degree of social acceptance, in the course of the eighteenth
century. The story ended tragically, however, in most
instances, as we saw with J. S. Oppenheimer. Finance
ministers, like those who lived by moneylending, were
never popular figures. Thus, once the minister ceased to be
indispensable, or once his royal benefactor died and was
succeeded by a prince of a different outlook, he invariably
fell from power—a fall that usually entailed the forfeiture
of his wealth and his life, and was often followed by a
general massacre or expulsion of his fellow Jews. One of
the most interesting and reliable portions of Sombart's
book is his presentation of the role of Jewish ministers of
finance in rebuilding the state apparatus of power and
administration that had been so crippled in the dynastic
and religious wars of 1500 to 1648. Having functioned as
catalysts in the initiation of commercial and banking enterprise, Jews came to be notable as midwives at the birth of
the modern state, centralized, efficient, financially stable,
and run by a corps of trained civil servants.

The Medieval Jew

Generally speaking, the medieval Jew was poor, often miserably so. The one exception to this generalization was Spain, where the freedom and prosperity Jews enjoyed under the Moors carried over in the Spanish Christian kingdoms to as late as 1391. Not compelled as elsewhere to abandon handicrafts, Jews remained prominent in them, particularly in the production of textiles. They were likewise extensively engaged in commerce, and it is instructive to find that Jewish moneylenders were few and far between in Spain, thus underlining our contention that they entered the loan business only by force of external circumstances.

Outside of Spain, where the wealthy Jew was the exception, he was characteristically a philanthropist, dispensing much of his wealth in the form of charity among his co-religionists. Not infrequently he was a rabbi, such as the great biblical and talmudic scholar Rashi. One extremely interesting phenomenon of medieval Jewish life may be noted here parenthetically: that is the remarkable degree of economic emancipation of women. Not only did they engage in business as widows continuing the work of their late husbands, but also in their own right during their husband's lifetime. This was the origin of the widespread practice of a later day by which women won the family's livelihood in order that their husbands could have sufficient leisure for scholarship, that jewel beyond price. (The practice has the special sanction of Proverbs 31:10–31, where the ideal wife is described as the family breadwinner.)

Sixteenth and Seventeenth Centuries

In the sixteenth and seventeenth centuries Jews played an important part in the economic life of the Netherlands, then in the vanguard of European economic development. The commercial and financial center of Europe as well as the capital of an overseas empire, the Lowlands were enormously productive, enterprising, and prosperous. Sombart explains this economic shift from the Iberian peninsula and the Mediterranean to the Low Countries and the north in terms of the Jewish refugees expelled from Spain and Portugal in 1492 and 1496 respectively. "Israel," he wrote, "passes over Europe like the sun; at its coming new life bursts forth, at its going all falls into decay."

Though the Jewish contribution was important in the Netherlands, it would be an exaggeration to say that it was decisive. After all, the foundations of Dutch prosperity were laid before the arrival of the Jews on the scene and subsequent developments would probably have been much the same with or without them. This conclusion is confirmed by two further considerations. First, most of the refugees made their way elsewhere—to Turkey, North Africa, and eastern Europe—where their settlement was not followed by any blaze of capitalist enterprise. Second, when in the later seventeenth century the economic hub of Europe shifted again, from the Netherlands to England, Jews had nothing much to do with it. There were Jews back in England since Oliver Cromwell's time. They engaged in financial operations, but interesting and significant though these contributions were, they were neither decisive nor indispensable. A very careful study of *The Early History of Banking in England* by R. D. Richards concludes, contra-Sombart, that "it is inaccurate to say that the Jews had a very great share in the establishment of the Bank of England, that English finance in the seventeenth century was very extensively controlled by Jews, that Jews were the principal participants in the first English loan, or that a very large part of the capital of the Bank of England came from Holland."

The Present Day

Thereafter, the story is very similar. Jewish economic activity is interesting and important to the economic historian of the development of Europe, but the role of Jews as initiators of economic activity steadily diminished. For example, Jews participated here and there in the various stages of the Industrial Revolution; in the annals of its financing, organization, inventions, etc., one runs upon Jewish names, but they did not initiate or dominate its development. Today Jews in Western Europe and America tend to be found in certain zones of economic endeavor. Broadly speaking, the majority of them gain their living in commerce, industry, the professions, and the so-called white-collar occupations, and, within these classifications, they tend to be concentrated in certain subdivisions. In the area of commerce, for example, the majority of Jews are engaged in retail trading, while in industry they are primarily to be found in the manufacture of textiles, clothing, furs, shoes, and food. (At the same time, they are practically unrepresented in the heavy industries of steel, coal, automobiles, oil, etc.) As for the professions, there is a concentration in law, medicine, dentistry, pharmacy, and the academic world.

Jews today are underrepresented in agriculture (although this is not true in the new state of Israel, where there has been a significant return to the land) as well as in banking and stock brokerage. This is particularly remarkable (and may come as a surprise) in the light of the prominence and influence Jewish international bankers and financiers had during the nineteenth century. For example, the Rothschilds of England financed Benjamin Disraeli's acquisition of the Suez Canal in 1874 and floated large loans in behalf of the North during the American Civil War. Germany affords an example also. Jews were prominent as bank directors and in maritime shipping. Bismarck's friend Gerson Bleichröder was a Jewish banker through whom he made capital loans to Russia and thus maintained the Russo-German alliance that was fundamental to German diplomacy down to 1890. The four largest banks of Germany were frequently headed by Jewish presidents. Today, by contrast, great banking houses are not in the least notable for the number or prominence of Jews among their executives; particularly in New York City are they underrepresented.

What explanation, then, can we offer for Jewish concentration and importance in certain ages in certain capitalistic enterprises? Sombart's explanation that Judaism is a highly legalistic and rational religion, and thereby induces in Jews a special capacity for the kind of rational and shrewd calculation which leads to the making of profit, simply does not stand up. It is untenable because he overlooked the profoundly mystical and non-rational aspects of Judaism which are expressed, as we have seen, by Solomon ibn Gabirol, Judah Halevi, and, above all, in the Kabbalah. ("The course of Jewish history," it has been observed, "is a long series of struggles between rationalistic and mystical elements.") In the calamitous sixteenth and seventeenth centuries the Jewish temperament and cast of mind were shaped far more decisively by the Kabbalah's mysticism and messianic hopes than by the Maimonidean rationalistic conception of calculable cause followed by predictable effect. Similarly, Hasidism in the eighteenth and nineteenth centuries and the writings of Martin Buber in the twentieth century testify to the pervasiveness of the anti-rational, mystical element in the Jewish faith. There exists, moreover, an enormous number of prophetic and other texts warning the believer against the accumulation of riches as an end in itself. So that, taking all these factors together, the only possible conclusion is that Judaism neither encourages nor represses economic activity; rather it accepts such activity as a human necessity, and seeks to regulate it in accordance with Scripture.

In the medieval world, the critical formative period for the whole question, first trade and then banking were thrust upon Jews as a result of their exclusion from other fields. Their success was a mark of their adaptation to the circumstances of their environment, hostile though that environment usually was. A further question suggests itself: What was the origin of the skill and acumen that enabled the Jews to take advantage of economic opportunties? Partly, as we have seen, it was because they brought the required techniques with them from the Islamic world, where such practices were commonplace. More decisive, and the key to the whole question, was education. Medieval education, when it existed, was for the monastery and the spiritual life. The Protestant Reformation, with its emphasis on reading and knowing the Bible, did much to introduce education for the laity. Yet it was not until the eighteenth century that popular education can be said to have begun, while it was only in the nineteenth century that national systems of education for all were inaugurated. At a period when most Christians were illiterate, the synagogue flourished as a center of popular education and of scholarship, for the Jews insisted, as a religious duty, upon a system of education of remarkable thoroughness.[3] Such mental training, which began at a quite young age, was intended to gain a mastery of the Torah, but it also sharpened the faculties for winning a livelihood. Other important factors that have been mentioned include the Jews' wide dispersion within a nexus of credit and international contacts, the necessity to keep their wealth in as liquid a form as possible, etc.

All these factors, it should be noted, are environmental ones and have nothing to do with race or religion. There is every reason to believe that when Jews are permitted, as they are in a democratic society, to enter any economic field, they will be scattered, once the traditions of the past have worn themselves out, more or less proportionate to their numbers throughout all the occupations and will cease to constitute a distinct economic group, as they still do, for example, in the clothing industry.

For lack of space I cannot pursue the question any

further. Suffice it to say that the long-standing ascription of certain invidious economic traits to the Jews has no basis in fact and is simply wrong. Yet the Shylock stereotype has penetrated to the marrow of our cultural bones, as anyone may see by taking a look at an unabridged dictionary. There he will find that the connotations of the word *Jew* are "to cheat in trade," "to Jew one out of a horse," "to Jew down the price," "to get the better of someone in a bargain," "refers to the proverbial shrewdness of Jewish traders," "a person who drives a hard bargain," "as an adjective it is taken to be offensive," etc. On the other hand, *Christian* has such associations as "a decent, civilized, or presentable person, characteristic of Christian people," "kindly," etc. The same kind of automatic prejudice will often come forth in attempts to explain the business success of two men, one Jewish, the other not. Of the first all that needs to be said, it seems, is that he is a Jew; his Jewishness explains his success and is inevitably associated with cunning, sharp practice, hard dealing, as in our dictionary quotations. A Christian's success, however, even though achieved in the same business and in the same way, will tend to be explained as a Horatio Alger saga of "rags to riches," or as "Yankee ingenuity," "American know-how," "frontier determination and hard work," etc. Hopefully these wrongheaded notions, fundamental as they are to the vilest kind of anti-Semitic prejudice, will ultimately die. Hopefully, too, the truth will one day triumph, and a new edition of the unabridged dictionary will show that our society thinks and feels differently about the issue.

NOTES

[1] The situation depicted here was not unique. Speaking of Protestant Nonconformists to the Established Church in her book *Eighteenth Century England,* Dorothy Marshall concludes: "Because they were [legally] debarred from so many activities,

both Quakers and Dissenters frequently turned their energies into opportunities offered by industry, and later by banking." Other parallels suggest themselves in her observation that "many disliked the Dissenters because they were different and did not conform to the established norm," while "others were jealous of their worldly success"; hence it was easy to inflame mobs against them: "To storm their meeting-houses and to break their windows with the cry of 'The Church in danger' was a delightful occupation."

2 Shakespeare is no mere anti-Jewish propagandist, for he asks, "Hath not a Jew eyes? Hath not a Jew hands, organs, dimensions, senses, affections, passions? Fed with the same food, hurt with the same weapons, subject to the same diseases, healed by the same means, warmed and cooled by the same winter as a Christian is?"

3 The notion of the Dark Ages, when the lamps of scholarship burned low or went out and men were abysmally illiterate and ignorant, is altogether inapplicable to medieval Jewish history.

9. Emancipation

France

The great milestone in the European age of Jewish history is the French Revolution. One of its early leaders was the Comte de Mirabeau. He had visited Prussia, knew Mendelssohn, and was much impressed by a book inspired by him, the non-Jew C. W. von Dohm's *On the Civil Amelioration of the Jews*; on his return to Paris he published a book on Mendelssohn and advocated in its pages fundamental changes in the Jews' status. These ideas were taken up by the Revolutionary Assembly and resulted in legislation in September, 1791, granting full equality to Jews. The Marranos in Bordeaux and Bayonne—a small, prosperous élite—caused no difficulty, but the Jews of Alsace-Lorraine (annexed from the Holy Roman Empire in 1738) constituted a large downtrodden proletariat. Hence the example of the American Constitution of 1787, granting full equality to Jews for the first time since the Roman Empire, carried little weight in the debates, since Jews were so few in number in the United States. Two years of debate finally carried their Emancipation, for, as the Abbé Grégoire argued, "If you must consider the past crimes of the Jews and their present degradation, do it to contemplate the work of your own hands. You made their vices, now make their virtues."

The price of equality and liberty, reminiscent of Frederick the Great's decree, was a great curtailment of Jewish autonomy, even in matters of religion. They had to become Frenchmen—if they refused, "let them be banished," one of the debaters had declared—and dismantle most of their judicial and administrative structure in favor of the national system. Under the Civil Constitution of the Clergy rabbis ultimately became paid officials of the state.

With the arrival of Napoleon the price of Emancipation became even clearer. In the same spirit that he styled himself Emperor, successor to Caesar and Charlemagne, he revived the ancient Sanhedrin and fashioned a hierarchal system of consistories and grand rabbis. His chief concern was to break down Jewish segregation and autonomy; he was satisfied of their loyalty when he learned from the Sanhedrin that Jews were as patriotic as anyone, willing to pay taxes and serve in his armies, although the Sanhedrin balked on the issue of intermarriage with non-Jews, what Napoleon thought an obvious gateway to integration.

Napoleon seems also to have been interested in founding a Jewish national state and resettling the world's Jewish population there. Where this was to be is not clear. Possibly his famous Egyptian expedition of 1798, had it succeeded, was linked to some plan of resettlement in Palestine. There is, however, much truth in the sardonic observation long after that one finds in Theodor Herzl's *Diaries;* there it is reported that any such design was intended to add a cubit to Napoleon's power, rather than to serve a humanitarian cause: the conqueror was more concerned "to convert the scattered peoples of the globe into his agents," and the espousal of their cause would have been simply a means to that end.

The emperor is less important for his reorganization of Jewish life in France (most of which did not survive him) or his flirting with Zionism than for bearing the banner of

Emancipation throughout Europe. In the Netherlands (the Batavian Republic) equality dated from as early as 1795. Italy's ghetto walls were pulled down by the revolutionary armies and the blessing of equality bestowed. So, too, in Germany, the whole of which west of the Rhine was incorporated into France, while the rest of the German states came under French influence, directly or indirectly. Even benighted Prussia, once it suffered a thumping defeat in 1806 at Jena, swept practically the whole of its Jewish disabilities into the dust heap. Polish Jews doubly revered Napoleon: as Poles because he resurrected a Polish state in the form of the Grand Duchy of Warsaw, and as Jews because he brought them the priceless gift of Emancipation. A Polish legion that included many Jews was part of the French army, and a fascinating figure in it was Colonel Joselowicz Berek, who died fighting for Napoleon against Austria in 1809; he had been Kosciuszko's lieutenant in the Polish revolt of the early 1790's against Russian domination, when he commanded the "Polish Jewish Regiment" of thirty-five hundred men in that lost cause.

Throughout the vast area ruled either by Napoleon, or by his brothers, or where his influence made itself felt, Jewish disabilities, in greater or lesser degree, disappeared. Jews began to participate in civil life, sometimes holding local offices or seats in municipal councils; they fought in all the armies and even rose into the officer corps. In France, naturally, their integration into the national life proceeded furthest, but everywhere it was underway. Jews began to extol the Revolution and Napoleon in little less than messianic terms, especially in the period of reaction after 1815. Heinrich Heine never ceased to adore Napoleon as his idol, and German Jews, still adopting surnames in the Napoleonic and Metternich eras, frequently took that of *Schöntheil*, a translation of *Bonaparte*.

Napoleon's defeat and overthrow in 1815 appeared, at least initially, to be a Waterloo for the cause of Jewish

Emancipation as well. Throughout Europe the clock was turned back, or the attempt was made to turn it back, in the name of "legitimacy" and "restoration." Yet in the quarter century since 1789 Emancipation had become part of French national life and was so widely accepted that the restored monarch, Louis XVIII, did not dare to tamper much with the revolutionary and Napoleonic legislation. In 1817 a Napoleonic decree that had partly restricted Jewish economic activity was due to expire, but such was the acceptance of Emancipation by the nation that no one proposed extending the restrictions and so they fell by the wayside. Thereafter a few small measures completed and rounded out Jewish equality; e g., as of 1831, rabbis were paid salaries out of the state treasury as Catholic priests and Protestant ministers had been—a situation that lasted until abolition by the law separating Church and State in 1905.

Jewish assimilation went faster, was more frictionless, and more fully completed in France than anywhere else. Looking back to 1789, French Jews referred to "our immortal Revolution" and declared that liberty, equality, fraternity, were first proclaimed to the world "in the voice of our Prophets" and by "our Holy Scriptures." Especially notable was Jewish entry into the national political system. From the 1830's on a number of Jews held high government posts. The Liberal Adolphe Crémieux (1796–1880) was the minister of justice who abolished slavery in the French colonies and secured legislation that did away with the death penalty for political prisoners; he was the leading figure in the educational and philanthropic institution, Alliance Israélite Universelle, founded in 1860 to render assistance to non-French Jews; he worked closely with his English counterpart, Sir Moses Montefiore, and the Board of Deputies of British Jews. Achille Fould was minister of state and minister of finance to Napoleon III. Léon Blum was premier several times under the Third French

Republic. Concomitantly, French Jews were in the vanguard of banking: Emile and Isaac Péreire built the first railway in France; an outstanding figure in banking, public finance, railway construction, politics, and much else was James Rothschild.

With the rise of French Jews to economic affluence and political power, anti-Semitic writers began to appear, clamoring against what they claimed was Jewish domination of the economic and political life of France. It was in such circumstances that was born the notion that Jews had invented capitalism and were the arch-capitalists who sat in the smoke-filled rooms or manipulated matters on the back stairs where all the reins of power, whether financial or political, lay in their hands. This caricature was very much a part of the early socialists' outlook in France and in much of Europe; indeed some of the most vitriolic attacks on Jews were made by socialist labor leaders. Nineteenth-century anti-Semitism, especially in its early stages, stemmed in large measure from this supposed equation of Jews and capitalism, and, as a consequence, there was to some degree a segregated Jewish socialist movement. On the other hand, toward the end of the century, it began to be asserted that Jews were the inventors of socialism and communism: Karl Marx was a Jew, etc., etc.

In France, however, Jews were much more prominent in the ranks of the establishment than among those aligned against it. Hence the anti-Semitism that began to emerge was of the socialist, anti-capitalist variety. E.g., Charles Fourier referred to Jews as parasites and one of his disciples, Toussend, sounded the tocsin in his Jew-baiting book, *The Jews, the Kings of Our Era.* Much fuel for anti-Semitic fires was provided by the bankruptcy of the Union Générale in 1882: it had been founded as a distinctly Catholic banking institution by a man once employed by James Rothschild; its collapse was blamed on the Jews' stranglehold on finance and invoked as proof of a deep dark conspiracy of Jews to take over France. The classic best seller of nineteenth-century anti-Semitism, the Catholic journalist Edouard Drumont's *La France Juive,* 1886, gathered in all these strands (we should add the racial anti-Semitism that derived from writers like the Comte de Gobineau) and presented them in what appeared to be plausible scholarship and in what certainty was an eloquent literary style; this enormous book, with conspiracy bursting forth on every page, went through a hundred editions in one year and was quickly translated into German, English, Spanish, and Polish.

The explanation of its frenzied reception in France may be seen in the difficult circumstances that the Third Republic found itself in. Parallel to the German Weimar Republic of 1918, it was born of humiliation and defeat in the war of 1870–1871; its liberal, democratic, anti-clerical, and perhaps semi-socialistic tendencies generated a profound revulsion and antagonism in conservatives, monarchists, Catholics, the officer corps, etc., who sought time after time to topple the Republic. In the fanatical nationalism that became the national mood after 1870, Jews were made very uncomfortable because their nationality could be assailed as defective or incomplete; the more intense the national spirit and the more grievous the national plight, the more readily were Jews singled out as dangerous, disruptive, treasonable, etc. Drumont's paranoid accusations and allegations came at a time when France, especially the anti-Republicans, desperately needed a scapegoat. Truth and logic are, of course, troublesome encumbrances to someone fabricating a scapegoat: hence Drumont is full of errors, lies, and exaggerations. Hundreds of Catholics, Protestants, secularists, atheists, freethinkers, etc., appear in his pages as "scheming Jews" in the seats of power; one can only conclude that his definition of "the Jews" was simply everyone whom he hated or envied, regardless of his religion or ethnic background. As might be expected, pointing up errors, whether big or small, had no effect on him, or on the sale of his book, or on the long series of similar books this most vituperative and inveterate Jew-baiter published in succeeding years. His anti-Semitic crusade gained added momentum from 1892 on, when he began to publish the newspaper *La Libre Parole*; he did not have to convince, but only to cater to a will to believe any anti-Jewish accusation, no matter how flimsy or ludicrous or crude. His remedy was expulsion of the Jews from France, but in the long run he thought the only solution was that all the European powers combine to deal the Jews "a big and simultaneous blow."

In 1894 Captain Alfred Dreyfus of the French General Staff was accused of treason; he was the first Jew to have attained a General Staff post, and his appointment had occasioned some muttering in the army. When it was ascertained that French military secrets were being transmitted to the Germans, a list of possible culprits was drawn up; but, upon coming to Dreyfus' name, it was unnecessary to go further: so great had been the impact of Drumont that Dreyfus' Jewishness convicted him. Amid agitations and near riots (in the forefront of which was Drumont), Dreyfus was tried, convicted, publicly degraded from rank, and sentenced to life imprisonment on Devil's Island. Dreyfus' brother pursued the matter further and turned up evidence of forgeries that vindicated the captain, and the case had to be reopened. Without much regard for the evidence, France divided into Dreyfusards—liberals, republicans, anti-clericals, democrats, socialists—and anti-Dreyfusards—conservatives, Catholics, monarchists, reactionaries, all those for whom the issue of Dreyfus came as a Heaven-sent weapon to overthrow the Third Republic. The novelist Emile Zola came forward at the head of the "Twelve Sane Men of France" with his celebrated pamphlet *J'accuse*, and he did much to win the cause for "the most infamously abused Jew of modern times." Yet it was 1899 before a retrial opened, when Dreyfus was again found guilty, but given a much reduced sentence, on grounds of "extenuating circumstances" (presumably there is no such thing in a case of treason) ! The president of the Republic "pardoned" Dreyfus, however; by 1905 the appeals courts had quashed the proceedings, acquitting him of all charges and reinstating him in the army. He was promoted to major and decorated with the Legion of Honor; he fought bravely in World War I and lived until 1935.

There had been a conspiracy, as Drumont said; but it was, as Zola said, a conspiracy of the army high command against Dreyfus; it was a "crime of high treason against humanity." One of the heroes was Georges Clemenceau, the Tiger of World War I, in whose newspaper Zola's plea was published. The greatest hero was Colonel Picquart, a professional soldier and a devout Catholic. Despite threats, obstruction, demotion, he persisted in his efforts to prosecute the real culprit (Colonel Esterhazy) ; truth and justice meant more to him than "the honor of the army" or the position insisted upon by Catholic spokesmen.

Thus in the early twentieth century France had an unsavory reputation as a benighted citadel of anti-Semitism. Yet the anti-Dreyfusards so discredited themselves and their anti-Semitic and anti-democratic cause that, once Dreyfus was acquitted and out of the spotlight, the whole thing began to look in retrospect like a huge aberration. Above all, the Republic had not been overthrown, for when the test came the liberal, republican, democratic forces were strong enough to sustain it; since the cause of Jewish Emancipation and social equality was bound up with the victorious forces, the ultimate outcome of the Dreyfus affair was to confirm and strengthen the free status of the Jews. The sequel, a clear indication that it was a pathological episode that had passed, may be seen in the political career of Léon Blum (1872–1950) [1] several times premier in later French governments. The fate of the Third French Republic at the turn of the century thus contrasts, after some initial parallels, with that of the German Weimar Republic in 1933: the liberal and democratic forces in Germany, favorable as they were to Jewish rights, were not strong enough to sustain the Republic, with the tragic consequence that it was overthrown by the intensely nationalistic, anti-liberal, anti-democratic, anti-Semitic forces gathered together under Hitler. French Jews remained in full possession of the rights of man and citizen, both in law and in life, until the German conquest of 1940; it is a mark of their acceptance and assimilation that Hitler's S.S. could track down only about 30 percent of the quarter million French Jews.

Let Marc Bloch (1886–1944), one of the greatest historians of the twentieth century, offer his moving testimony to the consummation of French acceptance of Jews and Jewish acceptance of France. Professor of medieval social and economic history and the world's foremost authority on feudalism, he had served in the French army in both world wars; he was active in the French Resistance, was caught, tortured, and shot by the Nazis. In his will he wanted to affirm, "in the face of death, that I was born a Jew: that I have never denied it, nor ever even attempted to do so. In a world assailed by the most appalling barbarism, is not the generous tradition of the Hebrew Prophets, which Christianity at its highest and noblest took over and expanded, one of the best justifications we can have for living, believing and fighting?" He went on to say, "I have, through life, felt that I was above all, and quite simply, a Frenchman. A family tradition, already of long date, has bound me firmly to my country. I have found nourishment in her spiritual heritage and in her history. I can, indeed, think of no other land whose air I should have breathed with such a sense of ease and freedom. I have loved her greatly, and served her with all my strength. I have never found that the fact of being a Jew has at all hindered these sentiments." A great and good human being, the soul of kindness, he exemplifies the observation half a century earlier of Bernard Lazare: "Being a Jew is the least difficult way of being truly human."[2]

Holland, Belgium, Italy

The period of the French Revolution saw the establishment under French auspices of a "Batavian Republic" in the Netherlands, the area outside of France which came most directly and permanently under the influence of the Revolution. It required little prompting there to incorporate in the constitution and to enforce liberty, equality, and religious freedom for all. By 1798 some Jews had been appointed or elected to important government posts. Under Napoleon the situation changed little beyond the incorporation of the Batavian Republic into the French Empire. And while Napoleon's downfall in 1815 was Waterloo for Jewish Emancipation in much of Europe, it was not so in the Netherlands. The Congress of Vienna re-created the Netherlands as an independent state in 1815, and its constitution preserved without impairment the earlier legislation. Nor was this undone by the Revolution of 1830 (which began in an opera house), when the country was divided to form Belgium and Holland. For both countries perpetuated (under international guarantee in Belgium) Jewish Emancipation. This noble experiment was so thoroughly successful—in law as well as in life—that over the next half century Belgium and Holland set the standard as compelling models of Jewish Emancipation for the rest of Europe. There is nothing in the annals of either country comparable to the Dreyfus frenzy, pogroms, or anti-Semitic press elsewhere. This happy state of things lasted until Hitler's invasion of 1940.

Second only to the Netherlands, the French impact was greatest in Italy, particularly the northern half of the peninsula, which was incorporated into the French Empire. A dramatic moment was Napoleon's capture of Rome, followed by torchlight ceremonies that saw with great jubilation and enthusiasm the proclamation of liberty, equality, religious freedom to Jews and everyone; all over Italy the ghettos were destroyed, the Inquisition abolished, and "citizen rabbis," as they were addressed, began to dedicate part of the synagogue service to prayers for the great liberator. With his overthrow the clock was turned back. Yet there were obvious limits to such a reaction after Emancipation had been experienced for not much short of a generation, especially in the country where the freer atmosphere of the Renaissance had never quite died out. Thus, while the old code of the *status quo ante* returned, practically nowhere in Italy were all its prescriptions enforced.

The principal exceptions to this rule were the kingdom of Sardinia-Piedmont, the duchy of Modena, and worst of all, the Papal States. The Papal States were the most obscurantist regime of western Europe, and down to 1870 the post-1815 reaction was most complete there. This included the restoration in all its shame and gloom of the Roman ghetto, although reaction stopped short of the reimposition of the yellow badge or the crimson hat. The explanation of the papacy's attitude lies partly in its humiliation at the hands of Napoleon and its great fear of the revolutionary program. In a larger sense the Church was more on the defensive than ever. Since the Reformation and the sixteenth century it had been a party to the conservative alliance of "throne and altar," and it could not afford to turn anything but a face of stone to the forces of change. The quarter century after 1789 saw the Church besieged in body and mind. For the papacy, subjection to Napoleon was a renewed Babylonian Captivity. The Revolution brought, from the viewpoint of the Church, only calamity, persecution, and martyrdom, the loss of property and of educational institutions and functions, while the temper of the age was increasingly secular, skeptical, democratic. The experiences of that quarter century were such as to confirm and deepen Catholic defensiveness, making it a kind of complex.

In the years after 1815 modernity appeared more than ever the enemy. In the revolutions that spluttered off and on until the 1850's, many of them in Italy, ephemeral regimes came into existence that re-enacted the revolutionary program of 1789, including Jewish Emancipation. Jews flocked to Mazzini's banner and were prominent in his "Young Italy" movement. A converted Jew, Daniel Manin, proclaimed a Venetian Republic in 1848. The next year, the Roman Republic was proclaimed by Mazzini, and like others that initiated a democratic government which guaranteed Emancipation it proved shortlived. Its ephemeralness did nothing to soften Pope Pius IX's deep-seated fears of revolution, democracy, or modernity. Under his leadership the Church became the rampart of conservatism. His indictment of liberalism and modernity in the *Syllabus of Errors*, 1864, is the peak of the Catholic obsession against change, and conferred upon Catholics a mentality that has been characterized as "a Maginot line of impenetrable defense." This meant that biblical studies except of the most traditionalist kind were brought nearly to an end through the first half of the twentieth century; and in the wake of papal threats the scholarly career of someone like Father Marie-Joseph Lagrange came to grief and the mystical faith of even so intense a Catholic as Baron von Hügel fell under papal suspicion. Such fears for the Catholic faith made it readily possible for the Vatican to become an ally of and reach concordats with governments that were the bodyguards of reaction, a practice that had grim results in the twentieth century and that made the hierarchy tolerant of such a regime as that of Perón in Argentina. Some change in outlook came with Pope Leo XIII, but the new era of *Aggiornamento* came only with the immortal John XXIII.

In the meantime Italian unification had been effected by the kingdom of Sardinia-Piedmont. In the post-1815 era it had been one of the most reactionary and benighted domains of Italy. But in 1848 it grudgingly accepted the insurgents' demands for legal equality and religious freedom, and thereafter these rights were ungrudgingly enforced, especially after 1851 when Cavour became premier. He was a liberal and constitutionalist on the English model, and did much to imbue the kingdom of Italy—of which he was the chief architect—with the spirit of English parliamentarianism and French egalitarianism. As Sicily, Naples, Milan, Florence, Venice, were annexed to the Italian kingdom (often through the efforts of Garibaldi, whose army numbered a significant proportion of Jews), so too was Jewish Emancipation extended into these areas. The climax came in 1870 when Italian armies broke into Rome and extinguished the pope's temporal power and domain. Rome, its infamous ghetto gone, became the capital of the new Italy. To this development Pius IX could not reconcile himself: rather than conclude a peace settlement with the constitutional monarchy of Victor Emmanuel, he became "the prisoner of the Vatican."

The year 1870 is thus a great milestone in the progress of Emancipation. A year later Bismarck's Imperial Constitution for the new Germany embodied the same principle of legal equality and freedom of religion. As of 1867–1868 the Habsburgs granted the same constitutional rights. Elsewhere the dates are as follows: England 1858, Norway 1855, Sweden 1853, Denmark 1848; Switzerland, seemingly as medieval in this respect as Russia, granted Emancipation last, in 1874, and then only after having been goaded into doing so by diplomatic pressure and commercial threats from France, England, and the United States. The third quarter of the century is thus the high tide of the liberal movement in Europe: Jewish Emancipation was carried everywhere and sustained on that high tide (except in Spain and Portugal, where there were, presumably, no Jews to liberate). Emancipation seemed to have triumphed once and for all. Yet in the succeeding century the tide was ominously turned back in one country after another, so much so that the timetable laid out above seems to have been only preliminary and tentative. Moreover, Emancipation as enacted by 1874 applied only to a small minority of the world's Jews, ignoring those of Russia (where it came only in 1917), Asia, and Africa. Indeed historians of the future may well conclude that neither 1787, nor 1789, nor 1848, nor 1874, nor 1917–1919, but 1946, marks the real onset of the era of Emancipation, in life as well as law. E.g., unlike the peace settlement reached at Versailles in 1919, that of 1946 with Italy, Hungary, Bulgaria, Rumania, and Finland saw no difficulty made by anyone about the principles of equality and religious freedom for all citizens. Such principles were taken for granted, despite the fact that the Jewish delegations present at the negotiations had no levers of power politics at their disposal and that nothing had to be conceded to them to gain their support. Elsewhere, also, no one dared to proclaim a system of constitutional discrimination or inequality, although actual practice may leave much to be desired; thus even in the Arab states—the old ones as well as the newly created Syria, Jordan, Lebanon—a profession of full equality for all was made and still stands even if it is evaded by subterfuge. (South Africa and Rhodesia are grimly out of step with the world with their policy of *Apartheid.*)

In Italy, however, until the sorry day when Mussolini became junior partner to Hitler, the story of the Jews is a happy one: Emancipation as of 1870 was real and Jewish assimilation proceeded so rapidly that the leaders of the Jewish community (not much over forty thousand) became alarmed that the community would disappear. In the years before World War I Jews were prominent in Italian political life. Most notable was Luigi Luzzatti, a professional economist who became premier and had two other Jews in his cabinet; as finance minister he had sought to "spiritualize the power of gold" by establishing cooperatives and founding the People's Banks. The mayor of Rome was a Jew. Nearly a dozen Jews attained the rank of general in the army, while all the professions from academic to legal and financial were open to them. No cry went up against "Jewish domination," anti-Semitism was hardly known, and such books as the *Protocols of the Elders of Zion* did not sell.

Neither the war of 1914 nor the first decade or so of Mussolini's fascist reign made much difference in this state of affairs. Until he became Hitler's rather helpless partner in crime, Mussolini refused to send any Jews to the death camps, so much so that Italy became something of a refuge for French and Balkan Jews fleeing the S.S. Nevertheless, twelve thousand Italian Jews, a quarter, were eventually carried off to cruel deaths "Himmler style." Moreover, fascism went fundamentally against the grain of Judaism; its glorification of the state as the one absolute before which all else is relative and its despotic regimentation of political and economic life cannot be reconciled with Judaism. Long before Italy's fatal embrace with Germany, eminent Italian Jews began to lose their positions, because they could not in conscience take the required loyalty oath; they began to disappear from university faculties, government posts, the professions, arts, and sciences. One of these was the renowned physicist Enrico Fermi. It is strange to record that the two scientists who had most to do with developing the atom bomb for the United States were two Jews who fled from fascist tyranny, Fermi from Italy and Albert Einstein from Germany. Happily one may record that since 1946 Italy has been a genuine democracy and that Italians have resumed their old tradition of regarding Jews as fellow citizens and fellow human beings, equally in private and public life.

Germany

Napoleon incorporated much of Germany into his Empire. In the Rhineland, particularly, Jewish disabilities and the whole of the *ancien régime* were swept away; equality and freedom of religion as embodied in the *Code Napoléon* became the order of the day. Revolutionary reforms spilled over into other parts of Germany where Napoleon's influence was only indirect, and before long numerous German states adopted constitutions and civil rights on the French model; this was a development, however, which had been prepared for partly by Joseph II's Patent of Toleration of 1781. In Prussia, where the harsher tradition of Frederick the Great still prevailed, a thoroughgoing reform and "regeneration" was inspired by Napoleon's stunning and humiliating defeat of the Prussian army at Jena in 1806. In the next dozen years a great body of reforms changed the whole of Prussian life, and one of the principal measures was the sweeping decree of 1812 granting full equality and citizenship to Jews; they were still barred from holding public offices but it was understood that this would be the subject of a future decree. That keystone in the arch of liberties never appeared, however, because the spokesmen of the old guard succeeded in rousing the fears of the king that the reformers were "Jacobins" bent upon turning "good old Prussia into a new-fangled Jewish state."

Prussia's capital at Berlin—its new university was the greatest in the world in the nineteenth century—became one of the three or four principal intellectual centers of Western civilization, and to this remarkable efflorescence the Jews of Berlin contributed astonishingly. To some extent Berlin's cultural life was a resumption of what we have seen there in Mendelssohn's time. One of Berlin's famous literary salons was that of his daughter Dorothea; two others were maintained by the Herz and Varnhagen von Ense families. To read the guest books of these three Jewish families is tantamount to naming the outstanding figures, Jews and Christians, of German literature down to the 1850's—the greatest of them was the Jewish lyric poet Heinrich Heine, who for a while belonged to a fascinating group of Jews and Christians calling themselves the Berlin Society for the Study of Judaism. This tradition lapsed in the period of Bismarck, when there seemed to be no outstanding Jews in German literature. But in the twentieth century, Berlin, Vienna, and Prague were famous as the residence of Hofmannsthal, Schnitzler, Kafka, Arnold and Stefan Zweig, and a great many others.

German Jews were indebted to the Prussian reformers of 1807–1819 in still another way. The outstanding Prussian statesmen, Hardenberg the chancellor and Wilhelm von Humboldt the education minister, became the spokesmen for Jewish Emancipation at the Congress of Vienna in 1814-1815. With the backing of Metternich of Austria, they secured an article in the constitution of the Germanic Confederation (replacing the defunct Holy Roman Empire) that was favorable to Jews. Members of the Confederation pledged themselves to maintain the free status of Jews that derived from the Napoleonic period, to which were added the international guarantees of all the signatories of the peace treaty at Vienna. It thus happened that until about 1824 Austria, Prussia, England, and even Russia protested or intervened in behalf of Jews against attempts to renew Jewish disabilities by various German states. In the period after 1824 these provisions became pretty much dead letters. Nevertheless, it is a measure of a degree of progress that neither the Germanic Confederation nor states like Prussia dared actually to repeal the emancipatory legislation or to enact new disabilities. Moreover, Jews would not, in the face of reaction, simply retire into the shadows of the ghetto again. They joined the political opposition and furnished notable leaders to all the parties left of center, from the moderate liberals to the extreme socialists and communists. The new type of Jew is represented by Gabriel Riesser, the eloquent and persuasive champion of Jewish Emancipation who played a central role in the Revolution of 1848.

Self-governing Frankfurt-am-Main had a quite different tradition from Berlin and Prussia. It had long before forfeited its reputation of the middle ages and early modern period as a haven of refuge and fair treatment for Jews. The city was the home of the Rothschilds. The five brothers under whom the banking firm reached the zenith of its wealth and influence—Nathan in London, James in Paris, Solomon in Vienna, Amschel in Frankfurt, and Karl in Naples—were the sons of Mayer, the founder of the business. In his time Jewish disabilities in Frankfurt were stark. He could not live or trade outside the ghetto, an insalubrious strip of land between the city sewer and the outer wall; he had to doff his hat to any street urchin who required of him, "Jew, do your duty." He was, for all that, so successful in his second-hand clothes business that in 1785 he could move his family of ten children out of their two-room shack into something ampler. He began to be able to deal in antiques and coins, and numbered among his clientele aristocrats and businessmen outside the ghetto; eventually he became Crown Agent to the prince of Hesse-Cassel, William IX, for whom he arranged loans, discounted bills, changed money, etc. In the meantime Napoleon conquered Hesse-Cassel and the prince fled, leaving the Rothschilds to manage his investments, which they did profitably for him and for themselves. It was in this connection that the branches of the firm were established in other cities, that of London becoming particularly important because it was the one money market beyond Napoleon's reach. Nathan became an agent of the British government and utilized his family connections to evade Napoleon's prohibitions in conveying British subsidies to the allies fighting France and also in getting funds to Wellington to maintain the British army in Spain; he also handled many British government loans and gained a reputation as a wizard on the London Stock Exchange.

In the period of peace after 1815, dominated by Metternich of Austria, the Rothschilds reached the summit of their fame, when they were referred to frequently as "the fourth great power." They developed the most efficient system of communications of the day, centered on London and utilizing carrier pigeons; they kept a ship constantly ready in the Channel near Dover and sent their couriers on systematic rounds from capital to capital. Not only was it the quickest system, but the information it provided was the most reliable and authoritative. The Vienna branch became financial manager to Friedrich Gentz, Metternich's secretary, and Solomon, gaining the confidence of both men, transacted many loans for the Austrian government and was kept closely informed of Austrian policies and intentions. Such information was passed on to the other branches, and was particularly useful to those of London and Paris. James in Paris made his services indispensable to a succession of French kings—Louis XVIII, Charles X, Louis Philippe; enjoying great prestige and dignity in French society, James was a principal financier of French railways and helped shape many important political decisions.

The Rothschilds, like the "court Jews" of an earlier day, sought, and with considerable success, to alleviate Jewish disabilities and to have Emancipation re-enacted after the fall of Napoleon. Emancipation of their co-religionists, rather than moneymaking, was their great passion. E.g., by utilizing the leverage of their financial services and with the favor of Metternich, they were able by 1822 to compel the grant of citizenship rights to Jews in their native Frankfurt. Rothschild influence was never so great as it was frequently made out to be; it was never the "Hidden

Hand" that anti-Semitic writers evoked. Its power to grant or refuse critical loans to governments made it a great force indeed in politics and international relations, but even in the lifetime of the five brothers disagreement among the various branches was such that they often worked against each other: the London branch was pro-English, the Parisian pro-French, etc. In the second and third generations these divergences inevitably widened. More important, perhaps, by the mid-nineteenth century, most governments began to act as their own financial agent, raising loans by selling bonds through their own treasury office, etc., and thus dependence on international banking houses such as the Rothschilds greatly diminished. The English Rothschilds continue to flourish as a great banking house, and have an especially interesting history. One of them was the first Jew to sit in the House of Commons, another to sit in the House of Lords; they initiated the settlement in Palestine of Jewish agricultural colonists in the 1880's, and were influential in bringing the British government to make the Balfour Declaration of 1917.

Whether, then, by the methods of Gabriel Riesser or of the Rothschilds, the cause of Jewish Emancipation made slow if uncertain progress in Germany as mid-century approached. It had enormous obstacles. For one thing the Napoleonic wars had been a profound stimulus to German nationalism; since it had its origin (in great measure) in Francophobia, the more intense German national feeling became, the more anti-Semitic it tended to be, because philo-Semitism and Emancipation were associated with the French enemy. German nationalism, also, had a *völkisch,* or racial, tinge from the start, and this made the Jew's German nationality appear to be incomplete or defective. In Germany, moreover, an unbroken tradition of hostility to Jews came down from the era of the Crusades and the middle ages, and this continuity represents a most significant difference from conditions in France, England, Holland, and Belgium, where the late medieval expulsions had the effect of allowing the evil heritage of persecution and prejudice to die out, so that with the return of Jews several centuries later (e.g., the Marranos) , a fresh beginning in relations between Christians and Jews was possible. But not in Germany, where just the opposite occurred: Luther's diatribes deepened the old heritage of hatred and brought it forward to the modern age. Another major difference with western Europe was the great number of German Jews, and their greater visibility. Visibility was not only a function of numbers, but stemmed, too, from Jewish prominence among the leaders of liberal and radical movements; for as agents of change and "apostles of modernity" they antagonized the dominant traditionalists and vested interests. The prominence of banking houses like the Rothschilds' roused fears of "Jewish domination of the national economy." The fact that most German Jews were far less assimilated to the customs and mores of the host society than their co-religionists to the west also made them more visible, which is to say, readier targets for abuse and attack. Such circumstances will help to explain why it was that a virulent anti-Semitic movement accompanied and paralleled every step of progress toward Emancipation in Germany.

The lives of the writers Heinrich Heine (1797–1856) and Ludwig Börne (1786–1837) illustrate the difficulties confronting Jews in the era. Both men were important in the "Young Germany" movement which took French liberal and constitutional doctrines as its ideal and, while patriotic and hopeful for German unification, was critical of extreme nationalism, especially the *völkisch* sort; such a viewpoint was dubbed "un-German," and since the writers and philosophers in the group included a high proportion of Jews, it was castigated in an effort to discredit it as "Young Palestine." Heine, indeed, became a Christian in order to acquire "an entrance card to European culture," but it was of so little avail that in the wake of the tumults that came with the Revolution of 1830, he exiled himself to Paris for the rest of his life; he simply confirmed German antipathies for himself and his poetry when he declared, "Freedom is a new religion, the religion of our age. The French are the chosen people of this new religion. Paris is the new Jerusalem and the Rhine is the Jordan which divides the land of freedom from the country of the Philistines."

Börne suffered all the disabilities of being a Jew in his native Frankfurt. He was by nature a rebel spirit and iconoclast; inspired by French liberty, equality, and constitutionalism, he launched pungent journalistic attacks on the despotic rulers of the German states. When his patriotism was impugned, he made a classic reply:

No, the fact that I was born a Jew has not embittered me against the Germans and has never deluded me. I would indeed not be worthy to enjoy the light of the sun if I paid with scornful grumbling for the great act of grace that God has shown me of letting me be both a German and a Jew. Only because of the derision that I have always scorned and because of the suffering that I have long since ceased to feel . . . yes, because I was a bondsman, I therefore love liberty more than you. Yes, because I have known slavery, I understand freedom more than you. Yes, because I was born without a fatherland my desire for a fatherland is more than yours, and because my birthplace was not bigger than the *Judengasse* and everything behind the locked gates was a foreign country to me, therefore for me now the fatherland is more than the city, more than a territory, more than a province. For me only the very great fatherland, as far as its language extends, is enough.

He went on to say that he no longer would remain "the slave of princes" and demanded a genuine libertarian and democratic constitution, a "house of freedom" and not "a rotten political edifice with new tiles on the roof."

Jews were prominent in the leadership and on the barricades of the Revolution of 1848. The hopes that the

German question would be solved by liberal methods—a constitutional monarchy, parliament, full civil rights for all, a German state united along federal lines—came to grief when the Prussian king refused in 1849 to accept the crown and constitution for Germany offered to him by the delegation from the revolutionary National Assembly at Frankfurt. An indication of the malignity and crudity of anti-Semitism even in the Prussian king appears in his insulting question to Gabriel Riesser, the Jewish member of the delegation: "Is it true, Herr Doktor, that you are also convinced that I cannot accept the constitution uncircumcised?"

"Socialist anti-Semitism" made its German debut in 1848 also. Some of the radicals combined socialist and democratic programs with attacks on Jews as the founders of capitalism and the arch-agents of commercial, industrial, and financial exploitation of the masses. It was not peculiar to Germany, but appeared in France also, where the Rothschilds among others were said to prove the charge. It was also said in 1848 and long thereafter that the Jews were the founders and arch-proponents of socialism and communism. Karl Marx was a Jew from the Rhineland. Moses Hess, "the socialist rabbi," was condemned to death for his part in the events of 1848—he lived however to 1872 as a socialist and pioneer Zionist. Ferdinand Lassalle (1825–1864), founder of the Social Democratic Party of Germany, was a Silesian Jew. Jews, moreover, were prominent in the socialist ranks and in the leadership of the German Revolution of 1918. Kurt Eisner led a communist regime in Bavaria for a short time in 1918; another important figure, in Berlin, was the Spartacist Rosa Luxemburg—both were murdered in the counter-revolution.[3] At the same time, outside Germany, Bela Kun headed a similar movement in Hungary, and of course, Leon Trotsky was a Jew. But practically none of them were practicing Jews. Marx, in fact, though he was the descendant of a long line of rabbis, was an atheist and wrote two Jew-baiting essays; his father had been baptized a Protestant in order to attract clients to his law office, and the son was baptized in infancy and thus was a Christian of Jewish descent.

The whole idea of communism or socialism being of Jewish origin, or reflecting closely the spirit and tenets of Judaism, smacks too obviously of anti-Semitic propaganda. Jews were no more, if no less, the founders of socialism or communism than they were of capitalism, for the mere participation of Jews in a movement does not make it "Jewish." The prominence of Jews in the socialist movement was a reflection of their concern for social justice, which is fundamental to Judaism. It is quite illogical to have it both ways, viz., to say that socialism or communism, on the one hand, and their antithesis capitalism, on the other, embody the spirit and practice of Judaism. But false logic never troubles anti-Semites. More important than such considerations, the liberal-radical-socialist parties were the parties of movement and change, and it was quite natural that Jews should tend to join such parties in the unending quest to improve the status of their co-religionists. Moreover, Jews did also appear within the conservative ranks; e.g., Julius Stahl, a kind of German Disraeli, was a mentor of the Conservative Party and a chief supporter of Bismarck. During World War I and after, Walter Rathenau held several of the highest posts in the German government. The real question to ask is why Jews in Germany and elsewhere were prominent and eminent, all out of proportion to their numbers, in the liberal and socialist movements, in business and finance, in literature and journalism, the legal and medical professions, art and music, philosophy and science, scholarship and technology, etc. To some degree the answer lies in the traditional devotion of Jews to education (at a time when public systems of education for all were only beginning to come into existence) ; in large part, however, their manifold achievements must be explained by the kindling of energy and creativity by Emancipation or the prospect of Emancipation. Otherwise we should have to explain why the gentile world was so disproportionately lacking in creativity and energy!

By 1871 Bismarck succeeded in uniting Germany in three wars and on a tidal wave of nationalism. The constitution he drew up for the new Empire, while it was a fig leaf for Hohenzollern despotism and Prussian domination, did provide for universal manhood suffrage, freedom of religion, and legal equality. Jewish Emancipation was thereby settled once and for all, so it seemed. Bismarck himself was not anti-Semitic and numbered quite a few Jews among his friends, from Bleichröder the banker[4] to Lassalle the socialist. He was especially fond of Heine's poetry and quoted it on public occasions. He once replied in parliament that the best resolution of the Jewish issue would come by intermarriage and gradual assimilation, which is hardly the panacea of a racist or anti-Semite. In 1878 he presided as "honest broker" over the Congress of Berlin, which brought the Russo-Turkish war to an end and erected an independent Rumania on territory that formerly was Turkish; Rumania had a large Jewish population and Bismarck (together with Disraeli, whom he greatly admired) was instrumental in including in the treaty a provision guaranteeing equal rights to Rumanian Jews. Although the constitutional provision was ultimately to no avail, Bismarck moved at least once to require the Rumanian government to adhere to the treaty stipulation.

On the other hand, Bismarck was quite willing to use anti-Semitic prejudice as a weapon against his political opponents, as when from 1879 onward he opposed the National Liberal Party, his former allies, led by the Jew Eduard Lasker. Such electioneering tactics not only utilize anti-Semitism but have the inevitable effect of fomenting it. Moreover, Bismarck was quick to brand his opponents as "enemies of the Empire," e.g., the Catholics (in the *Kulturkampf*) and the socialists; and while he never applied the epithet to Jews, he set bad examples and precedents that made it easy to do so in an age of strong national feelings, especially as he was quite willing to refer to Lasker as "the sickness of Germany." Thus, while Bismarck personally was not anti-Semitic and in some respects distinctly friendly to Jews, the tactics and policies of his long reign as chancellor, buoyed up as they were on a wave of intense nationalism, were ominous for the well-being of German Jews.

The economic panic of 1873 was another significant turning point for German Jews. There, as elsewhere, the depression was blamed on Jewish financial manipulations and intrigue. "Socialist anti-Semitism" reappeared, but it was not long before the intellectual leader of the Socialist Party dismissed it as "the socialism of fools." Anti-Semitism at the other end of the social and political spectrum was, however, greatly strengthened. Wilhelm Marr's vitriolic pamphlet, *The Victory of Jewry over Germanism*, informed the comfortable classes in 1879 that the seats of power had already been wrenched away from them by "the wholly dominant Jews." In dilating on "the great historical triumph of Judaism" and on "the beaten army" of Germanism, he minted the term *anti-Semitism*. By the very act of giving it a name he did much to beget the phenomenon the term expressed; by giving it a morally neutral, Latinizing name, he conferred on this vicious attitude a scientific air of authenticity and objectivity. Hence, the term was speedily adopted, especially by the pseudo-scientists of race, nationality, and religion.

If Marr did not quite make anti-Semitism respectable, the Lutheran chaplain at the imperial Hohenzollern court in Berlin, Adolph Stöcker, did. Imbued with the "new Pietism" of the Romantic age, he became a Christian socialist; he argued for "a healthy social reform" that would re-establish a society that was "Germanic and Christian." "That's why I am fighting Jewish supremacy." He was the stormiest political agitator and demagogue in Germany before 1914; his Christian conservatism, demagogic mass meetings, assaults on capitalism and his association of it with Jews and Jewish domination point to the very similar configuration of the Nazi era. Taking a cue from the Frenchman Drumont that the nations of Europe deal the Jews "a big and simultaneous blow," he went so far as to organize international congresses for his anti-Semitic purposes. Yet within Germany the party that he founded in 1878, the Christian Social Workers, was small and ineffective, not far removed from the lunatic fringe.

What was a more foreboding evolution was the adoption by the Conservative Party of much of its program, if not its demagoguery. "Positive Christianity" had long been a plank of the Conservative Party, and Bismarck and most of its members (Prussian junkers with large agricultural estates) were imbued with the same new Lutheran pietism that appears in Stöcker. We might note parenthetically that any combination (such as in fifteenth-century Spain or sixth-century Persia) of intense religiosity and strong nationalism inevitably diminishes tolerance and spells difficulty and danger for the Jewish community. In the course of the 1880's the Conservatives officially declared themselves "opposed to the increasing and destructive Jewish influence in our national life"; agrarians that they were, they identified capitalist exploitation with Jewish influence, and sought to keep Jews out of the officer corps (which had been partly open to them in the half century following the Prussian reforms of 1807–1819), the civil service, the academic professoriate, and all high appointive offices, though they could not keep them out of elective office and parliament. The upshot was—as Helmuth von Gerlach, a one-time follower of Stöcker ruefully put it—anti-Semitism "made the greatest gain in prestige it could hope for." Previously it was the stock-in-trade of a few splinter groups and parties; now it became "the legitimate property . . . of the party nearest to the throne and holding the most important positions in the state. Anti-Semitism had come close to being accepted at the highest level of social responsibility." And if Bismarck, the idol of Germany, did nothing to further this insidious development, he certainly did nothing to hinder it. Emperor William II (1888–1918), was much influenced by Stöcker, although he too was rather friendly to Jews.

The Catholic equivalent of Stöcker was August Rohling. He revived all the medieval rubbish about the Talmud's contempt for Christianity, Host profanation, and ritual murder for the "sacrifice" at Passover, etc. Under his influence there was a recrudescence of blood accusation trials in Austria-Hungary, where his influence was paramount; one of these was initiated by no less a personage than a Hungarian member of parliament. The link between Rohling and Hitler was Rohling's disciple Karl Lueger, the Viennese politician who founded a party whose alpha and omega were anti-Semitism; and on the strength of it he rode into power as mayor of Vienna and dominated its municipal life as a "boss" in the years before 1914, when the admiring Hitler lived in the city; Lueger's party, moreover, became the largest group in the Austrian parliament and remained so until 1938. In Germany Catholics were not in a majority, as they were in Austria. Hence the "Christian Socialist" Bishop of Mainz, Emanuel von Ketteler, and the Catholic Center Party after 1871 fought for minority rights, their own and Jews' alike; as victims of the *Kulturkampf*, German Catholics could not afford to tolerate discrimination against another minority.

As the century wore on, the forces of anti-Semitism were gathering strength in other areas of German life. Richard Wagner, though he probably had a Jewish father and certainly had help from Jews in getting his operas performed, pointed up in a polemical essay what he thought the dangers of "Judaism in Music"; he became high priest of the Nordic racialist cult. The obtuse biblical scholar Paul de Lagarde, among several others, found a parallel to the supposed Jewish economic "parasitism" in the supposed ancient Hebrew religious borrowings from the Sumerians and Babylonians; his findings, masquerading as science, "proved" that Jews were "parasitic," "derivative," "uncreative," etc. The transplanted Englishman H. S. Chamberlain went him one better, declaring Jesus to be of "non-Jewish Galilean" birth or, as Hitler was to have it, that Jesus was "Aryan"; St. Paul's role in the formation of Christianity was a Jewish plot and its effects had to be purged away. Though the exact opposite proved to be the case, the conclusion to his historical studies reached by Heinrich von Treitschke was that "the Jews are our misfortune"—a slogan much used by the Nazis.

Another propellant of anti-Semitism in Germany was the influx of Jews fleeing the Russian pogroms after 1881. One response in Germany was a gigantic petition presented to the government demanding that no more Jews be admitted, that none be allowed to hold political office or teach in the public schools; no official action was taken, although the petition could not but have an unfavorable impact on the status of Jews. Anti-Semitism reached its peak in the election of 1893, when the various parties that made hatred of Jews their political staple elected sixteen members to parliament. Thereafter anti-Semitism steadily declined. For example, a dear aunt of mine, who lived in Berlin as a young lady in the years after 1900, immigrated to the United States shortly before the war; her most vivid recollection of a visit in the early 1920's was a prevailing anti-Semitism that was radically unlike anything she had witnessed before 1914, at least in Berlin. Nevertheless, German Jews never ceased being second-class citizens, despite the provisions of the law and the stipulations of the constitution. The most that can be said is that anti-Semitism was declining in the twenty years before the war, that no anti-Jewish legislation was passed or contemplated, that no pogroms were triggered officially or unofficially. "Here in Hamburg, there is no open anti-Semitism, but latent anti-Semitic feelings," the Jewish banker Max Warburg wrote to his brother in 1913, and so it was throughout most of the country.

The reign of the emperor William II, 1888–1918, is, in fact, an enigma, "Germany's Tragic Era," as John L. Snell called it in an essay where he wonders whether it was the "Threshold to Democracy or Foreground of Nazism." William himself, in regard to Jews and in several other ways, was peculiarly ambivalent. Towards Jews there is much testimony that he was "in no way" prejudiced against them; but he seems to have felt it necessary to echo—rather than to discredit—the antipathies of his Prussian courtiers, military officers, and civil servants by an occasional barb or joke in his letters and conversations at Jewish expense. He was easily angered by criticism, but he and his government got prolonged barrages of it from the socialists and journalists, in both of whose ranks Jews were especially prominent, and so he lost no love on them.

Nevertheless, William was distinctly favorable to Jews like Albert Ballin, 1857–1918, the self-made director of the world's largest steamship company, the Hamburg-American Line (HAPAG). He frequently had the ear of the emperor in commercial and fiscal matters, and, though to a lesser extent, in political and diplomatic policy. Once or twice he was a candidate for the chancellorship, but, being Jewish, had "obviously" to be passed over by William. Jewish he remained all his life, and he was contemptuous of newly successful Jews who climbed on the bandwagon of assimilation and turned their backs on Judaism, although his own practice was limited to rare visits to a synagogue, donations to Jewish causes, and a certain sympathy for Zionism. He served William somewhat as Bleichröder had Bismarck: he too was a source of sound information, had many important contacts in many fields, especially in banking and journalism, and in the ports and capitals of the world; not infrequently he served the emperor as an unofficial ambassador. Something of an Anglophile, Ballin tried to dissuade William from some of the outrageous antics and the policies (e.g., the naval program) that alarmed England; he sought peace and even an alliance with England, arguing that the world was large enough for both states to have ample naval and merchant marine strength, great commercial and colonial domains, etc.; he was instrumental in initiating, with Sir Ernest Cassel, the Haldane Mission of 1912, an unsuccessful attempt to iron out naval and other differences with England. Ballin's attempt to deflect William from his bellicose course in 1914 failed, as did several other of his efforts to inaugurate peace negotiations during what he called "the stupidest of all wars." His several attempts with Cassel, an English Jew of German extraction, to avert hostilities between their countries should be pointed up. For in such libels as the horrendous *Protocols of the Elders of Zion,* Jewish profiteers are blamed for deliberately unleashing the beasts of war in 1914; and here we have presumably two such Jewish capitalists, one a great shipping tycoon and the other an enormously wealthy banker with great influence at the English royal court and in the government, seeking desperately to the last moment to keep the terrible beasts chained up.

The long-term decline of anti-Semitism that we have noted in Germany, the high point of which was perhaps Ballin's career, stemmed in part from Jewish attempts to build bridges, intellectual but also social, to the world outside their own ambit; this represented a continuation of similar efforts by Mendelssohn and his friends in the eighteenth century. For example, there developed in Galicia, the Austrian portion of what had once been Poland, a circle of Jewish scholars and thinkers who had several links with the Mendelssohn group at Berlin and represent the second stage of the Jewish Enlightenment, or Haskalah. The outstanding figure was Nahman Krochmal (1785–1840), who, inspired by Maimonides, wrote a *Guide for the Perplexed of Our Time*; this work makes him the most original Jewish philosopher of the nineteenth century. His thought is cast in a much more secular mold than any previous Jewish writer's, and in his philosophical and historical works he went far to accept the Kantian and Hegelian canons of scholarship. In a manner reminiscent of Azariah dei Rossi of the Renaissance, he interpreted Jewish history against the background of world history, and emphasized many close parallels between movements within Judaism and the outside world, e.g., the growth of nationalist sentiment.

Krochmal's influence flowed over into Russia, where a similar Haskalah movement developed, the most notable expression of which was Leo Pinsker's Zionist work, *Auto-Emancipation,* 1882. Krochmal's influence in Germany was of greater significance, for he became the spiritual father of the *Wissenschaft des Judentums.* This is a term difficult to translate. Literally it means "the science of Judaism," but it is better rendered as "the intellectual discipline that takes Jewish history, religion, and culture for its subject"; more important is the outlook that animated this school of Jewish thinkers—to see their subject in the context of general history, and to approach it with the scholarly thoroughness and scientific objectivity associated with the name of the greatest historian of the century, (the non-Jew) Ranke. As latter-day disciples of Azariah dei Rossi, it was especially appropriate that one of them, Leopold Zunz (1794–1886), republished *The Enlightenment of the Eyes* and also (posthumously) Krochmal's *Guide;* Zunz's own work on Jews in the middle ages was superb history. His younger friend Moritz Steinschneider revealed for the first time the contribution which Jewish scholars and translators made to the Latin Renaissance of 1050 to 1350, a theme we have treated earlier. The most successful figure in the group was Heinrich Graetz (1817–1891), whose classic *History of the Jews* in eleven volumes was published between 1853 and 1875; though it falls somewhat short of the high standard of objectivity set by the school (some of whom criticized it sharply, saying "Klio would blush"),[5] it was and remains a widely read work and is eloquent in its rendition of Jewish suffering and of the triumphs of Jewish scholarship. A learned journal, *Monatschrift für Geschichte und Wissenschaft des Judentums* (imitated by similar reviews in France and England) was, until its abolition by Hitler, the vehicle of the group. In hopes of providing a more disinterested treatment of Jewish subjects in the academic world, Zunz and others pressed for the establishment of chairs of Jewish studies in the universities. But in this attempt to build bridges they made no headway.

In coming now to the twentieth century and Hitler it is necessary to state that the long history of intolerance of Jews in Germany should not be overemphasized. Most of it Germany shared with other countries of the Western world. And as the nineteenth century gave way to the twentieth the citadels of anti-Semitism were France of the Dreyfus affair, Russia of the May Laws and pogroms, and Austria-Hungary, where anti-Jewish riots and racial phobias appeared to be the chief ingredients of culture and politics —so much so that they even caught the attention of Mark Twain and are the subject of one of his essays. These three countries had the reputation, and rightly so, as the worst offenders. What made the German situation less like that of western Europe and more like that of Russia was, as we have noted, the greater number of Jews living in Germany and that the medieval tradition of persecution had not lapsed, but been preserved.

On the other hand, nineteenth-century German Jews

were rapidly being assimilated into the national life. They entered into the national spirit and extolled the triumphs of Bismarck as much as anyone. What Gabriel Riesser had said several decades earlier was eminently true by 1900— German Jews were but "a group of people who do not wish to have a national existence of their own, such as formerly was imposed upon them by their enemies, but who think and feel as Germans." It is clearly a vindication of the patriotism of German Jews that twenty thousand of them died in the trenches of World War I for the German cause. And despite the resurgence of anti-Semitism after the war—owing to defeat, the influx of Russian Jews fleeing the communist regime, the economic distress, etc.— the prospect in 1929 was, according to Koppel Pinson, that Jew-baiting was definitely on the wane, and we have Hitler's testimony in 1941 that "ten years ago, our intellectual class hadn't the least idea of what a Jew is" and they should not, he added, be blamed for intermarriage with Jews before then. Thus, if Germany was undoubtedly the classic land of Jewish suffering since 1095, there was no real precedent in the German past for the Nazi holocaust of Europe's Jews.

Hitler's anti-Semitism—to the extent that it was not native with him—was imported to Germany, as he himself was, from the Vienna and Austria of Georg von Schönerer, Karl Lueger, and Lanz-Liebenfels, with their demonic brew of race phobia, demagoguery, irreligion, and paranoia; beyond that the chief intellectual justification of Hitler's anti-Semitism was the infamous *Protocols of the Elders of Zion* from Russia. No doubt the ugly plants imported from Austria and Russia would have died had there been no anti-Semitic roots in Germany to graft them on to. But such roots existed elsewhere than in Germany and, *mutatis mutandis*, a comparable nightmare would have followed upon a similar importation and grafting operation. I conclude, then, that the fatal element in the situation as of 1933 was Hitler and the macabre doctrines of which he was the bearer, rather than the native tradition of anti-Semitism, grim though it was and reinforced as it was by the iron-shod petulance of Oswald Spengler. To put it more simply, I do not think that, given the German past to 1933, it was inevitable that a genocidal regime would, sooner or later, have come to power.

Hitler, the greatest demogogue in all history, found a wide appeal for his notions throughout his "struggle" from 1920 to 1933. The Weimar Republic was born of defeat and was tarred with the brush of the stab-in-the-back myth. Jews were among the most enthusiastic supporters of the Republic; its constitution had been drawn up by the Jewish political scientist Hugo Preuss, and made full provision for democratic equality and minority rights. Jews, as mentioned earlier, had been prominent in the Revolution of 1918 that brought the Republic into being, and some, such as the brilliant Rathenau as foreign minister, were among its principal leaders. Treated as a stepchild by the victorious allies, especially in the matter of reparations and the occupation of the Ruhr, the Republic was proven in Hitler's demagogic oratory of the "big lie" to be equally "Jewish," "treasonable," and "corrupt." Thus Germany was politically dominated by Jews, as Preuss had "arranged for" in the constitution, and all her difficulties stemmed from that.

Economic domination of Germany by Jews was another idea exploited to the hilt by Hitler. As in the panics of 1847 and 1873, so now in the huge inflation of 1923 and again in the depression of 1929, economic dislocation pointed an accusing finger at Jews, who, however, suffered at least as much as anyone else. It may be true, as one of my uncles recalls of the 1920's, that there were too many cases in which the bankruptcy laws were evaded by Jews who passed through the courts and reappeared in business without apparent loss, but, as he also recalls, they were not confined to Jews. It was the sort of thing, together with the prominence of Jews in small retail businesses, that Hitler twisted and inflated for his own ends, as he did the notion of the Jews as capitalists. He drew a distinction between "rapacious" and "creative" capital: commercial and financial capitalism was "derivative," "parasitic," "Jewish," and therefore "rapacious"; while industrial capitalism was "genuine," "German," "Aryan," and, accordingly, "creative." The doggerel rhyming in German of *"raffendes versus schaffendes Kapital"* suggests the demagogic method of Hitler's crusade to "sunder the bonds of interest slavery," i.e., Jewish domination. But he also had it the other way, viz., that the Jews and Bolshevik communism were synonymous. Playing on German fears of communism and Russia (the way a virtuoso plays his instrument, it has been said), Hitler's harangues always ended with "the Jewish menace."

In fact anything that Hitler or his German audiences might hate, fear, or distrust was equated with Jews or Judaism. Modernity in the arts, e.g., was designated "cultural Bolshevism" and thereby associated with Judaism. Irrationally, as the Jewish winner of the Nobel Peace Prize in 1935 and victim of a Nazi concentration camp Karl von Ossietzky wrote, "when Klemperer takes tempi different from Furtwängler, when a painter uses a color for a sunset not seen in Lower Pomerania, when one favors birth control, when you build a house with a flat roof, when you admire Charlie Chaplin or Albert Einstein, when you follow the democracy of the novelist Thomas Mann, and when you enjoy the music of Hindemith and Kurt Weill—all that is cultural Bolshevism."

Hitler's intense nationalism, imbued as it was with the Nordic nonsense of Wagner, H. S. Chamberlain, and others, was reflected in his concern for German racial "purity." Accordingly, the 1935 Nuremberg laws, passed there unanimously by a special session of parliament, forbade marriage between Jews and Germans, and the employment of German servants in Jewish households; coupled with them was the law barring Jews from public office and denying them most of a citizen's rights. Thereafter increasing pressure was brought to bear that "Aryans" divorce "non-Aryan" spouses. All kinds of other restrictions followed: the "Jew ban" from residential sections, theaters, museums, the "Exclusion of Jews from German Economic Life," expulsion from public schools, and compulsion to shop at only certain stores at certain hours. The next step was the formation of huge ghettos and the mass deportations to them. Jews were required to use only Jewish names; those who already bore "Teutonic" names had to add *Israel* or *Sara* to them. The edict's intent was to make Jews more visible, and it testifies to the fact that in external matters there was little distinction between Jews and the rest of the population. The edict on names was a prelude to that of 1941 requiring Jews (throughout the whole of conquered Europe as well as Germany) to wear "a hexagonal star, the size of a palm, bordered in black, made of yellow material, bearing the inscription *Jew* in black letters, affixed to the left side of their garments at the height of the breast"; thus the sacred symbol, the Star of David, became a stigma. Later it had to mark the houses of Jews. Jews could not keep pets, own bicycles, typewriters, etc., nor could they have their hair cut by "Aryan" barbers. This whole program has been recognized as a piece of medievalism, and, as in the middle ages, its accompaniment was spoliation of property, riots, burning of synagogues, massacres, etc. It is, at best, only one part of the dual medieval policy, under which as we have seen, Jews were also officially tolerated by law, recognized as having an autonomous communal life, and enjoying religious liberty. In practice these rights were frequently infringed, but the Hitler regime recognized neither in theory nor in practice any rights or immunities as appertaining to Jews; Hitler's "medievalism" is only the first step to "the final solution."

All that has been spoken of so far—Hitler's idea about,

attacks and restrictions upon, mistreatment and robbing of, Jews—has roots in the German past and the European-Christian tradition, a fact that Hitler understood perfectly and exploited fully. The primary significance of pre-1933 anti-Semitism is, in my judgment, that it made harsh treatment of Jews so much a matter of course that it weakened, if it did not nullify, the Christian conscience, whether Catholic or Protestant, stilling what ought to have been its outrage and cancelling out what should have been the strongest source of resistance to Nazi bestiality. One of the saddest and most incriminating moments in the long history of the Church is Hitler's assertion to two bishops in April, 1933, when they raised the issue of his policy toward the Jews. As reported in Hitler's *Table-Talk*, he had said up till then, and would do, now that he was in power, only what Christian teaching and preaching had been saying for nearly two thousand years. And the bishops could not deny it, for there was an age-old Catholic-Christian tradition of hatred and vilification of Jews; had not St. John Chrysostom declared that the Jews "are a pest and plague to the human race" from whom Christians "should turn away," that "God has abandoned them," and denied them "the hope of salvation"? The German Cardinal Bea, in recommending the Declaration on the Jews to the Second Vatican Council, stated that anti-Jewish ideas in the Christian interpretation of history that had prevailed since time out of mind had done much to help Nazism. Certainly there were Catholics and Protestants who spoke out publicly and strongly against Hitler, e.g., the intrepid Cardinal Faulhaber, but they were exceptional and could have no impact on public opinion so as to restrain Hitler. Nothing—unless it was the decision to hold the Olympics in Berlin in 1936—went so far as to confer a stamp of approval on the Nazi regime as the Concordat of 1933 with the Vatican.[6] Moral support was clearly not the pope's intention in subscribing to the Concordat, although it was Hitler's

intention to gain it as cheaply as he possibly could; not surprisingly, he made no pretense of abiding by the agreement,
violating it from the start. Pope Pius XI's denunciations in
1937 and his assertion in 1938 (anticipating Vatican II) that
"spiritually we are all Semites" came too late to affect the
situation in Germany and were laughed to scorn there.

It might plausibly be argued that it is virtually impossible to recognize in time the wolf who masquerades in
sheep's clothing. The truth was, however, that Hitler
never so masqueraded, but poured forth an unending and
venomous stream of hatred and threats, in speeches and
books, from the moment he embarked on the quest for
power in his "struggle." His war on the Jews was the most
persistent aim pursued by Hitler from his Vienna days to
his will of April, 1945. (His will directed his successors to
"hold fast to the racial laws above all else" and continue
the inhuman assault on "the universal poisoner of all nations—international Jewry.") Before Hitler came to power
a group of Jews presented to President Hindenburg an
impressive indictment of what the Nazis were really up to,
but that senile old Prussian soldier was unmoved; it is true
that he did restrain some of Hitler's most outrageous intentions in the first year of Nazi power, down to 1934 when he
died and Hitler became president as well as chancellor. By
1937 it was crystal clear—as the Englishman Stephen Rob-
erts said in *The House That Hitler Built*—that the dictator
was embarked upon "a campaign of annihilation—a program of the crudest form, supported by every state instrument." It was then too late to stop Hitler from within
Germany, for he had captured the state apparatus, fashioned it into an unassailable despotism, and crushed all
opposition. To give witness to the truth by resistance or
martyrdom was almost impossible.[7] For it was a relentlessly efficient tyranny, with an elaborate technological network of control and surveillance. Hence martyrdom went
by unseen, unheard, unrecorded. A pebble dropped into

the waters of righteousness made no ripples. "The final solution" could thus be carried out with impunity, for no one could resist it and few Germans beyond the fifty thousand to one hundred thousand engaged in it would know of it.

The arch-executioner was Heinrich Himmler, but he was the subordinate in every way of Hitler. It is difficult to fathom Himmler's mentality and temperament. As described by H. R. Trevor-Roper, he was enormously "stupid, devoted, ruthless, efficient, mystical." Apart from his death camp operations, he carried out such absurd projects as prolonged laboratory efforts to "isolate pure Aryan blood," and he sent scientific expeditions to Tibet to discover the pure Teutonic stock that he believed had preserved there the runic mysteries of the ancient Nordic religion. To the Nordic theological gibberish that he adhered to as a pedantic true believer, Himmler added executive-administrative efficiency of a high order; combining this with unalloyed faith in and loyalty to Hitler, we have the modern Grand Inquisitor who calmly and righteously sends to death millions upon millions of the human race in the name of his abstractions. It is important to understand that neither Himmler nor Hitler utilized anti-Semitism as a Machiavellian stalking horse for other aims; for there can be no doubt that they both (and Goebbels equally) believed what they said of the Jews. Hence, even when it was obviously contrary to the German war effort, e.g., in the production of munitions, the extermination camps went on full blast and the death-dealing exploitation of slave labor persisted as crudely as ever.

Cruelty was institutionalized. As a matter of course prisoners were humiliated, starved, beaten, kicked, exposed to severe weather for days, etc.; wholesale torture in the form of inhuman medical experiments by S.S. doctors had the usual result of death, permanent maiming, or mental illness, the disclosure of which in the "Doctors' Trial" at

Nuremberg in 1946 is perhaps the most grisly page in the whole barbaric business. Bureaucratic procedures, careful auditing and accounting, a complex transportation network, and "rational" use of the human by-products were parts of the system. Such crude fanaticism and overwhelming bestiality joined with the technological efficiency and scientific precision of a huge slaughter house defy the mind's ability to grasp or imagine. The S.S. gangsterdom worked up a "table of yield per prisoner" that expresses as well as anything can how the Nazis reduced the Jewish people to the status of "animals" (a term much employed by them), thereby exempting themselves from all moral law, and enabling them to exploit the resources and by-products as in any economic undertaking. The tidy chart informs us that the productivity of a prisoner is 6 marks per day; he is calculated to work 270 days before he drops dead, whereupon his gold teeth, clothing, money, miscellaneous articles of value such as hair or eyeglasses, yield an additional 200 marks; from this has to be deducted 2 marks for cremation and one-tenth mark for amortization of clothing; the total profit then is 1,631 marks, not including, it is noted, what may still be realized from the bones and ashes, which commercially valuable items were bought up by German industry, like Krupp or I. G. Farben. Other Jews deemed not fit to work were gassed to death, a "humane" method devised by Himmler, who did not think himself a sadist and had been nauseated by the sight of mass shootings; "out of love for our people" ten thousand persons per day were disposed of without leaving a trace at the Auschwitz camp. Having set out to destroy Europe's eleven million Jews, the Nazis killed, according to Gerald Reitlinger's very careful analysis, between 4,200,000 and 4,600,000; a more recent estimate by a German scholar places the figure at 5,978,000 or 72 percent of the Jews to whom the S.S. had access. In some countries, e.g., Denmark, Holland, and Bulgaria, the native population resisted and managed to save a fairly high proportion of the Jews; and in fact every country possessed some of that saving remnant who regarded themselves as their "brother's keeper." In Russia, Poland, and Rumania, however, the Nazis fanned long-standing local hatreds and thus enlisted the cooperation of some natives with the S.S. extermination contingents. Trailer truck units speeded up the holocaust by taking the gas chambers to the victims.

One of the great epics of human courage is the rising in 1943 of the Jews who had been herded together in the Warsaw ghetto; there were as many as six hundred thousand Jews piled up together there as "animals" or "things," but they were reduced to less than forty thousand—either by the frightful methods outlined above, or sent out as slave labor gangs to German munitions and armament factories. Without the remotest hope of success the remnant decided to make a fight of it. Via the underground they accumulated arms, improvised grenades, swung shut the gates, and for thirty-six days held off a blitzkrieg attack of artillery, tanks, and infantry; on the thirty-seventh day the ghetto was a lifeless mass of smoldering ruins. It is an episode worthy of comparison with Bar Kochba's revolt against Rome in A.D. 135; rather than as a feat of pointless courage and symbol of death and oblivion, the Warsaw uprising is a fitting prelude to the rebirth of a nation in the Holy Land five years later. If I might apply the metaphor of Isaiah 6:13 to the fate of the Jews under Hitler: the millions of lives he took were but the leaves of the tree, and though the tree shed its leaves it remained alive.

One of the most widespread errors and illusions is that Hitler's target was solely the Jews and Judaism. Certainly they were his principal victims. But he regarded all peoples except the Germans as *Untermenschen* (inferior beings) and set about enslaving and annihilating them, especially Slavic peoples, by the same methods. Here is

Himmler in 1943 informing his S.S. underlings on what spirit should animate them; together with the "table" referred to above, it expresses the depravity and nihilism that were at the core of Nazism:

An S.S. man must adhere absolutely to one principle: he must be honorable, decent, faithful, and comradely to members of his own race, and to no one else. What happens to the Russians, what happens to the Czechs is to me a matter of total indifference. . . . Whether other nations live well or die of starvation interests me only in so far as we need slaves for our culture—other than that, it holds for me no interest. Whether during the construction of a tank trap 10,000 Russian women die of exhaustion or not, interests me only in so far as the tank trap for Germany has been constructed. We shall never be tough and pitiless where it is not necessary, that is clear. We Germans are the only nation in the world with a decent attitude toward animals; we shall also be decent toward these human animals. But it is a crime against our own blood to worry about them or to bring ideals to them so that our sons or grandchildren have more trouble with them. When someone comes to me and says: "I cannot build tank traps with women and children, that is inhuman, they will die," I shall say to him: "You are the murderer of your own blood, because if the tank trap is not built, German soldiers shall die, and they are the sons of German mothers. That is our blood." That is what I would like to inculcate in the S.S. . . . our care, our duty, is our people and our blood. . . . Everything else is of no importance. . . .

I turn now to the evacuation of Jews, to the extermination of the Jewish people. This is one of those things that is easily said: "The Jewish people will be exterminated," a party member says, "of course, it says so in our program, we shall eliminate, exterminate the Jews." And then they all come, the brave 80 million Germans, and each one of them has his decent Jew. Yes, of course, the other Jews are swine, but this one is a first rate Jew. Of all those who speak so, none has witnessed it, none has experienced it. Most of you know what it means when 100 corpses lie next to each other, or 500, or even 1000. To experience this, and—apart from human weaknesses—to remain decent, that has made us hard. This is a glorious page in our history. . . .

Moreover, Christianity had to be dealt with also, since it "is merely whole-hearted Bolshevism, under a tinsel of metaphysics, . . . fabricated with diabolical cunning" in a Jewish plot by St. Paul, who had vitiated the "Aryan" teaching of the "Aryan" Jesus. Accordingly, Christianity had at the very least to be "de-Judaized" and "Germanized," after which there would be, presumably, very little of Christianity left. But Hitler's intention as reported in *The Secret Conversations* for December, 1941, is far more ominous: with the conclusion of this "victorious" war, his "final life's task will be to solve the religious question." Having equated Christianity with Jewishness and with Bolshevism (as he repeatedly did), Hitler concluded that there was no possibility of a "synthesis between Nazism and Christianity . . . the obstacle is in Christianity itself." He therefore looked to the establishment of some pagan neo-Nordic deity by the *Übermensch* (superior man) on the bloody altar of racism—a botched up Nietzschean religion of ethical hardness and barbarian manliness (*barbarian* was a word Hitler delighted in: "We are barbarians. We want to be barbarians. It is an honorable title"). The Jews, communism, and Christianity constituted the trinity of his greatest hatreds, and a "final solution" was in store for each in turn. Only time stopped him.

Particularly the new Nordic deity, with Himmler as high priest, would have required the "extirpation" of Christianity and unquestionably would have kept the extermination camps going for a long time. In any event, Nazism was as fundamentally opposed to and inconsistent with Christian doctrines and ethics as it was toward those of Judaism. Yet Christians, whether Catholic or Protestant, were slow to see that Hitler intended literally the extermination of the Jewish people; they were still slower to recognize the danger that he represented for their own churches, beliefs, and their very lives.[8] Hitler was, as Alan Bullock's definitive biography concludes, a nihilist. "His career did not exalt but debased the human condition, and his twelve years' dictatorship was barren of all ideas save one—the further extension of his own power and that of the nation with which he had identified himself. . . . The great revolutions of the past, whatever their ultimate fate, have been identified with the release of certain powerful ideas: individual conscience, liberty, equality, national freedom, social justice. Nazism produced nothing. Hitler constantly exalted force over the power of ideas. . . . The sole theme of the Nazi revolution was domination, dressed up as the doctrine of race, and failing that, a vindictive destructiveness" or nihilism. For all his fanatical nationalism, the German people and nation were only instruments to use in attaining his ambition of world power, since he thought that in defeat there was no need to preserve "even the most primitive existence," that it was "better to destroy Germany and to destroy it ourselves."

In the nature of things the grim chronicle that I have recounted cannot have a happy ending. Yet the Bonn government since 1947 has done what it can—inevitably not much in comparison to the magnitude of the suffering and loss—to redeem the German people from the injustice committed in their name and to make material restitution to Jewish survivors in so far as it is possible. In some respects Bonn's attitude and policies reflect the views set forth in a famous book by the Heidelberg philosopher Karl Jaspers in 1946, *The Question of German Guilt*, "a question of life and death for the German people." He distinguished between (1) criminal guilt, which is to be punished in courts of law, (2) political guilt, for which, as Bonn acknowledges, there is responsibility and obligation to make restitution by official action, whether freely taken or enforced by the victorious occupying powers, (3) moral guilt, for which expiation is possible to the private individual only by repentance, (4) metaphysical guilt, which has for its basis that no man is an island: the solidarity of mankind makes each individual "co-responsible" for all injustice in the world, particularly crimes committed in his presence or with his knowledge. Jaspers, who strongly endorsed the Nuremberg trials, concluded that every German was guilty under at least one of these categories.

Partly in keeping with Jaspers' outlook, the government of Chancellor Adenauer proposed to pay reparations for the Jewish properties seized by Hitler to the state of Israel, since it was the representative of world Jewry and the haven of many who had escaped the death camps. Bonn undertook in the treaty of 1952 to pay three billion marks over a period of twelve years to the Israeli government, which proved to be of inestimable value to Israel for her tremendous economic growth. On a smaller scale, similar agreements were concluded with other countries, granting redress to their residents who had suffered Nazi tyranny. A Jewish Claims Conference was also set up to handle restitution to Jews other than those covered by the treaties. When East Germany rejected out of hand a Polish request for indemnification to some Jews who had survived the death camps, Bonn took it upon itself to accept responsibility and make restitution. Within Germany restitution to everyone (Jews and non-Jews) who had suffered on political, religious, or ethnic grounds, who had lost relatives, their health, income, or property, began under Allied direction in 1945, and much of these reparations were paid to Germany's thirty thousand surviving Jews; (of the 525,000 German Jews of pre-1933, roughly half fled, half were killed, and thirty thousand either survived and remained or returned). By the mid-1960's nearly thirty billion marks had been disbursed, most of it going abroad.

Some critical observers sneeringly called such payments "conscience money," but Bonn recognized clearly and publicly that mere economic restitution could not expiate moral and metaphysical guilt. The treaty of 1952 especially, I think, was a laudable attempt to repair what could be repaired; it was passed unanimously by the German parliament and had the approval of the overwhelming majority of German citizens. Stringent laws against anti-Semitism have been passed and are enforced—to judge by the few overt cases that have appeared (and West Germany is, as far as I can ascertain, the only nation in the world where anti-Semitism is an indictable offense). The most notorious were the swastikas that were painted on a synagogue in Cologne in 1959 by delinquent juveniles who were soon caught and punished. The incident, inevitably, caught world-wide attention and, equally inevitably, raised fears about the recrudescence of the horrors of the past.

Yet West Germany is one of the truly democratic countries in the world and has a genuine parliamentary system of government. There is far less anti-Semitism there than in many other countries. This is not saying much perhaps. Nevertheless, such symbolic acts of Bonn as the memorial to Walter Rathenau in 1967 on the forty-fifth anniversary of his assassination by anti-Semitic thugs, or the official German celebration of Israel's twentieth anniversary in 1968, and the proclamation of an annual "Israel Week" at Stuttgart in the spring of 1969, augur well for the future. On the Israeli anniversary Chancellor Kiesinger said, "The day on which, twenty years ago, the state of Israel was called into being, is for us Germans a day of rejoicing." The spirit of the Bonn republic is also expressed in Foreign Minister (as he was then) Brandt's remarks. Noting that German intentions at home and abroad can readily be defamed in propaganda, e.g., by Russia, as a recrudescence of Nazism, he said he repudiates such defamation: "I do this as a person whom nobody can associate with the crimes of Hitler [since he fought in the resistance movement in Germany] and who in spite of this bears his share of the national responsibility. We have learned from history." That a new spirit is abroad in Germany may be seen in her greatest historian's plea of

1946, to re-examine and judge the aims and methods of German policy not only since 1933 or 1918 but as far back as Bismarck; a reflection of Friedrich Meinecke's concern is clearly to be seen in the more recent works of the historian Fritz Fischer on why liberal democracy did not take permanent root in Germany after 1815 and on the German "grasp for world power" in World War I. Moreover, in contrast to the France of de Gaulle, Germany is a center of mutualism and internationalism, of European cooperation and unity—it is a proponent of the admission of England and Israel, among others, to the Common Market.

A German history book for high-school students by Hannah Vogt, published in 1961 and covering the period 1914–1945, concludes: "Who will believe that we want to respect all that is human if we treat the death of nearly six million Jews as a 'small error' to be forgotten after a few years? The test of our change of heart should be not only the dead but the living. There are 30,000 Jewish fellow-citizens living among us. Many of them have returned only recently from emigration, overwhelmed with a desire for their old homeland. It is up to all of us to make sure that they live among us in peace and without being abused, that their new trust in us, won after much effort, endures."

The younger generation seems to have taken such words to heart; it is part of the generation gap in Germany that many older people would like to forget it all as though it never happened. For this they are frequently taken to task by German cartoonists; e.g., one shows the pater familias reading his paper in the study where the history books on the wall show a conspicuous lacuna for 1933–1945, and one shows a prosperous businessman hearing with great perplexity that Nazis are being prosecuted for crimes against humanity committed "before 1948," i.e., the currency reform that is the basis of his prosperity and beyond which his memory does not extend. Such minimizing, glossing over, forgetting, are not characteristic, however.

The Jews in Germany today can, understandably, neither forget nor forgive. It is hard, especially for the younger ones, to be happy there even though the government protects and supports them, even though they are prosperous, even though they are respected by the public, and even though they are conscious, in many instances, of debts of gratitude to individual Germans who shielded them in the years of the holocaust. Their favored treatment often places them in the invidious position of feeling themselves to be "Germany's figleaf for Germany's shame." A further explanation of their being ill at ease in the Federal Republic is that well over half of Germany's Jews are not natives, but exiles who fled from Eastern Europe. Most of those who emigrate are young, and only the old remain in Germany. They are exceedingly old, so much so that the death rate is eight times the birth rate. There are about forty-five synagogues, and there are numerous Jewish libraries, museums, cultural programs; but there is no vital community life, with the one possible exception of West Berlin (of its 6,000 Jews, 3,750 are over fifty and no more than 750 are under thirty).

These dismal statistics and impressions come from Leo Katcher's recent book *Post-Mortem*; he quotes one elderly Jewish leader lamenting that "we are dealing with shadow, not substance . . . we can give lectures. We can have exhibitions of Jewish history and culture. But we have no Jews, and there is no prospect that we will have them in the future." Thus the grim outlook is that Germany will be entirely devoid of Jews at some statistically predictable point in the near future, that Hitler, though overwhelmingly defeated and destroyed, will have succeeded in attaining one of his aims. There may yet be a turnabout, as so often in history. Should that happen, historians may someday quote as a harbinger of the ultimate reconciliation of Jews and Germans Chancellor Kiesinger's public expression of gratitude for "the confidence which Prime Minister

David Ben-Gurion [of Israel] had in us Germans during his time in office," for it made possible the treaty of 1952 and eventually the exchange of ambassadors. "No man can forget the frightfulness of the crimes committed. Therefore, we have accepted the out-stretched hands of the Jewish people with thankfulness." Shortly afterward, David Hacohen, leader of a delegation of members of the Israeli parliament on a visit to Germany, acknowledged the fact that "there is a realization in Israel that the German people are undergoing an inner transformation."

Russia

The partitions of Poland brought a great many Jews, perhaps a million, to Russia in the reign of Catherine the Great. Although Russia was from 1815 to 1917 the classic country of Jewish persecution, it was nevertheless there that Jews were given for the first time in Europe *political* rights; Catherine permitted them to vote in municipal elections. She also initiated a program of agricultural colonization, by which Jews were permitted to hold land and encouraged to enter agriculture as a means of livelihood. Yet the sovereign fact was that an archaic medieval ethos pervaded the court and government, the Russian Orthodox Church and society at large, an ethos by which Jews were still regarded as "the enemies of the Savior," as eternal pariahs, as perpetual conspirators against the Orthodox faith, etc. This antiquated and repugnant superstitiousness persisted throughout the nineteenth century, not least in the time of the pietistic last czar, Nicholas II; it was progressively reinforced by the pseudo-scientific racial anti-Semitism that came out of Germany and France.

Catherine's agricultural colonization of Jews was continued by the czars of the first half of the nineteenth century, Alexander I and Nicholas I. The scheme was little more than a method of coercion and interference, intended less to get Jews into agriculture than out of other economic occupations. Catherine herself had inaugurated the policy whereby Jews were restricted to the Pale of Settlement, confining the Jewish population to a narrow belt of territories extending from the Baltic to the Black Sea. Emancipation of Jews was as remote as it is possible to imagine, although the Napoleonic armies had trod the soil of Russia as far as Moscow. That fatal campaign of 1812 marked the farthest point to which the Revolutionary program was carried, but was of ephemeral significance for the cause of Emancipation: the only result was a temporary suspension by Alexander of the eviction of Jews from village communities. Neither Russian serfs nor Russian Jews savored Emancipation, even for a moment, before Napoleon's fall; nor were they to do so, the serfs for another half century, the Jews until a full century had passed.

In the meantime the policy of successive czars was, as it were, to make Jews pay the price their co-religionists were paying for Emancipation in Western countries, viz., their absorption and assimilation into the Russian society's legal and administrative structure, and the abolition of the traditional autonomy and self-government—without, of course, conferring the precious boon of Emancipation. The accompaniment—usually brutal rather than subtle—was an unrelenting effort to bring them to renounce Judaism in favor of Orthodox Christianity. As in the medieval period of western Europe, all would have gone swimmingly for them had they subscribed to apostasy.

Alexander I promulgated the *Constitution of Jews* in 1804. Its real intention is revealed by its provision that Jews be admitted to the national schools and universities, with the impossible qualification, however, that they attend classes for Christian instruction and religious formation. Hidden behind all the *Constitution's* fine phrases were such requirements. More than anything else it pared down

Jewish self-government to zero, particularly in judicial matters. When Jews continued voluntarily to appeal to the traditional rabbinical authorities to adjudicate disputes, Russian officials and churchmen became more determined than ever to sunder the Jewish community.

Nicholas I sought, as a soldier might well do, to de-nationalize and Russify Jews by drafting them at a tender age into the army. Ordinarily military service for twenty-five years began at age eighteen, but for Jews the czar stipulated that it would begin at twelve. For six years and entirely removed from home and synagogue, Jewish lads would undergo military training and Christian brow beating that ranged from flogging and ice-water baths to mandatory pork consumption and equally mandatory attendance at conversionary sermons. After these preliminaries the twenty-five-year stint began. Sometimes children were kidnaped in the streets by official "catchers," but increasingly it became the terrible responsibility of Jewish leaders to round up recruits for the army. Nothing could have been better calculated to break the spirit and rend the Jewish community than to require its leaders to make the invidious choice. Jewish parents were sorely tempted and sometimes kidnaped Jewish boys to substitute for their own sons, or they maimed their sons so as to render them unfit for military life, while some depressed lads committed suicide on the way to the military camp and apostasy. The tyrant Nicholas fashioned for those who eluded the military forcing house of Christianization an educational one—a system of schools in which the teachers and religious instruction would be Christian and the aim baptism. Expulsions —such as that from Kiev in 1835—and the threat of expulsion were part of the age. So, too, was the burning of the Talmud by illiterate censors. Another piece of medievalism that flourished was blood accusation, supported especially by high churchmen.

Alexander II came to power in 1855 as "the liberal

czar." He abolished the old military system: no more inductions at twelve, and the term of service was reduced to six years. He also permitted Jews (the relatively few who met the stipulated property qualification) to travel and reside outside the Pale of Settlement. Within the Pale they could vote for and sit upon the new local councils (zemstvos). Their economic rights remained as circumscribed as ever, and this generated great poverty, especially as the Jewish population had tripled since 1800; increasingly in the second half of the century Jews tended to fall into the category of *Luftmenschen* (literally men of air), i.e., vagabonds and peddlers. Whatever goodwill Alexander earned by his half-hearted reforms was dashed by his failure to grant Emancipation to Jews once he had bestowed it upon the serfs. Soured by the Polish Revolt of 1863, the czar renounced his liberalism as a grand mistake and issued no further reforms.

In Alexander's reign blood accusation raised its ugly head again and there was a spate of anti-Jewish rioting. A hodge-podge of forgeries and of snippets from the Talmud entitled *The Book of the Kahal* (1866) proclaimed the existence of a globe-girdling Jewish plot to overthrow Christianity—Latin, Greek, and Russian; the *Kahal* was the name for the Jewish institution of local self-government, in their villages and municipalities, which had been linked together to form a parliament comparable to the old Polish Council of the Four Lands; written by an apostate and product of Nicholas I's military forcing house, Jacob Brafman, *The Book* appeared as an official publication and was placed in the hands of every bureaucrat. When a riot broke out against the Jews in Odessa during the Easter season of 1871, the government only inquired whether it was part of the Kahal plot. Unrestrained, the violent bloodletting spread until it ran its course; in retrospect it stands out as the first of the atrocious pogroms that went on so relentlessly over the next forty years.

Alexander II's assassination in 1881 was officially blamed on the Jews, although the charge is a complete fabrication; thus the accompaniment of Alexander III's ascent to the throne was a wave of officially inspired pogroms. It is true that the failure to grant Emancipation had led more and more Jews to the conclusion that they would never be free until the hateful tyranny was toppled, and consequently Jews began to appear prominently in the various revolutionary, radical, socialist movements. As they did so, the government became progressively more persecutory and repressive toward them. The new severity was spelled out in the May Laws of 1882. They undermined Jewish life even in those villages of the Pale where Jews had lived for centuries. A local personage could petition the village functionaries to evict the so-called undesirable elements, yet the evicted could not betake themselves to another village or found a new village; their only recourse (other than the prolonged and degrading bribery of petty local officials) was to tumble into the overcrowded towns of the Pale as urban *Luftmenschen*. The same result might follow if a Jewish villager went off on business, family matters, or to visit a doctor, etc., and then tried to return to his home village. He might also find himself barred from visiting relatives in another village than his own. Other items in the May Laws greatly restricted Jews from practicing a profession or craft, and severely limited the number that could enter the schools and universities. So seriously handicapped were Jews in earning a livelihood that, by 1900, 40 percent of them depended on their co-religionists' charity.

The May Laws were duly enforced throughout the reigns of Alexander III and Nicolas II. Their reigns were punctuated by savage pogroms, blood accusations with public trials and medieval inquisitorial fanfare, and systematic terror by a band of vigilantes under the patronage of Nicholas and worthy of comparison with the S.S.—the "Black Guards" of the "Union of the Russian People."

There were expulsions, as from Moscow, Kharkov, and St. Petersburg (the capital then; now called Leningrad). The evil genius of both czars was the Procurator of the Holy Synod (the governing body of the Russian Orthodox Church), who replied to a Jewish delegation urging restraint upon him and the government, that what was intended was that a third of the Russian Jews should die, a third be Christianized, and a third emigrate.

Emigrate they did by the tens and hundreds of thousands from 1881 to 1914 and after; they went to western Europe, England and her Empire, South America, and above all, the United States. But emigration was not easy and required extensive bribes of officials, frontier guards, guides, etc. Russian Jews were greatly helped by their co-religionists throughout the Diaspora, who were true to the tradition that dated from the days when Jews went to great lengths to purchase back the freedom of their enslaved brethren in the Roman Empire. In these decades Russia went from calamity to calamity on the way to its tragic destiny: frequent famines, the defeat in the Russo-Japanese war of 1904–1905 and the revolution that followed it, strikes, anarchist assassinations, defeats in World War I—all were officially blamed on the Jews, the czars' perpetual scapegoat.

The German government in 1914–1916 sought to further its aims against Russia by proclaiming itself sympathetic to Emancipation of Russian Jews and even to Zionism. A proclamation to this effect was issued, but the long tradition of German anti-Semitism coupled with the condescension of the German military and officials made the Jews (most of whom were Polish Jews) very wary. Thus, if after a brief hesitation, Jews remained loyal to Russia, serving in her armies and suffering great casualties. But the Russian government and the circles responsible for the pogroms before 1914 found in the German moves justification for their suspicions and hatred of Jews, who were now declared to be "enemies of Mother Russia." The upshot was renewed persecutions and mass deportations, a resumption of terror and suffering.

The medieval period was notorious for the forgery of legal documents and the fabrication of history; they are a form of wishful thinking. One such piece of medievalism in nineteenth-century Russia we have seen in *The Book of the Kahal*. A more insidious example is *The Protocols of the Elders of Zion*, a document whose capacity for evil has not yet been exhausted. Embodying the anti-Semitism that had become so deeply engrained a habit of the Russian mind by 1900, the *Protocols* throws a flood of light on the official designation by the czar's government of the Jews as "enemies," "international conspirators," "subverters of Christianity," etc. Its predecessor was *A Plan for the Conquest of the World by the Jews*, concocted in 1903 by the Russian editor Paul Krushevan; this instigator of a murderous pogrom shortly before in the town of Kishinev illustrates Tacitus' dictum that human nature is such that a person must hate those he has injured. In 1905 the strangely mystical "monk" Serge Nilus published his own version of the same conspiracy, one which purported to be an exact transcription of the meeting of "the elders of Zion" in 1897: twenty-four points or "protocols" are spelled out by which Jews are called upon to disrupt Christian societies, provoke wars and revolutions, corrupt education and the press, and utilize their economic power as capitalists to throttle Christians, reducing them to poverty and slavery under a Jewish despotism. In keeping with the "big lie," as it has been called, the *Protocols* specifies that the conspiracy is already under way—no doubt this accusation was a reflection of Nilus' perturbation with the war and revolution of 1904–1905. Much to Nilus' chagrin, Nicholas II—filled to overflowing though he was with anti-Semitic phobias—interdicted for a while any further publication, because he learned that the whole thing was a forgery. This came to light apparently when the czar required his officials to ascertain precisely who the elders were. Nilus, who was influential at court but no Rasputin, admitted to the forgery when he said in their defense: "Let us suppose that the *Protocols* are false." Yet he, acting as God's instrument, thought they should be accepted as though they were true: "Is it not possible that God should nevertheless make use of them?" As justification he quoted St. Paul on God's will being done through human weakness. It is, once again, that wrong theology and a parody-plagiarism of St. John Chrysostom: Jews are eternally hateful to God, His will is that they suffer agony and destruction, their persecutors are His instruments, and so forth.

The Russian Revolution of 1917 was taken by many of its anguished victims to be proof of the *Protocols'* validity. Trotsky, of course, was a (non-professing) Jew, and to suit their wishful thinking Lenin was fashioned into one. When such refugees fled to western Europe they carried the *Protocols* with them and it was widely read, being translated into German, French, and English. It led a significant number of western Europeans to refer to World War I as "a Jew war" and "a Jew harvest," as another stage in the unfolding of the global conspiracy, and as proof positive of the *Protocols'* authenticity. In the editions of 1920 the Zionist leader Theodor Herzl was announced as the arch-elder: the incongruity of the choice of a man who inaugurated a Jewish nationalist movement that would transport Jews out of Christian society to a homeland of their own—that incongruity was not lost on Philip Graves.

The brother of the scholar and poet Robert Graves, he was an English journalist serving as reporter for *The Times* of London in Constantinople. A book in French which had no indication of its author or title came to his hands. It turned out to be a satire of 1864 by Maurice Joly on Napoleon III of France. It had nothing to do with Jews, but had been adapted for his Jew-baiting purposes by Nilus, who followed literally and pedantically the sequence of subjects, the lines of thought, and even the very phrasing of Joly. Three articles by Graves appeared in *The Times* in August, 1921, demonstrating conclusively and unanswerably that the *Protocols* was a hoax, and not a very clever one at that; his articles, reprinted and translated, circulated widely in Europe.

One of Graves' readers was Hitler, who nevertheless proclaimed the *Protocols* in *Mein Kampf* and from the rostrum to be absolute truth; he fashioned them into a mandate for genocide. Moreover, it is thought that his own bombastic style owes much to the *Protocols*; he himself boasted that he had learned from them "political intrigue, the technique of conspiracy, revolutionary subversion, as well as prevarication, deception, and organization"—or what he called in other connections the technique of "the big lie." The murderers of the German foreign minister Rathenau in 1922 testified that they were urged on to the crime after having read the *Protocols*. Today the *Protocols* are still with us—the power of reason and logic seems to be as weak against them as against accusations of ritual murder and Host desecration in the middle ages; particularly in the Arab countries are these crudest of all libels on the Jews utilized as a guide to Jewish or Israeli aims and policy. (The absurdity of anti-Semitism is patent in the fact that the most vociferous anti-Semites in the world today are the Semitic Arabs!)[9] A professor in a Catholic college will sometimes find his students invoking the *Protocols* as "proof" of a conspiracy to take over New York City. The principal importer to these shores of the *Protocols* was Henry Ford, who sought to rouse Americans to the menace of the plot in the book entitled *The International Jew*; it is usually noted that Ford called history "bunk," and as he practiced it in *The International Jew* it was precisely that. What the *Protocols* do "prove" is man's infinite capacity to deceive himself about someone he may not like, and his inhumanity to his fellow man. One is reminded of

Thomas Hobbes' remark of three centuries ago: "If the human being were truly humane, there would be no Jewish problem."

As of 1917 the *Protocols* had no official standing in Russia and, as far as I can tell, have no influence there at present (though some pronouncements in the last year or so appear to echo in a rather literal way parts of the *Protocols*). The Lvov-Kerensky government that came into power in March, 1917, took at last the momentous step of Emancipation, as did some of the newly established states, particularly Ukraine, where Jews were granted full equality. The communist regime of Lenin, dating from November, 1917, confirmed Emancipation and recognized Jews as constituting a distinct nationality in possession of extensive minority rights. Lenin went so far as to declare anti-Semitism to be "counter-revolutionary" and he outlawed it in the Russian constitution. But law is not life, and in Stalin's time the deeply ingrained tradition of anti-Semitism reasserted itself, a strange atavism indeed. Though the laws remained unchanged, discriminatory practices became visible. Minority rights have crumbled and something akin to the old efforts to de-nationalize Jews has reappeared. The critical question is the transmittal of Judaism to the young, and this has become practically impossible in an atheistic regime that forbids absolutely any kind of religious education and frowns upon the normal practicing of one's religion. As Russia became intensely nationalistic and totalitarian under Stalin, Russian Jews, having still a real sense of kinship with all Jews of the Diaspora, seemed suspect and unreliable. Stalin's vendetta against Trotsky, who was assassinated in 1940, undoubtedly helped to rekindle the fires of anti-Semitism. At the height of the Cold War there was report of a "Jewish doctor's plot" that seemed to presage, as under the czars, a renewal of persecution, but whatever immediate danger there was disappeared with Stalin's death in 1953.

In the period since Stalin and the growing rapprochement with the West, the anti-Jewish trends have been greatly toned down. Nevertheless, there are stirrings and traces of a harsh attitude now and then; and while the visit to the United States of the chief rabbi of Moscow in the spring of 1968 was a hopeful sign, it is far from convincing that all is well. The position of the Jews in Russia today invites comparison with that of the Iberian Marranos, whom we described earlier. I am not sure whether that is a comforting or troubling comparison. It may be true, as Kremlinologists estimate, that 10 percent of Russia's scientific, technological, and scholarly élite are Jews, although Jews account for only one percent of the total population; that is a kind of Marranic proportion. Yet, as Salo W. Baron has written, "apart from anti-Semitism, the totalitarian system of education and the overpowering pressures of its one-track ideology have already sapped the vitality of Russian Jewry to such an extent that many keen observers have expressed doubts as to the possibility of its survival for many more generations."[10] It only remains to add that Hitler had tried to settle the fate of Russian Jews by exterminating them, and he succeeded in killing 1,250,000, or 40 percent.

Poland, Hungary, Rumania, Czechoslovakia

Poland regained her independence in 1918 after nearly a hundred and fifty years of partition among Czarist Russia, Austria-Hungary, and Germany. Thus, the re-created Poland became a signatory of the Minorities Treaty of 1919. Under its provisions all of Poland's minorities, including the three and a half million Jews, were guaranteed civil rights, political equality, cultural autonomy, and a government subsidy for education and similar purposes. According to the new Polish constitution, the Jewish population was guaranteed equal rights with other citizens and enjoyed them in many areas of political, economic, and cultural life.

Nevertheless, the Jews in Poland were often exposed to anti-Semitic manifestations from right-wing political parties and organizations. These reactionary groups, which included elements of the Catholic Church, were also responsible for inciting anti-Jewish riots in rural and urban areas of the country. It is equally true that the Polish socialist and peasant parties and various intellectual groups advocated cooperation and understanding with the Jewish population. Under Pilsudski, the military hero and dictator of Poland, there was some deference to the Minorities Treaty and restraint in treatment of the Jews. But after his death in 1935, the new leadership, apparently not uninfluenced by the Nazi example in Germany, pursued an avowed policy of overt anti-Jewish discrimination. The Jews of Poland lived under extremely difficult political, economic, and social conditions, but they nevertheless formed a vital and often thriving community. There were more than two hundred Jewish periodicals in Yiddish, Hebrew, and Polish, a network of Jewish theaters, schools with Hebrew and Yiddish as the language of instruction, and a number of prominent religious institutions. Many Jews took an active part in Polish cultural life as well, in literature, historiography, art, music, medicine, law, and science.

Hitler set about extinguishing the two and a half million Polish Jews that fell to him in the partition of 1939; Stalin transported many of his million to Siberia where they were "to work and to die." Hitler's invasion of Russia in 1941 and the alliance with the Western powers led to a change of Russian policy. Jews were allowed to return to Poland, but it was by then, 1944, a Communist Poland. Those who survived or returned were for the most part not happy there, and some of them managed to emigrate and make their way to the United States, Canada, and other places of refuge.

The situation in Poland today, until recently under Gomulka (whose wife is Jewish) parallels that in Russia: legally there is no distinction between Jews and non-Jews. There has been, however, an expulsion of Jews from public life which has been especially notable since the 1968 upsurge of anti-Semitism. Official pronouncements are made insinuating that Jews are responsible for faults of the regime in problems such as economic shortages. A significant number of Polish Jews came or returned from Russia, and, moreover, Russian Jews have been prominent in Polish affairs, so that anti-Semitism gains new strength as a form of anti-Russian feeling. Of the approximately 30,000 Jews in Poland just after World War II, almost half have emigrated to Israel. The anti-Jewish campaign in Poland started with the beginning of the Israel-Arab War. A familiar pattern reappeared: Jews were dismissed from their jobs, expelled from colleges and universities, and the government moved to dismantle the remnants of Jewish institutions. The Jews have become the scapegoat of the official Polish newspaper, radio, and TV. Millions of copies of anti-Jewish books and pamphlets have been printed and distributed. The country's Jewish population continues to shrink, there are now no more than eight or nine thousand left. Yet even "without Jews," as Paul Lendvai convincingly shows, there is still much official anti-Semitism, although it usually masquerades and follows the Moscow line in using the rubric "anti-Zionist." Such things have prompted an English specialist in Polish studies to deplore how "the Jews, indeed, have shown again their unrivalled capacity for being made universal scapegoats."

The vicissitudes of Poland's Jews since 1919 parallel approximately those of their co-religionists in Hungary and Rumania. At the time of the Versailles settlement, all three had great minority problems, were backward economically, and were bound by the Minorities Treaty. The three fell into Hitler's murderous grip. Each today has only a minuscule Jewish population that is declining rapidly; they exhibit in common the ancient anti-Semitic hatred even though it is usually concealed under circumlocutions. Hungary conforms to the pattern with the difference that a communist regime had been established there by Bela Kun, "an opportunist scoundrel" according to Abram Sachar, amidst the rubble of defeat in 1919. Bela Kun and some of his colleagues were of Jewish extraction, and this fact was much exploited by the government of Admiral Horthy. Under that despotic reactionary, a frenzied nationalism, anti-communism, and anti-Semitism reinforced each other. Jews were exposed to every kind of abuse, from legal chicanery to physical assault. In 1938 a new law set severe limits to the percentage of Jews eligible to practice a profession or economic calling, with the result that two-thirds of Hungary's Jews forfeited their livelihood. That was the culmination of a mounting offensive against Jews; the frightful sequel under Hitler and then under Stalin has already been mentioned.

Rumania made its Jews, nearly a million strong, scapegoats for the problems and difficulties that beset it after 1919. Anti-Semitism was blatant and crude, and came close to being a formal government policy, no matter what the Minorities Treaty required, no matter which group or party was in power. Jew-baiting was an indoor sport for university leaders and ecclesiastics, among others. Rumania followed much the same policy as Poland and Hungary in forcing Jews out of their places in the economic structure and reducing them to beggary. But it was done by legal subtlety rather than arbitrary force: protracted legal inquiry was made into the status of Jews with a view to denying the validity of their citizenship and thereby barring them from the universities, professions, commerce, etc. By the time the war broke out in 1939, one-third of the Jews were declared to be "stateless"; the emigrant's path was about the only escape, but it was no more open to them than to other refugees at the time. An episode told by James Parkes suggests how the opportunities to make a new beginning were ignored: a wealthy Jew donated a social center to a university; once the university had posses-

sion of the building, it announced that its statutes forbade
Jews to use it!

   Czechoslovakia's was the most fortunate Jewish community, a prosperous and highly cultured group of about three
hundred and fifty thousand during the period between the
wars. A truly democratic state, under the leadership of
Masaryk and Beneš, the Czechoslovak government treated
all its minorities in a fair and enlightened way, and the
Jewish communities flourished. Here too, and through the
same forces, a glorious tradition has, since 1938, practically
come to an end.

England

   Since no Napoleonic army conquered England, the Jewish question there was, like much else, untouched by the
revolutionary ferment on the Continent. English Jews
enjoyed in life, if not in law, a far freer status and degree
of acceptance than any of their co-religionists across the
Channel (except in the "Dutch Jerusalem") up to 1789.
There had been a small but significant immigration of Jews
to England in the eighteenth century, so that by 1800 the
Jewish population went up to perhaps twenty-five thousand, or four times what it had been in the 1730's. In
1714, and long before Mirabeau's book calling for the
Emancipation of French Jews or C. W. von Dohm's *On
the Civil Amelioration of the Jews* in Germany, an English
Deist, John Toland, had advocated full Emancipation in
his *Reasons for Naturalizing the Jews in Great Britain and
Ireland on the Same Foot with All Other Nations.* A
remarkable number of Englishmen in the eighteenth and
early nineteenth centuries—such as James Finch in the
1720's—came forward with projects for the restoration of
the Jews to the Holy Land. Another indication of toler-

ance of Jews was the custom, dating from the 1690's, of reserving 10 percent of the seats on the English stock exchange for them. English-born Jews ordinarily could, if they met property qualifications required of everyone, vote in parliamentary and local elections. And if Pelham's measure of 1753 for Jewish naturalization had to be rescinded owing to mob tumults, a similar step taken by Parliament in 1740 in regard to the Empire—the Naturalization Act for the North American Colonies—stood.

Popular antipathy for Jews, such as the virulent outcry against Pelham's act of 1753, was slow in dying, but it was almost unknown in the nineteenth century. The change by the 1830's stemmed not from legislation, of which there was practically none, but from what contemporaries called "the reform of morals and manners," and the consequent improvement in the tone of English public life. The transition is caught up most interestingly in the *Improvement of the Working Classes,* written in 1834 by the political reformer and friend of Jeremy Bentham, Francis Place. He recalled how several Jews in 1771 had committed a horrible murder in Chelsea, then outside of London. Thereupon,

every Jew was in public opinion implicated, and the prejudice, ill will and brutal conduct this brought upon the Jews even after [the murderers] had been detected and punished for it, did not cease for many years. "Go to Chelsea" was a common exclamation when a Jew was seen in the streets and was often the signal of assault. . . . Dogs could not be used in the streets in the manner many Jews were treated. One circumstance among others put an end to the ill-usage of the Jews. . . . About the year 1787 Daniel Mendoza, a Jew, became a celebrated boxer and set up a school to teach the art of boxing as a science, the art soon spread among the young Jews and they became generally expert at it. The consequence was in a very few years seen and felt too. It was no longer safe to insult a Jew unless he was an old man and alone. . . . But even if the Jews were unable to defend themselves, the few who would now be disposed to insult them merely because they are Jews, would be in danger of chastisement from the passersby and of punishment from the police.

Sir Walter Scott's best known novel, *Ivanhoe* (1820), includes a sympathetic and, in general, historically accurate depiction of Jewish life in late-twelfth-century England. With an eye on his own era, Scott's heroine is Isaac the Jew's beautiful daughter, Rebecca. The novelist points up a parallel between the "disinherited" Saxons and the "disinherited" Jews: both peoples were strongly dedicated to preserving an ancient way of life; both were despised and persecuted by the Norman rulers. But, he wrote,

except for the flying fish, there was no race existing on the earth, in the air, or the waters, who were the object of such an unremitting, general, and relentless persecution as the Jews of this period. Upon the slightest and most unreasonable pretences, as well as upon accusations the most absurd and groundless, their persons and property were exposed to every turn of popular fury; for Norman, Saxon, Dane and Briton, however adverse these races were to each other, contended which should look with greatest detestation upon a people whom it was accounted a point of religion to hate, to revile, to despise, to plunder, and to persecute. The kings of the Norman race, and the independent nobles, who followed their example in all acts of tyranny, maintained against this devoted people a persecution of a more regular, calculated, and self-interested kind. It is a well-known story of King John that he confined a wealthy Jew in one of the royal castles, and daily caused one of his teeth to be torn out, until, when the jaw of the unhappy Israelite was half disfurnished, he consented to pay a large sum, which it was the tyrant's object to extort from him. The little ready money which was in the country was chiefly in possession of this persecuted people, and the nobility hesitated not to follow the example of their sovereign in wringing it from them by every species of oppression, and even personal torture.

Scott's inspiration for the fair Rebecca, remarkable for her intelligence and courage, came to him through the

American writer Washington Irving, a dear friend; Irving greatly admired Rebecca Gratz (1781–1869), a celebrated beauty of a family prominent in Philadelphia as merchants and philanthropists. She was a teacher, and distinguished herself in the founding and direction of orphanages, schools, and various civic projects. There is no absolutely incontrovertible evidence for the belief, but it is reasonably clear that Scott was so moved by Irving's description of her virtues that he sought to preserve her name, beauty, and sterling character in the heroine of *Ivanhoe*.

The years intervening between Scott's historical novel and Place's book saw the English Liberal Reform movement get into high gear. Catholic disabilities were struck down in 1829, those of Protestant Nonconformists (that is, dissenters from the established Anglican Church) were also repealed; and the next logical step—as the pressure built up that finally carried the famous Parliamentary Reform Bill of 1832—appeared to be the abolition of "the civil disabilities and privations affecting Jews in England." The great English historian and member of Parliament, T. B. Macaulay, lent his support to the Jewish bill in a famous essay of 1831. As a Liberal and Whig he could not conceive that a man was unfit to vote for or sit in Parliament because "he wears a beard, because he goes to the synagogue on Saturdays instead of going to the church on Sundays"; and he argued that "on all questions of police, of finance, of criminal and civil law, of foreign policy, the Jew, as a Jew, has no interest hostile to that of the Christian." As an Anglican, Macaulay thought it appropriate that Parliament take up the bill on Good Friday: there was "no day fitter for terminating long hostilities," "repairing cruel wrongs," "blotting out from the statute-book the last traces of intolerance" than "the day on which the religion of mercy was founded."

Yet despite the eloquence of Macaulay in and out of Parliament, such a measure was not passed until 1858, a generation later; having been repeatedly passed in the

House of Commons, it was each time rejected in the Lords. The obstacle barring Jews from sitting in Parliament was a grand technicality, viz., that the form of oath required of an M. P. before he could take his seat was couched in Christian terms, to which a professing Jew could not subscribe. Except for that "incidental necessity," it was remarked by the Tory leader Lord George Bentinck in 1845, Jews could have held any post in the cabinet, including that of prime minister. Lionel de Rothschild was elected five times consecutively, but barred by the Commons on the score of the oath.

In the meantime other avenues had been opened to English Jews. In 1831 they could study but not receive a degree at Cambridge. The City of London (the financial district of the metropolis) for the first time granted Jews its "freedom," thereby enabling them to open retail businesses and enter the commercial associations known as the Livery Companies. In 1833 Jews were admitted to the bar and thus enabled to practice law before the courts; for the first time a *hereditary* title was granted to a Jew when Isaac Lyon Goldsmid received a baronetcy in 1841. The prime mover behind most of these events, however, was David Salomons (1797–1873). A Freeman of the City, he got himself elected as its sheriff in 1835, and Parliament went so far as to modify the required oath, thus permitting him to enter upon the office. It took a decade of squabbling before he could become an alderman, but he made it, and topped it off by becoming lord mayor of London in 1855. This meant that Jews were eligible for all municipal posts; only from Parliament were they still excluded.

Lionel de Rothschild tried but failed to overcome that last legal hurdle in 1847. In 1851 the pertinacious Salomons was elected for the City and ignored the oath in taking his seat in the Commons, participating in debate and casting his vote; he was, however, ejected from the House and heavily fined. The anomaly was at last disposed of in 1858 when the Lords agreed to an act permitting the Commons to amend the oath, and in 1866 a similar measure opened the Lords to Jews. Thus Lionel de Rothschild was finally allowed to take his seat for the City; interestingly, his son was ennobled by Queen Victoria and was the first Jew to sit in the Lords, 1885.

Prime Minister Gladstone was the first to include a Jew in the Cabinet, Sir George Jessel as solicitor-general in 1871. In the Liberal government that came into power in 1905, Sir Rufus Isaacs served successively as attorney general, lord chief justice, ambassador to the United States, and viceroy for India; he was joined by Herbert Samuel at the Home Office, and both men were subsequently ennobled. But the most famous English Jew of the past century was Benjamin Disraeli (1804–1881). Born of an Italian immigrant of the 1780's who became a Christian and had his son baptized, Disraeli was thus a Christian and free to enter Parliament. In the 1840's he embarked on the reconstruction of Conservatism as the party of "Tory democracy"; he was a chief figure in the "new imperialism," having acquired the Suez Canal for England in what was one of the great diplomatic coups of the age, and was a great favorite of Queen Victoria, who ennobled him as Lord Beaconsfield. For all that Victorian England was supposedly narrow, stuffy, prejudiced, hidebound, and respectable, it nevertheless saw fit to have the flamboyant Disraeli as its price minister twice and as leader of the Tory Party for thirty-five years. It is true that he was a Christian, but he always represented himself as a loyal Jew, even if it is not clear what he meant by that assertion; in most countries of the world—whether now or then—racial prejudice would have sufficed to close him out from the remarkable career he attained in England.

Another indication of the growth of a humane and tolerant society in England is the life of George Eliot (Mary Ann Evans) and her novel *Daniel Deronda* (1876), in which she depicts sympathetically and tenderly the life of a Jewish family in England.[11] She had departed far from her narrowly Evangelical upbringing—at one point she had protested against a Jewish tenor singing scriptural passages from an oratorio. She went on, however, to become learned in the Bible and in biblical criticism; by 1856 she had translated Spinoza's *Tractatus Theologico-Politicus* and his *Ethics*. In the novel she sets about demonstrating to Victorian society that prejudice is absurd. In justification of Jews living lives that are both apart from and integrated with English society, she wrote that "the strength and wealth of mankind depend on the balance of separateness and communication," or, as we might say, a balance between exclusiveness and assimilation. She would have her readers understand that Jewish qualities are precious to the human family, that the world would be the poorer without those qualities. Her sympathetic rendition of the hero's Zionism is especially interesting in the light of England's contribution from the 1880's on to the birth of Israel; she has Daniel say at one point that "the idea that I am possessed with is that of restoring a political existence to my people, making them a nation again, such as the English have, though they too are scattered over the face of the globe." He is the disciple of the enigmatic Mordecai Cohen, a pre-Zionist philosopher of Zionism, whose sister Mirah he marries; together they leave "for the East" to put her brother's philosophy into practice.

With the onset of the Russian pogroms in 1881, a mass emigration carried Jews to all parts of the world, particularly to England, the British Empire, and, above all, to the United States. By 1900, one hundred thousand refugees had made their way to England and caused considerable dislocation in London. A prolonged depression since the 1870's made English unions murmur about Jews flooding the labor market and causing wages to fall, especially among the unskilled. Most of the criticism, however, came from English Jews, prosperous and assimilated, who found it difficult to be sympathetic to the newcomers, not because they were paupers, but because they were such devout traditionalists as to be "superstitious"; to the immigrants the Anglo-Jews frequently appeared to be not loyal Jews but "apostates." The difficulties were such that a Royal Commission on Alien Immigration deliberated in 1902–1903 and heard everybody's complaints; its recommendations were incorporated in the Aliens Immigration Act of 1905, stipulating certain qualifications that excluded the down and out (on the grounds that their relief would become a burden to the Treasury). And if this lacked humanity, the traditional right of asylum was nevertheless preserved, so that by the 1930's England's Jewish population was nearly a half million or three times the figure of 1900.

For all the hubbub, it will be found, if one reads the commission's *Report,* that Englishmen were kindly disposed toward the strangers. Workmen were more notable for their admiration of Jewish pluck and perseverance than for xenophobia or anger with economic competition. It quickly became clear that Jews were assets to the economy in certain areas, introducing mass production methods in such trades as suit and dress making. They were admired for their intelligence; it was pointed out that "the Jews have always been a nation of students," and that "the Talmud sets the scholar above the king." English observers commended the lengths to which even the poorest parents went to assure a good education for their children, while the London School Board found its Jewish pupils were "sharper and more intelligent than the English, and carry off a large portion of prizes and scholarships." As for their defects, they "are fairly chargeable upon what they have been forced in the past to suffer," and it would require many years before the taints of the ghetto disappeared, as it had taken forty years in the desert under Moses to purge away the stains of Egyptian bondage.

Hence it is not surprising that James Bryce (an outstanding scholar and Liberal statesman) could boast truthfully

in 1901 that "England is now pretty much the only country
in which Jews are subject to no sort of disability, either
social or legal," that there had been a "recrudescence of
anti-Semitism everywhere except in England." With the
prominence of Jews in the circle of King Edward VII's
personal friends Jewish acceptance and Emancipation in
England may be said to have been fully attained. The
notable thing about the reception of *The Protocols of the
Elders of Zion* in England, in the 1920's, was that it was
there that it was first proved to be a forgery—by Philip
Graves of *The Times* of London. The fascism of Oswald
Mosely in the 1930's and after belonged to the lunatic
fringe, so too, the anti-Zionist phobias of Ernest Bevin (for
which see the last chapter). Since both Napoleon the
emancipator and Hitler the exterminator failed to conquer
England, its Jewish community was untouched by either of
the colossi who most fatefully shaped the destiny of the
Jews in the modern era.

The United States of America

In my account of Jewish history in the age of Emancipation, I have thought it appropriate and useful to organize
the presentation along national lines. There is, admit-
tedly, something artificial in doing so, because much that
was characteristic of Jewish life did not reflect national
boundaries at all. To a remarkable degree Jewish history
in the period since 1789, as before, is all of a piece, that
seamless robe which the historian does well not to tear
asunder. Moreover, some divisions within Judaism are ob-
scured by reference to national boundaries. In the nineteenth century Jews tended to break up into various group-
ings; some fell away from the practice of Judaism entirely,
becoming Christians, agnostics, freethinkers, etc. The heirs
of Mendelssohn and Krochmal became modernized and

secularized in varying degrees as Reform Jews, while others remained steadfast in the received beliefs and practices as Orthodox Jews. Nevertheless, as it seems to me, Judaism continued to possess much of the solidarity that has enabled it in the past to avoid sectarianism while still preserving a full measure of freedom of thought and conscience for all within its fold. As we have seen, e.g., in the Karaites, Jewish history has frequently been marked by much controversy but by no enduring divisions. Division usually has its source in practices rather than in beliefs; for, as Mendelssohn would remind us, Judaism makes it incumbent on the Jew to behave ethically rather than to believe strictly. "Curiously," as Professor Baron has said, "despite the fervor of theological debate the differences between Reform and traditionalism go much less deep in the realm of religious fundamentals than in that of ritualistic practice." Today, the paramount divisions among Jews are circumstantial and do reflect national lines. The Jewishness of a citizen of Israel is both in religion and nationality, of a Russian Jew it is primarily in nationality, of an American Jew it is primarily in religion. The distinctiveness of the three main bodies of world Jewry will probably last for a long time. It should not obscure the truth, however, that Jews everywhere belong in a significant sense to a single community.

The remarks above about the difficulties of treating the history of the Jews and of Judaism within a national framework are especially applicable to any discussion of the Jewish experience in the United States. Three strands of Judaism—Reform, Orthodox, Conservative, with several varieties of each—flourished here as in no other country. These divisions were partly owing to the traditional Jewish intellectual freedom and pluralism, which were given full scope in the libertarian and individualistic society of the United States; Jews express this tendency humorously when they say "where there are two Jews there are three opinions." More particularly, the United States was a melting pot of varieties of Jews as well as in the usual sense of all nationalities. American Jews were of greatly diverse national origins, and each new wave of settlers brought with it distinctive ways and customs, languages, rites, etc.

Another source of diversity within American Judaism has been the remarkable degree of assimilation and nationalization of the descendants of earlier Jewish immigrants to American life. Until the mid-nineteenth century Jews came in such small numbers that they were hardly noticed. No laws against them were passed, and since they found real justice in American courts they dispensed with their own; indeed, except in religious matters, they dispensed with the whole apparatus of autonomy and self-government as we have seen it in Europe and the ancient empires. The autonomous community, isolated from the host society, is an effective bar to integration, but that bar never existed in the United States. American Jews down to 1881 were frequently prosperous; they knew nothing of, or had forgotten, the ghetto and its grinding poverty, nor of discriminatory laws, massacre, expulsion; for them anti-Semitism was a "feeble" thing and no more than a "nuisance." Their forebears had come as early as the seventeenth century from Holland, England, and after 1848, from Germany; their memory of the Old World was, variously, of Emancipation or quasi-Emancipation, of the Jewish Enlightenment—that tradition of bridge-building to the modern world that went back to Mendelssohn and Krochmal. They spoke English and were forgetting Hebrew, wore no skull caps and grew no beards. They constituted the strength of Reform Judaism, which originated in Germany, where it was led by Abraham Geiger (1810–1874). In the United States its outstanding leader was Rabbi Isaac Mayer Wise (1817–1900), who came from Bohemia and founded Hebrew Union College in 1875, the first American rabbinical seminary. An especially notable practice of the Reformists was their frequent welcoming to their pulpits of

Christian clergymen of various denominations, and so receptive were they to, seemingly, outside influences that there were, according to Wise, "Episcopalian Jews in New York, Quaker Jews in Philadelphia, Huguenot Jews in Charleston, everywhere according to the prevailing sect of the locality."

Initially at least, American Reform Jews regarded—and were regarded by—the pauperized ghetto-bound Polish and Russian Jews that came in such great numbers after 1881 as being "no true Jews." By 1914 two million had arrived, fleeing the Russian pogroms that began in 1881. Bearded, hatted, wearing caftans and speaking Yiddish, these medieval apparitions seemed to come from another world. They were the strength of Orthodox Judaism (which had its American origin, however, in the Maranno settlements of the seventeenth and eighteenth centuries). One of its early champions, the contemporary and rival of Wise, was the newspaper journalist and editor of *The Occident*, Isaac Leeser (died 1868). A particularly strong disagreement between Reform and Orthodox was, especially about 1900–1920, Zionism. The Orthodox were, with a few exceptions, stalwart supporters of Theodor Herzl's "political Zionism," whereas the great majority of Reformists rejected it, one of them going so far as to refer to it as the "Zionist heresy"; to them America was almost the land of the promise.[12] "This country is our Palestine, this city our Jerusalem, this house of God our Temple," exulted a rabbi while dedicating a new synagogue in Charleston, S.C., in 1841. Nevertheless, and owing to the Dreyfus case and a world-wide resurgence of anti-Semitism, Zionism began to make more and more converts among the Reformists in the new century.

Conservative Judaism was an attempt—a typically American attempt, perhaps—to effect a compromise between the Reform and Orthodox. It may be defined as a synthesis, seeking to preserve the Judaism of the Old World, but to accommodate it to the conditions of the New World also. Its founder was the outstanding scholar Solomon Schechter (1850–1915), who had been born in Rumania in a time of severe Jewish persecution there; he was educated at Vienna and went to Cambridge University in England as Reader in Rabbinics in 1890. He gained fame, it has been said, for "introducing British wit into Talmudic discussions" and for his identification of a fragment of an original manuscript of Ecclesiastes and the discovery of another fragment of it in an ancient synagogue in Cairo. In 1902 he came to the United States to be president of the Jewish Theological Seminary, founded in 1887 and now a familiar landmark at Broadway and 122nd Street in Manhattan. Owing in large measure to his reorganization of it, this seminary for the training of rabbis became a central institution of scholarship and spiritual direction for the growing number of Conservative congregations; since its founding it has done much to set a high standard for Jewish scholarship and learning in the United States. But brilliant as the achievements of its seminary have been, Conservative Judaism's efforts at mediation have failed; there has never been in the United States an overall organization that incorporated all Jews and every strand of Judaism. Variety has been the spice of Jewish religious life in America. The Society for Ethical Culture, founded in 1876 by Felix Adler, although it has departed far beyond the pale of what can be recognized as Judaism, is another expression of that religious diversity.

The history of the Jews in the United States has been a happy one; the theme that runs through those three centuries is, as S. W. Baron has remarked, "the well-nigh universal Jewish feeling of being at home in America." There was never an evil heritage of ghettos, massacres, expulsions, yellow badges, Inquisition, discriminatory legislation, etc., to overcome. If anti-Semitism in some form is co-terminous with the presence of Jews in America, so too, but more deeply rooted, is philo-Semitism. Philo-Semitism was as characteristic of Puritans in New England, where they set about building a "New Zion," as it was in old England. They greatly valued the Old Testament, compared their flight from England to the exodus out of Egypt, named their children after its heroes, and modeled their lives on it as fully as possible; they wanted to adopt the Mosaic code as their legal code to be enforced in the courts of law, there were proposals that Hebrew become their official language, and Harvard was a pioneer in making full provision for Hebrew in its curriculum.

Partly owing to their small numbers and assimilation, partly owing to philo-Semitism, the normal state of affairs in colonial America was for Jews to enjoy equal rights with all others. What a Swedish traveler noted in New York in 1748 was generally true: "They have a synagogue and houses, and great country seats of their own property, and are allowed to keep shops in town. They have likewise several ships, which they freight and send out with their own goods. In fine, they enjoy all the privileges common to the other inhabitants of this town and province." That there were exceptions—such as Rhode Island's refusal in 1762 to grant citizenship to Aaron Lopez, exemplary person though he was—cannot be denied; but they were exceptions to the rule, namely the Act of Parliament of 1740 allowing Jews to become citizens in the colonies after a residence of seven years. The provisions of the Constitution of 1787 guaranteeing religious liberty and equality before the law, while so momentous in one respect, only confirmed, broadened, and made uniform to all the states what had been ordinary practice for some time. With the nineteenth century, certainly from the presidency of Jackson onward, the American system of political democracy and social-legal equality—with which Jewish communalism and ethics have close affinities—has sustained and, let us hope, will sustain, this happy state of affairs. The example of America had its effect. E.g., an eccentric but kindhearted English authoress, Harriet Martineau, was so profoundly impressed by the superior position of Jews on a visit to the United States in the early 1830's that, on her return to England, she launched a vigorous drive to gain for them the same rights at home; in so doing she imparted additional momentum to the campaigns in England down to 1858 that we described earlier.

It is sometimes argued or feared that the United States will inevitably see the outbreak of the anti-Semitic mania of massacre and expulsion that has been the fate of Jews in every instance heretofore—after a golden age in Babylonia, Islam, Spain, Germany, etc. That some Jews should fatalistically search for signs of an approaching doom and remind us that cataclysm came unforeseen in past ages, like a bolt from a cloudless sky, is certainly understandable. But as long as we make our democracy last and make its ideals guide our actions more and more fully, there is no real danger of such an eruption of barbarism. It is true that anti-Semitism musters a good deal of force and commands a good deal of influence, but there have always been in our free society countervailing forces and influences.

E.g., by the turn of the century, some immigrant groups began to be notable for an anti-Semitism that they had brought with them from Europe; together with a milder native American anti-Semitism that went back to about 1870, it began to erode the unusually fortunate position Jews had enjoyed since the colonial period. The Populists preached against the money interest, which to some extent they identified with Jews, as did, from another vantage point, Henry Adams; an "American Anti-Semitic Association" was founded in Brooklyn in 1896 by recent immigrants. Jewish peddlers were often molested by beard-pullers, mostly Irish and German toughs. There was a riot in Manhattan's Lower East Side in 1902, when the funeral procession of an eminent rabbi was attacked by Irish factory workers; the police arrived, only to join forces with the Jews' assailants. A Greek immigrant began to translate Drumont's diatribes as early as 1888, but it is indicative of the American situation that, as Professor Higham writes in his essay "Anti-Semitism in the Gilded Age," "whereas Drumont created a sensation in France, his disciple in America fulminated in obscurity and neglect."

The later 1930's likewise saw a crescendo of anti-Semitism in the United States, partly owing to the dislocations that came in the wake of the depression of 1929, but much more to Nazi propaganda after 1933; there was a "ritual murder" accusation at Massena, New York, in 1928; Henry Ford was peddling a Model-A version of *The Protocols of the Elders of Zion* in his *The International Jew;* Father Coughlin waged a crusade that was a peculiar compound of anti-Sem-itism, Anglophobia, and inflationism. These calumnies and misrepresentations were countered and offset in large measure, however, by such things as a widely read article of 1936 by the editors of *Fortune* magazine on "Jews in America"; by fact and statistic they demonstrated, e.g., "that there is no basis whatever for the suggestion that Jews monopolize U.S. business and industry." We may note parenthetically that the old European habit of blaming economic panics and depressions on Jews did not occur in the United States—certainly not in 1873, 1907, or 1921, although 1929 is a partial exception.

On the whole, then, while American society is by no means immune to anti-Semitic outbreaks, anti-Semitism has not taken root here owing to the essentially democratic quality of American life and the absence of any long-stand-ing tradition of mistreatment or persecution. To the ex-tent that our treatment of Jews reflects the European heri-tage, it is the beneficent tradition of England. Much the same considerations apply to Canada, to which thousands of the refugees after 1881 made their way. To South Amer-ica, by contrast, the ancient heritage of Inquisition, persecu-tion, expulsion, had been transplanted in colonial times, as we have seen in the history of the Marranos; it was still something to reckon with after 1881 when tens of thousands of Jews sought to find new homes there, particularly in Argentina. At the present time in Argentina, anti-Semitism is not just a nuisance but a real danger. The Tacuara movement, made up principally of Catholic university students imbued with an extreme fascist nationalism, incites its members to go about the streets of Buenos Aires painting swastikas, firing machine guns at synagogues, and tossing bombs into Jewish business establishments; the group has carried out all sorts of violent crimes and kidnapings. The students have a Roman Catholic chaplain, Father Julio de Meinville, who gives the highest sanction to their crimes (despite the efforts of his bishop and the hierarchy to restrain him); in his book *The Mystery of the Jew in History* he invokes what I call in the Introduction an aberration, the false theology, the theology of prosecution, which he traces back to St. John Chrysostom and restates as the one to which the Church should return. The Tacuara combination of a narrow and intense religiosity with a narrow and bellicose nationalism is the same that has so often in the past been fatal to Jews. Whether the spirit and injunctions of Vatican II will make their way into Argentina is impossible to say; in the meantime we may note that our rendition of the long chronicle of Jewish sufferings is something other than a kind of academic sigh over what once happened but which cannot happen again, for that past is not dead and gone but still with us.

Jews in the United States, like all our immigrants, have had no picnic making the transition to a new mode of life, and mounting the ladder from poverty, ignorance, and ostracism to affluence, education, and acceptance. The Lower East Side of New York, a fashionable residential area at the time of the Civil War, first became infamous as a slum when, after 1881, Jews settled there in swarms. If not on the same scale, there were similar quarters in Philadelphia, Boston, Detroit, Cleveland, Chicago, and New Orleans. Conditions were atrocious, sanitation woeful; a dozen people lived in one room, a hundred used one privy. Tuberculosis, rheumatism, etc., flourished, but crime, dirt, ignorance, immorality, did not. If one looks into the explanation for the refusal to succumb to the temptations of the slum, it is not far to seek: the Jewish family stuck together through the thick and thin of slum degradation and squalor as it had through the thick and thin of the old world's ghettos, poverty, persecution. The family circle is the scene of the most touching religious services in Judaism, as readers of Eliot's *Daniel Deronda* will recall, and as such it has been a great source of strength to Jewish life. Venereal disease, illegitimate children, abandoned wives, were practically unknown. Ritual cleanliness and the change of clothes for the Sabbath warded off diseases and epidemics. Much-thumbed books lined the walls of dingy apartments, night schools were crowded, and a much-used public library card helped satiate the passion for learning and self-improvement.

Reinforcing the family was the synagogue, of which Anita Lebeson has said: "The transformation of a poor, insecure, awkward immigrant into a dignified patriarch on Friday evening and Sunday was a morale-building practice which fortified him for the long days of menial tasks and degrading rounds when both poverty and lack of linguistic skills made the immigrant the butt of jokes and the target of the buffoon." The synagogue was also a charity distribution center, and on the principle that we are our brother's keeper, a vast and efficient assistance system was developed, one in which the synagogue was only a cog.

Not content with waiting until the immigrant stepped off the boat or wended his way through Ellis Island, aid societies sought him out in Europe and saw him through all vicissitudes until he was able to dispense with charity and stand on his own feet, which ordinarily did not take long. The principal organization for this purpose was the Hebrew Sheltering and Immigrant Aid Society, founded in 1887; its picturesque headquarters building has been preserved as a Manhattan landmark. A characteristic grouping on a smaller scale was the *Landsmannschaften,* or mutual aid societies, comprising persons coming from the same town or village in the "old country"; they helped each other here, encouraged those who remained behind to come, and preserved the camaraderie and memories of the old days.

The organized system for the assistance of Jewish immigrants after 1881 is of the greatest significance as "welfare pioneering." Modeled in part on similar organizations in France and England, the immigrant aid agencies of the period down to 1914 are the foundations of the world-embracing structure created by American Jews in the twentieth century for aid, charity, and services of an immense range. Assistance to "displaced persons"—almost the chief product of the twentieth century so far—hospitals, sanatoria, homes for the aged, handicapped, orphans, health clinics, legal aid and guidance, first-rate medical schools, etc., are characteristic expressions of it. Jews have dug deep into their pockets to provide these philanthropies and services—which are by no means rendered only to Jews—largely through the Federation of Jewish Philanthropies. Such massive and sensitive philanthropy has become the most characteristic expression of American Judaism, so much so that it is sometimes criticized as "pocketbook Judaism"; the characterization is quite unfair if one remembers that the worship of God has always required such sacrifices and gifts in behalf of others, that they are not given as a surrogate for prayer or ethical conduct, that the sorrowful plight and tragic fate of world Jewry in the twentieth century demanded such an epic of philanthropy for their very survival. "The devil take the hindmost" has never been a proverb among Jews.

In this connection we may take note of the philanthropic and social service society that dates from 1843, B'nai B'rith.

Founded in part as a fraternal society and club for Jews who were not admitted to non-Jewish clubs, it dedicated itself from the start to religious and social aims of a high order. The original statement of purpose may well stand as the motto for Jewish philanthropy in the twentieth century: "B'nai B'rith has taken upon itself the mission of uniting Israelites in the work of promoting their highest interests and those of humanity; of developing and elevating the mental and moral character of the people of our faith; of inculcating the purest principles of philanthropy, honor, and patriotism; of supporting science and art; alleviating the wants of the poor and needy; visiting and attending the sick; coming to the rescue of the victims of persecution; providing for, protecting, and assisting the widow and orphan on the broadest principles of humanity." B'nai B'rith also sought to bring Reform and Orthodox Judaism into harmony, but, while it has a splendid record in other areas and has been a profound influence for good in American life, its efforts to unite American Jewry have failed.

B'nai B'rith's daughter institution, the Anti-Defamation League, was founded in 1913 to counter anti-Semitism; before long it became a pioneer in the field of inter-religious understanding. A.D.L. is not content to point out that anti-Semitism is wrong, ugly, undemocratic, un-American, and heretical, but demonstrates so by fact and statistic, logic and eloquence. Yet since all liberties stand together and all injustices are united, A.D.L. is, in its own words, "dedicated to translating democratic ideals into a way of life for all Americans in our time." Accordingly, it has been active in such areas as the Negro civil rights movement; in fact, in the perspective of the last hundred years, it is quite appropriate to speak of the American Jew as "the first friend of the Negro." I might observe parenthetically that the recent manifestation of anti-Semitism among several black civil rights leaders is a little disconcerting, not so much because it is a species of ingratitude for Jewish support in the past, which is perhaps understandable; rather because two minorities ought to be allies in the good cause and cannot afford to abuse each other. As Harry Golden said in a letter to *The New York Times* for November 9, 1968, "Basically, a Negro anti-Semite is about as convincing as a Jewish white supremacist."

Reference was made earlier to the immigrant, beneficiary though he was of a remarkable program of aid and support, earning a meager living at "menial tasks." A high proportion of the immigrants were *Luftmenschen*, vagabonds or people who live on thin air and by their wits, who had no industrial skills except as "needle workers" and cigar makers, about the only trades the czars' policies left open to them. There were openings for them in great numbers as unskilled or semi-skilled workers in the "needle trades"; they were "sweated labor," i.e., overworked in squalid conditions that brought pay that was only a pittance. Not infrequently a venerable talmudic scholar, frail and wan, worked at the sewing machine eighteen or twenty hours a day. By sheer persistence—self-help and community help— Jews made their way up; as a journalist reported in 1894, "They are anxious for work, intelligent, quick to learn our language, and promise, in the fullness of time, to become useful additions to our population." Some scraped together enough capital to open a candy-cigar-newspaper booth, a tailor shop, or a grocery store. Some as peddlers with their sack of items going about the countryside with a remarkable variety of goods became figures of American folklore; they followed in the footsteps of their German-Jewish predecessors and went from peddler's pack to "dry goods store" and then the department store and the mail-order catalogue, which last two are almost Jewish inventions. Some made fortunes, particularly the German Jews who had arrived just at the right moment, as retailers, meeting the needs of a mass market as it opened up in the period after the Civil War. Among others who made enormous fortunes were the Guggenheims, Warburgs, Strauses, Schiffs

—names which now, however, are synonymous with philanthropy and generous subsidization of the arts. Jews have long since graduated from the ranks of the unskilled, and by dint of education have entered the professions in great numbers; in keeping with their earlier economic occupations, however, they are still strongly represented in the manufacture and retailing of clothing.

Enrolled in the ranks of labor and animated by the sense of social justice that Judaism inspires, many American Jews have become prominent in the labor movement and the organization of unions. The great pioneer in the American labor movement was Samuel Gompers, who came from England in 1863 as young as he was poor; from a cigar maker he became leader of the International Cigar Makers Union. His conception was of craft unionism, viz., to organize the men of a particular trade and to charge relatively high dues in order to maintain an extensive program of insurance and assistance in the event of illness, injury, death, unemployment, etc. His union welfare program reflects many of the charitable practices and institutions we have seen Jews organizing in behalf of immigrants; in 1886 Gompers organized the American Federation of Labor. Sidney Hillman came from Russian Lithuania and in 1914 succeeded to the presidency of the Amalgamated Clothing Workers; over a long career he led the fight against sweating, was a pioneer in union health, welfare, pension, and housing programs, organized a union insurance company, and was an important adviser to President Franklin D. Roosevelt, both in shaping New Deal legislation and in preventing labor disputes during World War II. A third generation of Jewish labor leaders is represented by David Dubinsky, still active and resourceful. He came from Russia in 1912 and became president of the International Ladies' Garment Workers Union in 1932. Under him the union has been a pacesetter in employee welfare and adult education; it has been particularly notable for the promotion of cultural interests among its workers and has its own theatrical group, "Pins and Needles." For every Jew who became a millionaire businessman, another became a labor leader of vision and idealism.

In the United States, as elsewhere, Jews have been city dwellers. The free or cheap land in the United States did not attract them, partly because they came too late when the frontier was closing. Owing to the conditions of life in eastern Europe, they tended to be frail and not sufficiently robust for the life of a homesteader. Nevertheless, there was a trend among these traditional town dwellers to turn to the soil for a livelihood. By 1909 about thirty thousand Jews were engaged in agriculture, while about three thousand families worked their own farms. Characteristically, Jewish communities, or "colonies," were established on great tracts of land, suggestive in some respects of the *kibbutz* cooperative farms now in Israel. One of the proponents of such schemes was the wealthy German railway magnate Baron de Hirsch (1831–1896), who made huge sums available for the purpose of establishing agricultural colonies, principally in Argentina, but also in the United States. His Jewish Colonization Society continues his philanthropic projects today. He was an anti-Zionist and would assist Jews to settle on land almost anywhere except in Palestine. In the United States such efforts did not meet with much success, although four colonies did—Alliance, Carmel, Rosenhayn, and especially Woodbine, located in South Jersey, where an agricultural school was also founded; frequently a feature of such communities was small factories to meet local needs and to sustain the farms over the shoals of financial troubles.

The children of immigrants went forthwith to the public schools and, as we have seen among their counterparts in London, carried all before them in the competition for awards, prizes, and honors. Thence they began to make their way into the universities and colleges; their eminence in practically all the higher callings and professions is astounding. To tick off name upon name in a catalogue may not be very edifying, but it will confirm the view put forward earlier that Emancipation has had a profound impact on Jews in kindling a great range of creative powers. Among many, many novelists Saul Bellow is probably the best known of contemporaries; Sholom Aleichem, Russian-born and Yiddish-writing, was famous at the start of the century and his work seems to grow in estimation with the passing years as it gains a wider audience. In drama we have George S. Kaufman, Lillian Hellman, and Arthur Miller. In music Sigmund Romberg, Jerome Kern, Irving Berlin, George and Ira Gershwin, rounded out by the immortal team of Rodgers and Hammerstein. Virtuosos include Vladimir Horowitz, Alexander Brailowski, Artur Rubinstein as pianists; Mischa Elman, Jascha Heifetz, Na-than Milstein, Isaac Stern as violinists; Gregor Piatagorsky as cellist; Serge Koussevitzky, Bruno Walter, Fritz Reiner as conductors. If it is objected that all these virtuosos were European born and trained, we may mention the Ameri-can-born violinist Yehudi Menuhin, conductor-composer Leonard Bernstein, and jazz clarinetist Benny Goodman. The American motion picture industry was launched al-most entirely by Jews. In science the names are legion. The first American Nobel Prize winner (1907) was Albert Michelson in physics. Others include Isidor Rabi, Jacob Lipman, Hermann Miller; in medicine there are Selman Waksman, Casimer Funk, and Jonas Salk, whose vaccine did so much to conquer polio. Jews have served with distinction on the Supreme Court, where perhaps the great-est figures were Benjamin Cardozo and Louis Brandeis. Possibly the most eminent Jew in politics was Herbert Leh-man, four times governor of New York and United States senator (the first Jewish congressman was elected in 1841, senator in 1845, both in Florida). *The New York Times* was founded by Alfred S. Ochs; a more influential journalist was Joseph Pulitzer, founder of the *St. Louis Post-Dispatch*, the Columbia University School of Journalism, and the Pulitzer Prizes. Jewish scholarship has flourished in the United

States also, both the ancient rabbinic scholarship as well as the *Wissenschaft des Judentums*. The publication in New York of the *Jewish Encyclopedia* in 1906, largely an American-Jewish scholarly and financial feat, marked the coming of age of American Jewry as the leader of the Diaspora. Today the United States is second only to Israel as a center of Jewish scholarship.

Jews have participated in many of the critical or dramatic events in American history. They have fought in large numbers and bravely in all our wars. In the American Revolution they were divided, although most of them were strong for independence rather than for the loyalist cause. The somewhat legendary Haym Salomon of Philadelphia helped to finance the Revolution. In the Civil War also they were divided and in fact fought on both sides, attaining high rank in both armies (there were eleven Jewish generals in the Union army by 1865). The great majority favored the North for the preservation of the Union and the abolition of slavery. Jews such as Ernestine Rose were among the most outspoken of the Abolitionists. They liked to quote the words of Adolphe Crémieux, the French Jew who as minister of justice had effected the abolition of slavery in the French colonies; speaking to an Abolitionist gathering in London in 1840, he declared, "All liberties are united. All persecutions are associated."

Abraham Lincoln was revered by his Jewish compatriots. In 1862 General Grant issued a strange order that all Jews be expelled from the territories where his authority ran; Lincoln revoked the order after a plea from a Jewish delegation who said they came once again, as of old, seeking protection in "Father Abraham's bosom." His death was mourned deeply by Jews, and for the first time the prayer for the dead was recited in the synagogue for someone not of the Jewish faith. By the later 1860's Jewish equality and rights had been strengthened and acknowledged, partly owing to the yeoman service they had rendered in the Civil War. From an early time in our history they had, by insisting on their own rights and those of others, helped to strengthen American democracy and civil rights; more fundamentally, as the nineteenth-century English historian W. E. H. Lecky expressed it, "The Hebraic mortar cemented the foundations of American Democracy" and the whole edifice.

On the other hand, the United States has had a profound impact on the Jewish world, of course on those Jews who came to America's shores and entered into its life as citizens, but also on the whole of world Jewry. E.g., President Ulysses S. Grant, redeeming himself for his infamous order of 1862, sought to intervene in 1869 in Rumania to restrain the anti-Jewish persecutions that were then the worst nightmare of Jews. Successive presidents sought earnestly to check the outrageous Russian policies that began in 1881. Of greater significance, a strong sympathy with the re-establishment of a Jewish homeland and state in Palestine runs deep in the American tradition. This Christian Zionism is another manifestation of that philo-Semitism we have noticed in Puritan New England. President Benjamin Harrison received sympathetically a petition to the government to consider and act upon Jewish "claims to Palestine as their ancient home"; it was signed by a great many luminaries that included Cardinal Gibbons. The critical turn came in 1917 when President Woodrow Wilson signified his concurrence and support before its publication of the Balfour Declaration. As though in reproof of the seeming repudiation of the Balfour Declaration in the peace settlement reached at Versailles in 1919, President Harding signed a Congressional Resolution in 1922 officially proclaiming American support of the Declaration. In the events that led to the birth of Israel in 1948, President Harry S Truman was actively sympathetic to the Jewish cause[13] and solicitous toward the refugees from Hitler's Europe seeking to make a new home in Palestine.

So it has been in the two decades since, during which Israel has been able to purchase most of the military hardware necessary for her defense here. In the presidential campaign of 1968 almost all the major aspirants saluted Israel and pledged their support to her in adversity.

It only remains to say that the five and a half million Jews in the United States constitute by far the largest segment of the Diaspora. The only real danger to their existence is not their disappearance by the methods that have loomed so often in these pages. Perhaps toleration will accomplish what persecution has never effected: the American Jewish community may disappear through its complete absorption and assimilation into the host society. The nationality of American Jews, as European Jews used frequently to emphasize, is American. The Europeans have had difficulty understanding why Jews here have not demanded the minority rights of an autonomous community, and they have pointed out, critically, that except for religious purposes no such communal organization as the Council of the Four Lands ever existed here. Moreover, American Jews (unlike Catholics) have been slow to develop their own distinctive schools, which probably would have come into being quickly had there existed here the organs of self-government and administration that were basic to Jewish life in Europe. As Americans, Jews wanted to enter the public schools and only to supplement that with religious formation and the study of Hebrew at a Hebrew school a few hours a week. Resort to the public system of education seemed to open the way eventually to complete assimilation. An inauspicious parallel is sometimes suggested in the disappearance in China of its Jewish population by the seventeenth or eighteenth century, since the Chinese were, in matters of religion and philosophy, the most tolerant society in the world. But such dangers in the United States appear to be greatly exaggerated. The example of China is inapplicable, since the number of Jews there was infinitesimally small.[14] And there are counter-vailing tendencies. As a recent book by Jacob Katz, *Exclusiveness and Tolerance*, indicates, Jewish life has always followed, when it was free to do so, a middle course between the way of life of the host society and its own heritage. American Judaism appears to occupy that middle ground. There are some signs to suggest that Judaism in the United States is on the threshold of a great age of cultural creativity along the lines that we have seen in ancient Babylonia, medieval Islam, or nineteenth-century Europe. But that is prophecy.

NOTES

[1] At the time he was pursuing a brilliant dual career as literary critic and jurist, but was impelled by the Dreyfus affair, which he called "a crisis of humanity," to enter politics. Active in the Socialist Party, especially during World War I, he was elected to the French Chamber of Deputies in 1919; he became premier twice in the 1930's, a double milestone in that he was the first Jew and the first socialist ever to head a French government. Imprisoned and then sent to Nazi concentration camps by the Vichy regime, he was rescued dramatically from the clutches of the S.S. in 1945. As a grand old man he served again as premier briefly in 1946–1947; he was an outstanding example, in his biographer's phrase, of the "humanist in politics."

[2] France is, however, not immune to such irrational episodes as the baseless anti-Semitic rumors that raced through Orléans in May and June of 1969. It was believed that as many as twenty-six women, customers in six style shops and boutiques, had been drugged in the fitting rooms, spirited off through labyrinthine cellars to the port, embarked at night in a submarine that had come up the river Seine, and rapt away to the ends of the earth to be sold into "white slavery"—prostitution. Supposedly, the police and press did not interfere because they had been bribed by the Jewish "slavers," the authors of the plot; five of the six shops belonged to Jews, while the sixth had recently been purchased from its Jewish owners. At the height of this collective delirium, an aggressive crowd congregated men-

acingly in the street outside the shops. The rumor was finally demolished by strong denials from municipal officials and local associations, and derisive attacks in the Paris newspapers—that noted, for example, that there was absolutely no record of a single woman or girl disappearing from the city. Similar rumors, equally baseless, have been known in several other French towns, such as Rouen and Toulouse. But what is so disconcerting about the whole thing is the credulity with which the myth was accepted and propagated, not on flimsy evidence but on no evidence at all; even schoolteachers are reported to have warned their students away from "the Jewish shops." One is reminded again how deep, as I suggested in the Introduction, the anti-Semitic habit runs in Western civilization.

[3] It is well to mention the socialist thinker Eduard Bernstein (1850–1932), who turned out to be, perhaps, the most important figure for the later history of socialism and the German Social Democratic Party, in that he weighed Marx's doctrines and theories against economic fact and economic history (much as did the English Fabians, his acquaintances during a long exile); his "revisionism" removed much of the literalness from Marxism and defused much of the Marxian fireworks about inevitability, class conflict, ultimate collapse of capitalism, and so forth.

[4] Gerson Bleichröder (1822–1893), had served his apprenticeship as agent in Berlin for the Rothschilds; from 1859 to his death he was Bismarck's banker and financial adviser. He had much to do with enabling the chancellor to finance the Prussian government and the wars of 1864 and 1866 in the midst of the constitutional struggle, when the parliament sought to throttle Bismarck by refusing loans and taxes; he was in fact the financier of German unification. Later he went out of his way to place Russian securities on the German market, and in the 1880's warned Bismarck that maintenance of his Russo-German alliance depended much on the flow of German capital into Russia. His expertise, contacts, and discretion made him a frequent agent and unofficial ambassador in Bismarck's political and diplomatic moves, so much that he has been called a compound of a "traditional court Jew and a modern [diplomatic] trouble shooter." Despite the most truculent criticisms by anti-Semites like Stöcker against Bleichröder's power and wealth and influence, Bismarck ignored the abuse and stuck with his friend (allegiance to his friends was not a notable virtue of Bismarck, and the persistence of his regard for the Jew is practically unique); he went so far as to induce William I in 1872 to raise Bleichröder to the hereditary nobility, an honor which no

Prussian Jew had ever won without first apostatizing in favor of Christianity. Baron Bleichröder remained a Jew, and he never forgot his co-religionists; in a manner reminiscent of the Rothschilds, he used his influence and wealth to alleviate their condition, at home and abroad (as in 1878 at the Congress of Berlin in behalf of Rumanian Jews). Upon his death the history of the family follows the pattern, it has been aptly said, of "a kind of Jewish Buddenbrooks," for his descendants lacked the gifts he had possessed and, moreover, the day of the great private banks had passed. The family was buffeted about by the anti-Semitic storms of the twentieth century, and one of the most pathetic scenes one can imagine is their petition to Adolph Eichmann to remain in Germany and not be deported; today the family and the business live on in the United States.

5 Their objections to his occasionally passionate language and lapses from objectivity—on grounds that they were a disservice to Jewish studies and to the cause of toleration and acceptance of Jews—were graphically confirmed when Treitschke attacked the *History* in his *A Word on Our Jews*, 1879–1880; he accused Graetz of hating Christianity and of being biased against the people of Germany, supporting his view by seemingly plausible quotations. To Treitschke, who was read widely, the *History* was "proof" that Jews could not assimilate themselves to German society and culture.

6 Technically speaking, a concordat confers no moral approval on the regime with which it is concluded, for it is usually intended to protect the threatened Catholic community in the particular country; world public opinion, however, does not judge such matters on technical grounds.

7 The enormous difficulties of resistance to the Hitler regime are illustrated by the enigmatic career of Kurt Gerstein (1905–1945), the subject of a fascinating book subtitled *The Ambiguity of Good* by Saul Friedländer and, less authentically, a character in Rolf Hochhuth's play *The Deputy*. Gerstein was a "typical" north German of the respectable middle class, of a Prussian family that had a tradition of entering the civil service, educated, Lutheran, nationalistic; he was, however, profoundly Christian and it was his opposition to Nazi attacks on the Protestant churches that got him expelled from the Nazi Party and landed him in jail for two terms. He did not oppose the anti-Semitism of the regime (he in fact shared the antipathy for Jews of most Germans) until his sister-in-law, a mental patient, was murdered in 1940–1941 for reasons of racial "hygiene." He then set out to oppose the system from within, becoming a lieutenant in the S.S. and responsible for the ship-

ment of poison gas to Auschwitz. Transportation schedules were delayed, some of the gas was destroyed, but his monkey wrench had very little effect in saving lives. He also tried to rouse and inform Christian leaders (including the papal nuncio), the neutral powers, members of the underground, and, in his desperation, any stranger he could buttonhole in the streets of the extermination butchery that was going on in their midst. But no one heeded his words, whether out of fear or incredulity. He was not understood by his father, a retired judge, to whom he wrote, "I am aware of ideas and values we can't transgress against, except with the most drastic results. However powerless the isolated individual, and however much he honors prudence as the crowning virtue, he should never give up those ideas and values he cherishes. He can never make excuses to his conscience by saying: that doesn't concern me, I can't do anything about it." It seems strangely symptomatic that this brave man, despite the great risks that he assumed, could accomplish so little, and that he should have committed suicide (though that is not definitively established) in a French prison after having turned himself in to the Allies. Had there been many— instead of very few—Kurt Gersteins, the extermination factories might well have been sabotaged. The failure of another kind of resistance, the well-known attempt of Colonel Stauffenberg to assassinate Hitler on July 20, 1944, was also perhaps symptomatic. Both men are worthy if somewhat "ambiguous" heroes, and are officially commemorated in West Germany; there are, unfortunately, few others to be thus honored.

8 The Christian blindness to the menace of Hitlerism appears perhaps more strange in retrospect than at the time; students of such subjects ought to beware of falling into the trap of wisdom and insight after the event—20-20 hindsight vision. The profound theological pessimism of Karl Barth about human nature—an extreme example of a tradition which, in the form of Pietism, has run through Lutheranism since the eighteenth century—may have done much to disarm German Protestantism's resistance to Hitler. On the Catholic side there is much controversy; until Professor Albrecht finishes his work in compiling the Vatican's notes to the German government, E. Duerlein his on the Concordat, and Professor Stasiewski his massive volumes on the "Actions of the German Bishops," it will not be possible to say much that is conclusive. In the present state of knowledge, one may hazard the judgment that recent findings do extenuate slightly, but do not justify, the Church's stance with regard to Nazi persecutions. In such intellectual enterprises as those of the three scholars mentioned,

one has to be on guard, as Lord Acton once said, against too much explaining, lest one explain everything away. Equally I am skeptical about works that place very much or all the blame for the Jewish catastrophe on religious or political leaders, e.g., Pope Pius XII, Prime Minister Churchill, or President Roosevelt —that they were guilty of grievous sins of omission I do not deny. There is a tendency among some Jewish interpreters of the holocaust, e.g., Hannah Arendt or Raul Hilberg (who, of all things, invokes a Jewish "death wish" as explanation!), to criticize the Jews for not having resisted their Nazi persecutors and made a fight of it. Apart from the fact that bare flesh does not have a chance against cold steel, overt and forceful resistance (which did occur) only elicited greater cruelty and suffering from the S.S. brutes. Passive resistance of the kind that Gandhi used so effectively will work against a liberal state like England, but not against a totalitarian despotism that does not flinch at any crime. Jews resisted in the only way open to them —by remaining civilized beings in the face of the most appalling barbarism.

9 Arab diplomatic pressure on the Second Vatican Council was great. Some of the anti-Semitic propaganda and pamphlets that bombarded the bishops originated with Arab governments, and attributed Vatican II's Declaration on the Jews to "Jewish machinations" that followed exactly from the *Protocols*.

10 In the short time since this was written, events in Russia point tentatively to different conclusions, viz., that Soviet treatment of Jews has been harsher than appeared—and it is getting harsher; that Soviet Jewry is not on its last legs, that it has a very keen sense of its identity, that it desires intensely to preserve that identity as a Jewish one, that it is conscious of its links with the Diaspora and with Israel.

11 One should not exaggerate the sunniness of English progress. If we have in Scott (1820) and Eliot sympathetic and even philo-Semitic portrayals of Jews and Jewish life, we have in Charles Dickens' Fagin in *Oliver Twist* (1838) the old libels in their crudest, most virulent form; e.g., Fagin's red hair recalls the medieval devil theory of the Jew; Fagin is the gangster version of Shylock. G. K. Chesterton and Hilaire Belloc, two influential writers of the twentieth century, also saw fit to vitiate some of their numerous writings with castigations of Jews and Jewishness; sad to say, both were famous as Catholics.

12 There were a considerable number of Zionist projects for America in the nineteenth century, the most interesting of which was that of Mordecai Noah (1785–1851). In 1825 he proclaimed the city of "Ararat," near Buffalo, as a "city of refuge

for the Jews"; through the aid of a Christian friend, he purchased 2,555 acres as the starting point of a new Jewish state under the American flag. As "judge and governor of Israel," he issued decrees and invitations to Jews all over the globe to migrate to "the new and better world." But they ignored him and the project collapsed; its foundation stone—still to be seen in the Buffalo Historical Museum—became its epitaph. From the start Noah had admitted that his new Zion was a way station to gather all his fellow Jews until the day came when they could return to the true Zion of Palestine; in later years he concentrated on the direct restoration to the ancient home, and did some notable preaching of that cause to Christian audiences.

13 Many scholars interpret President Truman's immediate according of diplomatic recognition to the new state as perhaps the decisive event in the creation of Israel. A pleasant anecdote is told of his partnership in a haberdashery with Edward ("Eddie") Jacobson, a Jew with whom he had served in the artillery in World War I. When Mr. Truman left the business to go into politics, he assured his old partner, "If ever I can be of assistance, don't hesitate to call upon me." In 1948, many years since they had seen each other, Mr. Jacobson called at the White House, and the president was as good as his word.

14 The comparison is, I conclude, encouraging rather than depressing. For the Jews of China dated from the first and second centuries A.D., having come probably to participate in the silk trade; later settlements continued possibly to the end of the period of Islamic expansion, down to perhaps 750. Chinese Jews possessed the Old Testament and, though the knowledge of it tended to disappear, the Hebrew language. They were, however, without the Talmud and were out of touch with Jewish life and thought in the Diaspora. If one considers their small numbers, the absence of the faith-sustaining Talmud, and above all, the Chinese Jews' isolation from the Diaspora communities, then, I think their survival for a millennium and more is as astounding, nay more so, than that of the Marranos. By 1600, when Christian missionaries reported Jewish communities there, Chinese Judaism was seemingly on its last legs. Yet as late as 1850, or even 1932, American and European Jews still thought it possible to "reclaim" their Chinese brethren, and they organized, e.g., the Society for the Rescue of Chinese Jews (1900). In the twentieth century a considerable number of Jews from Communist Russia and Nazi Germany fled to China, but little is known at present of their fate.

10. The Birth of Israel

Roots of Zionism

Zionism and the establishment of the state of Israel were sequels to Emancipation. Once they were free and equal, Jews were expected to be thoroughly integrated and assimilated into the national life amid which they lived. This meant the end of local self-government and the loss of many of the distinct characteristics of Jewish life. With its disappearance, the ghetto sometimes was looked back upon through the rose-colored glasses of nostalgia as the great bulwark of the distinctively Jewish way of life. There Jews had lived according to their own law enforced by their own officials, spoken their own language, and been subject to practically no assimilatory pressures. And the more the Jewish communities were absorbed by the host societies, the more threatened were the coherence and unity of the Jewish people. Paradoxically, Emancipation posed greater problems for the preservation of Judaism than persecution had, and increasingly the only possible resolution of the dilemma appeared to be an independent Jewish homeland and state.[1]

To the dangers of Emancipation has to be added the failures of Emancipation. The key figure in the Zionist movement was Theodore Herzl (1860–1904), a Hungarian journalist who came to Paris to report the trial of Captain Alfred Dreyfus. Revolutionary France had led the world in the Emancipation of the Jew, yet, as Herzl wrote, "after a century of full-fledged Jewish participation in French culture, the alleged disloyalty of a single Jewish army officer could set ablaze the ancient hatreds." The springboard for his famous book proposing *The Jewish State* was his conclusion that the Dreyfus affair had demonstrated the inevitability of a powerful anti-Semitic movement, sooner or later, in every country, regardless of what Jews did or did not do. The Russian Zionist Leo Pinsker had reached the same conclusion a dozen years before in his *Auto-Emancipation*: having witnessed the bloody pogroms in 1881 of Russian Jews —who were notoriously unemancipated—he asserted that anti-Semitism was a permanent pathological phenomenon in the Western world; the only hope for escape from the treadmill of persecution was an independent Jewish state. Thus Zionism increasingly commended itself to Jews, whether emancipated or unemancipated.

Herzl and others organized Zionist International Congresses, beginning with the first one at Basle in 1897, "to create for the Jewish people a home in Palestine secured by public law." He also took the initiative in entering into negotiations with the great powers with a view to persuading them to sanction and support "a national home" by international guarantee. His first discussions were with the ruler of Palestine, the Ottoman Turkish sultan, who thought in terms of the economic advantage Jewish settlement would bring his bankrupt state; yet he was willing to open every province of the Turkish Empire to Jewish settlement except the ancient homeland of Palestine. Herzl, a man of great charm and diplomatic skill, made some headway in discussions with the German emperor William II, but these came to nothing, as did those with the Russian government. A famous episode was his interview with Pope Pius X, whose secretary declared, "The history of Israel is our own. It is our foundation. But before, as you request, we declare ourselves for the Jewish people, it must first be converted." Since there was not the slightest possibility of such conversion, long officially prayed for by Catholics, Pius X said, "We cannot favor this movement." Herzl's only success came in England, but that was ultimately decisive. He fired the imagination of the brilliant colonial secretary, Joseph Chamberlain, who induced the British cabinet, led by Arthur James Balfour, to offer land for settlement in the Sinai peninsula, and El Arish (near the Palestinian border) over which Britain exercised jurisdiction by virtue of its control of Egypt as a protectorate since the 1880's. But since the arid desert could not be made to bloom, an offer was made of the highlands of British East Africa (Kenya) in 1903. Herzl persuaded the executive committee of the International Congress at Basle to consider the offer on the argument that the colony would be a stepping stone to Palestine. He died the next year, and although a Zionist delegation visited the site, the outcry of Jews and non-Jews against the proposal was such that nothing came of it. Nevertheless, Herzl had succeeded in gaining world attention and the sympathetic interest of the British government.

Role of Great Britain

British imperial concern over Palestine went back at least to the 1840's, when Foreign Secretary Palmerston compelled Mehemet Ali, the ruler of Egypt (who had usurped it from the sultan) to restore his conquests of Arabia and Syria to the Turkish Empire. Palmerston had received a delegation of English Christian Zionists urging a course other than restoring Palestine to "the unspeakable Turk": it "was bestowed by the Sovereign of the Universe upon the descendants of Abraham as a permanent and inalienable possession nearly 4,000 years ago, and neither conquests nor treaties among men can possibly affect their Title to it. He has also decreed that they shall again return to their Country and that the Gentiles shall be employed as the means of their restoration." Thereafter in the Victorian age such moral or ideal aims were never entirely absent from British foreign policy.

The queen had knighted Sir Moses Montefiore (1784–1885), and her Foreign Office and consulates had assisted him in his efforts to alleviate Jewish suffering wherever it appeared. His greatest success was a mission—with the leader of French Jewry, Adolphe Crémieux—to Damascus to intercede in behalf of a Jew against whom the ancient charge of blood accusation had been leveled. With the diplomatic backing of the British government, the two Jewish spokesmen managed to have the charges withdrawn and induced the sultan to issue a proclamation that both affirmed Jewish civil rights and condemned blood accusation as entirely false. Other missions were much less successful—his several attempts to intervene with the czars in behalf of his co-religionists in Russia or his trip to Rome to expostulate with Pius IX over the surreptitious baptism and kidnaping of Edgardo Mortara—but he did succeed in rousing the British, and indeed the world's, conscience over the plight of the Jews. In a long life, he played a (minor) role in the Emancipation of English Jews between 1832 and 1858. His importance for Zionism appears in his seven pilgrimages to the Holy Land, coupled with his philanthropic efforts in behalf of Jews settled there, and his plans to establish agricultural colonies in Palestine for new immigrants and refugees on lands purchased with the approval of the Turkish government. Such efforts, reminiscent of those of Joseph Nasi at Tiberias in the sixteenth century, ran into political difficulties and came to very little; it is suggestive to learn, however, that Montefiore was the brother-in-law of the famous banker Nathan Rothschild, whose descendants carried out successfully very similar programs beginning about 1883.

The Rothschilds' efforts, with others, raised the Jewish population of Palestine to eighty thousand by 1914, three times what it had been in 1883. Herzl had no patience with colonization, or "practical Zionism" as it was called, and complained that it would take nine hundred years before the world's Jews could be brought to Palestine. But his failure to make headway with his political program and the indifference to Zionism of the new Liberal government (despite the presence of several Jews in the government) ruling Britain in the decade after 1905 left no other recourse except the "practical" one, as Chaim Weizmann argued.

The situation was radically altered by World War I. The desperation of a three-year stalemate induced the British government to cast about for additional strength to throw into the balance. Once the Turks entered the war on the German side, the Zionists found themselves in a strategic position to influence British and Allied policy. Such realism, tinged with the idealism that ran like a golden thread through British foreign policy for nearly a century before the Versailles settlement of 1919, led the British government to make a promise to carve a Jewish homeland out of the Turkish Empire. Thus it was that the Balfour Declaration was issued on November 2, 1917 (the Cabinet had given secret assurances several times previously to Jewish leaders) stating that "His Majesty's Government view with favor the establishment in Palestine of a national home for the Jewish people and will use their best endeavors to facilitate the achievement of this object." To this pledge the Allies, France, Italy, and particularly the newest member, the United States, solemnly bound themselves. Unfortunately, in their desperation British officials in Palestine made promises inconsistent with the Declaration in behalf of the Arabs, although such actions did not seem so radically irreconcilable at the time.

British intentions in issuing the Balfour Declaration have been subject to such misinterpretations that it is necessary to examine the question in some detail. It was far from being a cynical piece of spur-of-the-moment power politics, as is sometimes alleged. Chamberlain is the pivotal figure, and it was the policy he initiated in 1902 that was ultimately brought to fruition by Balfour. We have seen in the conversations between Herzl and Chamberlain that the British government was officially concerned at least fifteen years earlier to resolve the Jewish question. It was clearly sympathetic to Zionism in its proposals for settlement in the Sinai peninsula and the Kenya highlands, and it was not owing to any change of heart by Britain that neither of these plans came to anything. Chamberlain hoped, as he said in 1905, "to solve a problem the existence of which, in its present form, is a disgrace and danger to European civilization." Initially, his interest in Zionism was purely humanitarian, a reflection of his repugnance for the pogroms in eastern Europe and the Dreyfus affair. Reasons of policy, however, also drew him toward the Jews, who were still very important in British finance. Chamberlain's plans for the economic development of the British Empire depended for their realization on the support of the large financial houses in the City of London, many of which, led by the Rothschilds, were Jewish. By supporting Zionism, Britain, he thought, could enlist the sympathies of world Jewry on her behalf. She would also secure Jewish capital and settlers for the development of key parts of the Empire. A Jewish colony successfully organized in Sinai might open the way to British penetration into Palestine, as the Turkish Empire wilted and withered away. Chamberlain's (and the British) blend of motives is caught up precisely in his protest against Rumanian persecutions of Jews in 1902: "History shows that, while preserving with extraordinary tenacity their national characteristics and the tenets of their religion, the Jews have been amongst the most loyal subjects of the states in which they have found a home, and the *impolicy* of persecution in such a case is almost greater than its *cruelty*." Writing in retirement a few years later, he made the clearest statement of what his intention in the negotiations with Herzl had been: "to organize a great settlement on a sufficient area of vacant land somewhere under the British flag, where with the help of large funds at the disposal of Jewish organizations and under a system of extended municipal institutions which would allow full play for Jewish aspirations without actually creating an *imperium in imperio*, the Jewish refugees from tyranny and persecution might develop the resources of a British colony and find a home for themselves." (One may speculate how long it would have taken for such a colony to proclaim its independence *à la* 1776).

The decisive role was played ultimately by the prime minister, Balfour, with whose approval Chamberlain (and also the foreign secretary, Lord Lansdowne) negotiated with Herzl in the years 1902–1903. Balfour, in addition to being a superb parliamentary debater and politician, was a philosopher and an Anglican Christian. His interest in the Jews and their history was lifelong, deriving from the Old Testament training of his mother and his Scottish upbringing.[2] As a philosopher he was much drawn to Maimonides and Spinoza; he was deeply conscious of the immeasurable debt Christianity and Christian civilization owed to Judaism, and was in the habit of remarking that the debt was "shamefully ill paid." He could not fathom why the Jews refused the Kenya offer. Not, that is, until it was explained to him by Chaim Weizmann, who had taken the lead in the Basle Zionist Congress' "grateful but firm" rejection of the British proposal.[3] The famous conversation between Weizmann and Balfour took place in 1905. Weizmann recorded the encounter this way: "I began to sweat blood to make my meaning clear through my English. At the very end I made an effort, I had an idea. I said 'Mr. Balfour, if you were offered Paris instead of London, would you take it? Would you take Paris instead of London?' He looked surprised. He: 'But London is our own!' I said: 'Jerusalem was our own when London was a marsh.' He said: 'That's true!' I did not see him again till 1916." Balfour himself said of the interview, "It was from that talk with Weizmann that I saw that the Jewish form of patriotism was unique. Their love for their country refused to be satisfied by the Uganda scheme.[4] It was Weizmann's absolute refusal even to look at it which impressed me." What is clear beyond doubt is that Balfour's philo-Semitism and Christian Zionism took form long before the occasion of the Declaration that bears his name. It should be noted that he, much like Chamberlain, wished to further the interests of the British Empire, of which he took a somewhat mystical and rather exalted view. Both statesmen sought to draw Jewish resources into the development of the Empire. Both shared an ennobling humanitarian purpose. But it is in Balfour that one finds, what is most important from the point of view of this book, the profoundly Christian inspiration for the policy he pursued.

In the Cabinet which actually issued the Declaration, Balfour (he had been out of office from 1905 to 1915) was the foreign secretary, under Lloyd George as prime minister. Lloyd George's position was governed essentially by his concern that the Allies concur, that the question not become a source of discord among them. Their concurrence was relatively easy to procure. Balfour could exploit in Cabinet debates the fact that President Wilson, deeply sympathetic as he was to great moral causes, was very favorably disposed toward Jewish aspirations; he made much of the close friendship between the president and the outstanding Zionist leader in the United States, Supreme Court justice Louis Brandeis, with whom Balfour himself was in contact. Aside from his anxieties for the Alliance,

Lloyd George had a personal sympathy for Zionism, impressed upon him in large measure by an encounter with Weizmann. That brilliant chemist had contrived a means to synthesize acetone, which was basic to British munitions production. In refusing any reward from Lloyd George, the minister of munitions at the time, 1915, Weizmann simply expressed the hope that his services to Britain's war effort would help the cause of his suffering people. Lloyd George was much taken by the appeal.

An important member of the Cabinet was the South African Jan Christiaan Smuts, an ardent Zionist sympathizer over many years. Lord Milner, earlier a close associate of Chamberlain (who had died in 1914), was equally strong in espousing the Jewish cause. A Jewish Zionist enthusiast, Herbert Samuel, also sat in the Cabinet. Paradoxically, the opposition in the Cabinet was led by a Jew, Edwin Montagu, and hinged on the seemingly odd issue of anxiety for the civil status of Jews. He feared that once a Jewish national home came into being, Jews would be compelled to renounce their citizenship, forfeit all civil rights, and emigrate to Palestine—this was the chief stumbling block in Cabinet discussions and the explanation of a delay that was prolonged nearly a year. (Undoubtedly Montagu was correct in fearing that the existence of a Jewish state could be misused by governments to justify suspicion and ill treatment of Jews, as the plight of Russian Jews today bears out abundantly.) Power and politics? Yes, but of equal or greater moment were considerations of morality and justice, much of which had a Christian inspiration.

The Period of the Mandate

In the final year of the war General Allenby and a British army, in what has been called the "last crusade," conquered Syria and with it Palestine, and the Turks went down to defeat with their allies, the Germans. Allied ardor for the Jewish cause cooled noticeably at the Paris peace conference, where power politics and revenge went far to blot out the generosity and idealism of Wilsonian "national self-determination." Ultimately Palestine was constituted as a British mandate under the League of Nations. Jewish immigration mounted so rapidly after the war that by 1922 Jews accounted for one-ninth, by 1936 one-fifth, by 1945 one-third, of the Palestinian population. As it rose, so did the irritation, opposition, and bloody attacks of the Arabs; there were sanguinary clashes in 1920, 1921, 1929, and particularly 1936–1938. What no one could have foreseen was the Arab awakening, which, with its perfervid nationalism, filled the void left by the defunct Turkish Empire. Increasingly the British mandatory administration had difficulty conciliating the Arabs. The first high commissioner—a remarkable English Jew and important leader in the British Liberal Party, M.P., and Cabinet member, Sir Herbert Samuel, "the second Nehemiah"— had leaned over backwards to make accommodation for Arab interests. He convened a General Moslem Council, as a counterpart to the Jewish Agency, in the hope of facilitating the cooperation of both organs, but the Arabs had no policy but sheer negation and massacre.[5]

Until 1939 Britain, as the mandatory power, tended to favor, on balance, the Jewish cause. The visit of Balfour in 1925 to inaugurate the Hebrew University of Jerusalem (whose cornerstone had been laid in 1918 before the echoes of Allenby's conquest had died away) symbolized British solicitude; its high point came in 1937 when the royal commission headed by Lord Peel recommended to the government that a sovereign Jewish state be established, a step beyond the "national home" of the Balfour Declaration twenty years before. This meant partition of Palestine into two states, one west of the Jordan for the Jews and one east of it for the Arabs, a proposal repugnant alike to Arabs and Jews but ultimately carried into effect by the United Nations; by the later 1930's human wisdom probably could contrive no better resolution than the partition of what Weizmann once called "the twice-promised land."

Arab intransigence and violence led the British government—which had an eye to oil interests also—to try to limit Jewish immigration from 1939 on. A white paper of the colonial secretary laid it down that only seventy-five thousand would be admitted over the next five years; at which time Jewish immigration would become subject to Arab approval and Palestine would become independent under a constitution that was to be drawn up in the interval. What had been exacerbating the situation since 1933 was the rise of Hitler and the floodtide of German Jews seeking refuge in Palestine. (It should perhaps be recalled that since the 1920's many countries, particularly the United States, had drastically cut back their immigration quotas, thus practically closing themselves off as possible places of refuge.) So desperate was the plight of Jews in Hitler's Europe that illegal entry on a large scale was organized to save as many lives as possible. The exigencies of World War II led Britain to interdict the clandestine immigration as much as it could. And so far did Britain forget its humanitarian policies of the Victorian past, that when refugee ships were tracked down they were forced to turn back —to certain death or in the case of the *Struma* to shipwreck and the loss of nearly eight hundred lives.

The stance of Palestinian Jews during World War II is perfectly expressed in the epigram of David Ben-Gurion: they would support the war against Hitler as though there were no white paper, but would fight the white paper in Palestine as though there were no war. Palestinian Jews volunteered in great numbers for military service, but the British accepted only thirty thousand, the limit because that many Arabs volunteered. Independently of the British, a Jewish army was organized and trained, the Haganah. It figured in British strategic calculation as a reserve force should Rommel break into Egypt. Moreover, British campaigns against the Desert Fox owed something to food, medical supplies, and even war equipment from Palestine, which otherwise had to be brought in by a perilous sea route.

Israel Reborn

Once the war was over in Europe, Palestinian Jews declared war on the British administration and its "atrocities." Violence and terror broke out, begetting counter-violence and counter-terror, though it all seemed to loom larger in the reporting than it did in fact. It should not be understated, however. The Stern gang had assassinated Lord Moyne, the highest British official for the Middle East, in 1944, and thereafter British policemen and administrative officers were not infrequently murdered. Efforts went on, despite British policy, to bring in the survivors of the concentration camps. Ernest Bevin, the British foreign secretary, remained throughout implacably anti-Zionist, going so far as to order the *Exodus*, a ship full of Jews rescued at the threshold of the gas chambers, to be turned back: after a naval duel of three hours it was towed into Haifa; in three other ships the hapless passengers were taken to Marseilles, where they stewed in the ships for a month until Bevin ordered them to Hamburg, since he could not compel the French to compel the Jews to disembark. In Germany they were ushered at British bayonet point back into the concentration camps; the crowning piece of his irrational hatred was Bevin's telegram of official felicitation and thanks to the bayonet wielders. He took six months to say no to President Truman's request that one hundred thousand Jews be admitted to Palestine as a humanitarian gesture, and then repeated his negative to a second petition from the president. His conduct was, in the view of the world, the final proof of Herzl's argument, and he did as much as anyone, paradoxically, to make a Jewish state inevitable. There could be no guarantee of toleration of Jews anywhere if democratic England, which had not known anything beyond insignificant anti-Semitism for centuries, could be a party to such transactions.

In 1945 an Anglo-American commission conducted a careful inquiry and recommended partition of Palestine into two sovereign states, as in the report of 1937. Down to January, 1947, British proposals for a resolution of the issues were rejected by Jews and Arabs alike, and Britain, at her wits' end, threw the matter into the United Nations. A U.N. Commission declared for partition, and so it was voted in the United Nation's resolution of November, 1947; interestingly, Russia supported the measure, rather to get the British out of the Middle East than to create a Jewish state. Jews hailed the resolution as Heaven-sent. Arabs said they would fight it out. Bevin announced that Britain would have nothing to do with it and, in any event, would withdraw from Palestine by May 15, 1948—a fit of irresponsibility that does not sit well with a glorious imperial tradition.

In the last months Bevin did what he could to encourage Arabs to prepare for the melee that was coming and to prevent Jews from arming themselves. He seems to have thought that the Arabs in Palestine, joined by the invading armies of the surrounding Arab states, would have an easy time of it, scattering the Jews like autumn leaves before the gale. On May 14 the British departed, the last step in an ignominious withdrawal that constituted one more addition to what an English critic has called "the great scrapheap of British bungles." Within the space of that same day a provisional government was formed in Tel Aviv—whose name means "hill of spring"—by the Jewish leaders —principally David Ben-Gurion and Chaim Weizmann—the

State of Israel was proclaimed, and the United States and Russia accorded it official recognition. The next day saw the Arab invasions, but the invading Goliaths were thrown back David-like, for the Jews possessed in the Haganah a spirited and disciplined force, whose organization and training in World War II served it well. A U.N. cease-fire saved the Arab armies from annihilation.

Israel has defended herself several times since, with brilliant élan and brilliant success. Israel fights in a unique way, one that combines biblical inspiration and patriotism with the intellectual sophistication of the strategy of indirection, as expounded chiefly by Sir Basil Liddell Hart. A military analysis of the Arab-Israeli War of 1948–1949 by the Israeli General Staff takes its title from Proverbs 24:6: "For by wise counsel thou shalt make thy war"; the essay's references are about equally divided between those to the Old Testament, e.g., Esau's girding of his loins for battle, and to the works of the British strategist. Here are the two familiar hallmarks of Jewish history—faith and intellect. But for the non-Jew, especially if he has read Arnold Toynbee, the situation in the Middle East may be awesomely foreboding of tragedy. The Arabs may get themselves bludgeoned a dozen times, as in their experiences in the astounding June War of 1967, yet in the long run they must inevitably develop efficient military systems, especially as Russia is bent upon helping them in every way. Will that not spell Israel's doom? Would it not have been better to establish the Jewish state in a quarter of the world less fraught with danger? To the first question the ancient history of Israel affords a possible answer: Israel did not then, as she does not now, enjoy natural barriers or readily defensible strategic frontiers, yet she held her own against hostile neighbors, and succumbed only to super-powers like Persia or Rome that conquered everyone. My second question is an absurd one. For Judaism is equally inconceivable apart from the land of Israel as it would be without the people of Israel. "Next year in Jerusalem" is the age-old toast at Passover. Through all the agonies and dislocations since the first century A.D. and the destruction of the Temple, Jews have never ceased to live there in significant numbers; Jews were always in a majority (except for a short period during the Christian Crusader kingdom of the twelfth century) in Jerusalem, the sacred city. As the Psalmist (137) sings: "If I forget you, O Jerusalem, may my right hand forget its cunning, May my tongue cleave to my palate if I remember you not, If I place not Jerusalem ahead of my joy. Remember, O Lord . . . the day of Jerusalem."

NOTES

1 It is necessary to qualify these remarks in that it does not follow literally that the dangers of Emancipation would cause *all* Jews of the Diaspora to return to the homeland, once it became an independent Jewish state. Many, many Jewish families have struck deep-going roots in the various lands, especially in the tolerant and democratic ones, of the Diaspora, and are not likely to tear up those roots and break long-standing traditions. Since 1948 many Jews, particularly displaced persons and victims of persecution, have emigrated to Israel, but the great majority of Jews (not all are free to move) have remained in the lands of their birth. There is an instructive parallel in the Old Testament. The Jews "by the river of Babylon" wept bitterly and yearned passionately for their homeland, yet when King Cyrus in 538 B.C. permitted them to return home, although many did so, many had struck roots and chose to remain. Both in antiquity and in the present period, however, those remaining behind were and are ardently dedicated to the well-being of the ancient homeland.

2 Scots are very proud of the fact that—unlike "the kingdom to the south"—their homeland has never been desecrated by anti-Semitism, expulsions, confiscations, or ill feeling of any kind toward Jews; in a pleasantly whimsical way they attribute their tolerance to the ability of the proverbially thrifty Scot to

compete and out-compete with his Jewish commercial rival; Scotland's Calvinist heritage and the minuteness of its Jewish population are perhaps more to the point.

3 Those Zionists who wanted to accept the Kenya offer, or something comparable, broke away from the main Zionist body; led by the Anglo-Jewish novelist and dramatist Israel Zangwill, they formed the Jewish Territorial Organization and are referred to frequently as the "Territorialists." Never more than a minority, they believed that an immediate refuge for persecuted Jews could not be delayed.

4 How "Uganda" came into the picture is obscure. Chamberlain has been derided for offering an area considered uninhabitable for Europeans, when in fact what he offered was the most suitable site in all Africa, the Kenya highlands. The much used misnomer "Uganda scheme" may derive from Chamberlain's reference to land he had viewed "from the Uganda Railway" which ran through Kenya.

5 Samuel should loom much larger than he does in the accounts of the events that culminated with the birth of Israel in 1948. Jewish writers, such as Foreign Minister Abba Eban and Maurice Samuel (unrelated to him), tend to view the prehistory of Israel in the jaundiced light of British "repudiation" and "betrayal"—represented by the white paper of 1939—of the Balfour Declaration. But Samuel, and Britain as the Mandatory power, did a great deal to transform Palestine from a backward province of the Turkish Empire into a modern country. He was seeking to create the whole of Palestine into a flourishing, self-governing Dominion of the British Empire, "the Jewish Home," as he conceived of it; and there was some reason to be hopeful of the outcome when, in 1925, after five years as high commissioner, he retired. The fact that the State of Israel, and not the Dominion of Palestine, was the ultimate result should not blind anyone to the fact that Samuel did much to lay the material and, indeed, the spiritual foundations for the society that finally did emerge.

Epilogue

HAVING COMPLETED this sketch of Jewish history since the first century, I wish to round it out with some observations and generalizations. The Jewish odyssey is one of the greatest epics in world history. But what has been borne in upon me more forcefully by the preparation of this book is how closely integrated so much of Jewish history is with that of Europe (the area where my professional specialization lies). Frequently, I had to confess to myself utter innocence and ignorance of matters in which Jews had a profoundly creative impact, and gradually I came to see that Jews had a more decisive influence in shaping the European mind and the Western world than I was able, at the outset, to grasp. It is really a great disservice to historical knowledge and understanding to treat Jewish history the way one usually treats Greek history —the conquest by Rome or the first century A.D. is the cut-off date, and it is assumed that neither Greeks nor Jews had any significant part in the development of Western civilization thereafter. Byzantine studies have done much to repair such shallowness with regard to the later Greek world. But the academic walls that separate Jewish from Western or European history are not so easily surmounted. It has been my experience that even a small liberal arts college will offer an undergraduate course in Byzantine

298   A History of the Jews Since the First Century A.D.

history but none in Jewish history; or its religious studies
department will offer one and perhaps several courses in
Buddhism, Hinduism, and other Eastern religions, but absolutely nothing in post-biblical Judaism. Yet whether one
abides by the view that we should study those peoples and
cultures that have had the profoundest influence in the
making of our society and heritage, or, rather, those whose
attainments are of such intrinsic worth that they merit our
studying them as ends in themselves—by either of these
criteria Jewish history has a strong claim upon us and
should take precedence over those fields which I have mentioned, as well as a great many more. I cannot believe it is
possible to make much sense of European and Western
history without considerable attention to post-biblical Jewry
and Judaism. Such studies are not merely auxiliary and
peripheral, for, if my experience points to anything, Jewish
life and thought run like golden threads woven into the
very fabric of our history and culture.

What soon strikes the student who takes the plunge into
Jewish history is its magnitude and complexity, such that
no single scholar can master it in one lifetime. One source
of difficulty is the sheer length of Jewish history. Even if
one discards as legendary the traditional calendar—by which
1971 is designated 5731—the Jewish people have, nevertheless, a history verging on four thousand years! Such longev-
ity they share only with the Chinese and Hindus, with the
result that the historian of their experience is compelled to
think in terms of centuries and millennia, rather than
reigns or generations. Within that span of time the historian cannot keep his eye cast on one single place—although
Jerusalem and Palestine are the unique focus of Jewish
history. Throughout most of history Palestine has been,
not a Jewish state, but as one may say, a desire of the heart
and a province of the mind. Indeed, from the Roman
period on, more than half of the Jewish population have
lived outside of Palestine, scattered over the globe. Thus

Jewish history touches and mingles—to a greater or lesser degree—with that of almost every area and every people in the world. This means that their experience finds expression in a multiplicity of modes, institutions, and languages. The ordinary specialist in historical studies has to command two, three, or four languages. But pity the poor scholar who finds his materials in Hebrew, Aramaic, Greek, Latin, Arabic, all the European languages, Yiddish, and Ladino, and indeed all the major languages of the world. Yiddish, it is well to note, is an important cultural datum that preserves in itself an important strand of Jewish history and tradition: a vernacular language spoken by Jews of eastern Europe and by immigrants from there in the United States and elsewhere, it derives from medieval German, has absorbed many Hebrew, Aramaic, English, and other words, and is written in Hebrew letters; since the mid-nineteenth century a large body of popular literature and journalism has appeared in Yiddish, first in Poland and Russia, then (and still) in the United States. Ladino has a similar place in the life of Iberian Jews and Marranos in exile after 1492.

This unique time span and geographical dispersion have made Jewish history hard to make sense of for philosophers of history. "Generalization is even more difficult in Jewish than in general history," says Cecil Roth, the author of two dozen books of Jewish history. By all the ordinary historical canons, the Jews as a people should have disintegrated and disappeared over the historical horizon as of A.D. 70, just as the numerous peoples of the ancient Near East disappeared, e.g., the Assyrians and Lydians, and the medieval invaders of Europe, e.g., the Avars and Goths. The Jewish refusal to "disappear" has baffled and contradicted the laws and generalizations that some philosophers of history would like to establish. Oswald Spengler, a generation ago, conceived of historic societies as organisms which go through a natural cycle of birth, maturity, age, death, etc. But the facts of Jewish history do not fit into any such scheme, with the result that Spengler brushed the Jewish segment of history aside, adding some unfortunate anti-Semitic remarks in the course of his fuming. Jewish history deviates, in a different way, from Arnold Toynbee's concepts of universal history. He concludes that the Jews have been a "fossil" in Western Christian society. Actually the survival of the Jews through so many terrible vicissitudes can be construed as a vindication of Toynbee's central idea that a people's capacity to survive as a civilized society depends on their "response" to the "challenge" thrown up to them by their circumstances and environment.

Not being in any formal sense a philosopher of history, I will not hazard any grand scheme. Suffice it to say that we have seen a progressive displacement in Jewish history from Palestine outward. Thus the center of Jewish life was for a while in Babylonia, then in the Islamic Empire; then came the European age of Jewish history, and we are now in the phase when the Jewish community of the United States exceeds in numbers and in the eminence and distinction of its leaders any other in the world. In the meantime, Jerusalem, the Holy City, has become once again the center of a Jewish national state. Down the centuries, however, the Holy Land remained fixed in Jewish consciousness as an aspiration of the heart and a province of the mind. No matter how assimilated or content or secure the Jew came to be in the lands of the Diaspora, he never ceased to yearn for the homeland and usually thought of himself as an "exile." That tension, or polarity, between the center at Jerusalem and the various centers of the dispersed communities is the golden key, it seems to me, to explain the unique character of Jewish history. The dispersion saved the Jews from physical destruction, since they could be attacked in one or several but not all places at once. Parenthetically, it may be added that the dispersion also exposed them to other influences and peoples, so that

Jews became, characteristically, cosmopolitan, and Judaism was never allowed to become intellectually stale; cosmopolitanism and intellectual keenness are qualities which also enhance the possibility of survival. The danger was that Jews would be so thoroughly absorbed into the various host societies as to lose their identity as a people. The memory of the Temple and the yearning to return to the homeland, however, conferred on Jews an indelible sense of being a single and a sacred people. Confirmation of this interpretation will be seen in the history of the Chinese Jews, for their disappearance through complete assimilation to Chinese society is explained by their isolation from the rest of the Diaspora; as a detached segment, Chinese Jews never acquired the Talmud, their intellectual life languished, they lost Hebrew, and thus forgot the Temple; they ceased to be "exiles." The longing for the homeland was not mere patriotism or empire-building; rather it was the quintessence of Jewish religious ideas and beliefs. As was remarked earlier, Judaism is as unimaginable without the land of Israel as it would be without the people of Israel. We come back then to our point of departure, the Jew and his religion: the one is inconceivable without the other. This relationship prevails now, as in the past, and no doubt it will persist in the future.

Appendix

SECOND VATICAN COUNCIL
DECLARATION ON THE RELATIONSHIP OF THE
CHURCH TO NON-CHRISTIAN RELIGIONS

*Promulgated October 28, 1965
by Pope Paul VI*

1. In our times, when every day men are being drawn closer together and the ties between various peoples are being multiplied, the Church is giving deeper study to her relationship with non-Christian religions. In her task of fostering unity and love among men, and even among nations, she gives primary consideration in this document to what human beings have in common and to what promotes fellowship among them.

For all peoples comprise a single community, and have a single origin, since God made the whole race of men dwell over the entire face of the earth (cf. Acts 17:26). One also is their final goal: God. His providence, His manifestations of goodness, and His saving designs extend to all men (cf. Wis. 8:1; Acts 14:17; Rom. 2:6–7; 1 Tim. 2:4) against the day when the elect will be united in that Holy City ablaze with the splendor of God, where the nations will walk in His light (cf. Apoc. 21:23 f.).

Men look to the various religions for answers to those profound mysteries of the human condition which, today even as in olden times, deeply stir the human heart: What is a man? What is the meaning and the purpose of our life? What is goodness and what is sin? What gives rise to our sorrows and to what intent? Where lies the path to true happiness? What is the truth about death, judgment, and retribution beyond the grave? What, finally, is that ultimate and unutterable mystery which engulfs our being, and whence we take our rise, and whither our journey leads us?

2. [Treats of Hinduism, Buddhism, and other religions.]

3. [Treats of Islam.]

4. As this sacred Synod searches into the mystery of the Church, it recalls the spiritual bond linking the people of the New Covenant with Abraham's stock.

For the Church of Christ acknowledges that, according to the mystery of God's saving design, the beginnings of her faith and her election are already found among the patriarchs, Moses, and the prophets. She professes that all who believe in Christ, Abraham's sons according to faith (cf. Gal. 3:7), are included in the same patriarch's call, and likewise that the salvation of the Church was mystically foreshadowed by the chosen people's exodus from the land of bondage.

The Church, therefore, cannot forget that she received the revelation of the Old Testament through the people with whom God in his inexpressible mercy deigned to establish the Ancient Covenant. Nor can she forget that she draws sustenance from the root of that good olive tree onto which have been grafted the wild olive branches of the Gentiles (cf. Rom. 11:17–24). Indeed, the Church believes that by His cross Christ, our Peace, reconciled Jew and Gentile, making them both one in Himself (cf. Eph. 2:14–16).

Also, the Church ever keeps in mind the words of the Apostle about his kinsmen, "who have the adoption as sons, and the glory and the covenant and the legislation and worship and the promises; who have the fathers, and from whom is Christ according to the flesh" (Rom. 9:4–5), the son of the Virgin Mary. The Church recalls too that from the Jewish people sprang the apostles, her foundation stones and pillars, as well as most of the early disciples who proclaimed Christ to the world.

As holy Scripture testifies, Jerusalem did not recognize the time of her visitation (cf. Lk. 19:44), nor did the Jews in large number accept the gospel; indeed, not a few opposed the spreading of it (cf. Rom. 11:28). Nevertheless, according to the Apostle, the Jews still remain most dear to God because of their fathers, for He does not repent of the gifts He makes nor of the calls He issues (cf. Rom. 11:28–29). In company with the prophets and the same Apostle, the Church awaits that day, known to God alone, on which all peoples will address the Lord in a single voice and "serve him with one accord" (Soph. 3:9; cf. Is. 66:23; Ps. 65:4; Rom. 11:11–32).

Since the spiritual patrimony common to Christians and Jews is thus so great, this sacred Synod wishes to foster and recommend that mutual understanding and respect which is the fruit above all of biblical and theological studies, and of brotherly dialogues.

True, authorities of the Jews and those who followed their lead pressed for the death of Christ (cf. Jn. 19:6), still, what happened in His passion cannot be blamed upon all the Jews then living, without distinction, nor upon the Jews of today. Although the Church is the new people of God, the Jews should not be presented as repudiated or cursed by God, as if such views followed from the holy Scriptures. All should take pains, then, lest in catechetical instruction and in the preaching of God's Word they teach anything out of harmony with the truth of the gospel and the spirit of Christ.

The Church repudiates all persecutions against any man. Moreover, mindful of her common patrimony with the Jews, and motivated by the gospel's spiritual love and by no political considerations, she deplores the hatred, persecutions, and displays of anti-Semitism directed against the Jews at any time and from any source.

Besides, as the Church has always held and continues to hold, Christ in His boundless love freely underwent His passion and death because of the sins of all men, so that all might attain salvation. It is, therefore, the duty of the Church's preaching to proclaim the cross of Christ as the sign of God's all-embracing love and as the fountain from which every grace flows.

5. We cannot in truthfulness call upon that God who is the Father of all if we refuse to act in a brotherly way toward certain men, created though they be to God's image. A man's relationship with God the Father and his relationship with his brother men are so linked together that Scripture says: "He who does not love does not know God." (1 Jn. 4:8).

The ground is therefore removed from every theory or practice which leads to a distinction between men or peoples in the matter of human dignity and the rights which flow from it.

As a consequence, the Church rejects, as foreign to the mind of Christ, any discrimination against men or harassment of them because of their race, color, condition of life, or religion.

Accordingly, following in the footsteps of the holy Apostles Peter and Paul, this sacred Synod ardently implores the Christian faithful to "maintain good fellowship among the nations" (1 Pet. 2:12), and, if possible, as far as in them lies, to keep peace with all men (cf. Rom. 12:18), so that they may truly be sons of the Father who is in heaven (cf. Mt. 5:45).

Bibliographical Note

I MENTION HERE only those books that have been especially useful to me, those that have shaped my thinking decisively about Jewish history and thrown light for me on its problems and intricacies. There are a great many bibliographical guides available for the whole of Jewish history as well as for its specialized fields. One handy listing of which I made much use is *A Bibliography on Judaism and Jewish-Christian Relations*, compiled by Max and Isaac Celnik and published by the Anti-Defamation League.

The single most important book has been that edited by Leo Schwarz, *Great Ages and Ideas of the Jewish People* (New York, Knopf, 1956); it is rich with ideas, eminently suggestive, and authoritative for its interpretations and conclusions. Other general works are the very solid two volumes edited by Louis Finkelstein, *The Jews: Their History, Culture, and Religion* (New York, Harper, 1949), particularly for the historical essays contributed by William Foxwell Albright, Elias J. Bickerman, Judah Goldin, and Cecil Roth. The older great work on a large scale is Heinrich Graetz, *A History of the Jews*, in eleven volumes and completed by 1870. I have read in it here and there to savor its quality, for I have preferred Salo W. Baron's classic work, *A Social and Religious History of the Jews*, 2nd ed., 12 vols. (New York, Columbia University Press, 1960), which, so far, comes down to 1650. James W. Parkes is the outstanding Christian historian of Jewish life and a prolific author; his little book, *A History of the Jewish People*, (London, Weidenfeld and

Nicolson, 1962; rev. ed., Baltimore, Penguin, 1964), summarizes a lifetime of work and reflection. A well-known and popular book is Max I. Dimont, *Jews, God, and History* (New York, Simon and Schuster, 1962); it does undoubtedly contain many insights, but its author is too desirous of turning a dazzling phrase and propounding a startling conclusion; the book does not reflect a lifetime's devotion to scholarship as do those mentioned above. *The Legacy of Israel* (London, Oxford University Press, 1927), edited by Edwyn R. Bevan, has many a gold nugget in it. Dating from 1901 to 1906, *The Jewish Encyclopedia*, 12 vols., remains a great storehouse of sound information on Jewish history, biography, and related themes; I have made much use of it. I have also pillaged two books edited by S. Noveck: *Great Jewish Personalities in Ancient and Medieval Times* (New York, Farrar, Straus and Cudahy, 1959) and *Great Jewish Personalities in Modern Times* (Washington, B'nai B'rith, Department of Adult Jewish Education, 1960). One may follow the vicissitudes of Palestine and the coming and going of her imperial conquerors in Philip K. Hitti, *The Near East in History: A Five Thousand Year Story* (New York, Van Nostrand, 1961). Jewish historiography is well served by Salo W. Baron, *History and Jewish Historians*, compiled with a foreword by Arthur Hertzberg and Leon A. Feldman (Philadelphia, Jewish Publication Society, 1964). Not the best perhaps, but certainly the most attractive one-volume history is Abba Eban, *My People: The Story of the Jews* (New York, Knopf, 1968); it is full of marvelous photographs and conveys, in the person of her foreign minister, something of the dynamism and fortitude of Israel. Two other one-volume works that are very serviceable are Solomon Grayzel, *A History of the Jews* (Philadelphia, Jewish Publication Society, 1948) and Abram L. Sacher, *A History of the Jews* (New York, Knopf, 5th ed., 1965).

On the subject of Christian-Jewish relations and anti-Semitism, Edward H. Flannery, *The Anguish of the Jews: Twenty-three Centuries of Anti-Semitism* (New York, Macmillan, 1965), is a brilliant and eloquent book; I am immensely pleased that a priest of my Church should have written it and I like to think of this book as a companion to his. James Parkes, *Voyage of Discovery* (London, Gollancz, 1969), is the autobiography of

308   *A History of the Jews Since the First Century A.D.*

the Englishman who has authored a great many scholarly works on Jewish history and the Christian-Jewish encounter in history and in the present; he has done as much as anyone to promote mutual understanding between Jews and Christians. From the Jewish vantage point, the best book is Jacob Katz, *Exclusiveness and Tolerance: Studies in Jewish-Gentile Relations in Medieval and Modern Times* (London, Oxford University Press, 1961). On the Vatican II Declaration, I have consulted with much profit John H. Miller, ed., *Vatican II, An Interfaith Appraisal* (Notre Dame, Indiana, University of Notre Dame Press, 1966); Walter M. Abbott, S. J., ed., *The Documents of Vatican II*, with commentary and notes (New York, Herder and Herder, 1966); and Msgr. John M. Oesterreicher, "Declaration on the Relationship of the Church to Non-Christian Religions," in Herbert Vorgrimler, ed., *Commentary on the Documents of Vatican II*, vol. III (New York, Herder and Herder, 1969). My point of departure owes much to Myles M. Bourke, *A Study of the Metaphor of the Olive Tree in Romans XI* (Washington, Catholic University of America Press, 1947). A subject of particular interest to me, but to which I could give practically no space, is explored in Eric Werner's fascinating book *The Sacred Bridge: The Interdependence of Liturgy in Synagogue and Church during the first Millennium* (New York, Columbia University Press, 1959).

On classical antiquity, in addition to the general works enumerated above, Josephus, *The Jewish War*, is indispensable; in many editions, the handiest available is the Penguin paperback (Baltimore, 1959); the great Roman historian Tacitus wrote of the Jews in the Roman Empire in anything but a spirit of objectivity; for the earlier age William W. Tarn, *Hellenistic Civilization*, 3rd ed. (New York, St. Martin, 1952), contains much interesting material by the greatest authority on the subject.

On the Islamic age of Jewish history, I would add to the general works mentioned in the opening paragraph above Charles C. Torrey's stimulating, if somewhat speculative, *The Jewish Foundation of Islam* (New York, Jewish Institute of Religion Press, 1933). To those same works I would add, for the middle ages, the following: Cecil Roth, "The Jews in the Middle Ages," ch. XXII, vol. VII of The Cambridge Medieval History (Cambridge, Cambridge University Press, 1932, 1964);

Jacob R. Marcus, *The Jew in the Medieval World: A Source Book, 315–1791* (Cincinnati, Sinai Press; New York, Harper Torchbooks, 1965); H. G. Richardson, *Medieval Jewry under the Angevin Kings* (London, 1960); Michael Adler, *Jews of Medieval England* (London, E. Goldston, 1939); and Douglas M. Dunlop, *The History of the Jewish Khazars* (New York, Schocken Books, 1967). For the early modern period, a fascinating work is Cecil Roth, *The Jews in the Renaissance* (Philadelphia, Jewish Publication Society 1959; New York, Harper Torchbooks, 1965); he is the author of a shelf-full of books on Jewish history in the European age; his masterpiece is, I think, the unforgettable *A History of the Marranos* (Philadelphia, Jewish Publication Society, 1932). The story of *The Court Jew* (Philadelphia, Jewish Publication Society, 1950) is well told by Selma Stern. On the Enlightenment, Arthur Hertzberg, *The French Enlightenment and the Jews* (New York, Columbia University Press, 1968), is a major work, while a bright light is thrown on the age by Solomon Maimon's *Autobiography*, edited by Moses Hadas (New York, Schocken Books, 1967), a work which is so engrossing I could not put it down the first time I had it in hand.

On Jewish economic history the starting point ought still to be Werner Sombart, *The Jews and Modern Capitalism,* though it must be used with great care; the Free Press paperback edition (Glencoe, Ill., 1951) has an excellent introduction by Benjamin Nelson and notes that will arm the student sufficiently against Sombart's errors as well as give credit where it is due. Nathan Reich, "Capitalism and the Jews," *The Menorah Journal,* vol. XVIII, 1930, is a cogent critique of Sombart. A work of major significance is Richard W. Emery, *The Jews of Perpignan in the Thirteenth Century* (New York, Columbia University Press, 1959), while Richard David Richards, *The Early History of Banking in England* (New York, A. M. Kelley, 1965), will be of much more use for this theme than its title might suggest. The Richardson book mentioned earlier is also relevant. The few references to Jews in T. S. Ashton's *An Economic History of England: The 18th Century* (New York, Barnes and Noble, 1955) point up the small role they played in that stage of economic development.

For European Jewry since 1789, I must again refer the reader to the general works cited at the outset: many of them

concentrate on these last two centuries. For France three excellent books are central: Guy Chapman, *The Dreyfus Case: A
Reassessment* (London, R. Hart-Davis, 1955); Robert F. Byrnes,
Antisemitism in Modern France (New York, Howard Fertig,
1950); and the exceptionally interesting biography by Joel
Colton, *Léon Blum: Humanist in Politics* (New York, Knopf,
1966). German-Jewish history—the great sphinx of Jewish
historiography—is so complicated and sensitive a subject that
I feel it necessary to reveal my intellectual tracks as fully as
possible. The general works I have relied on most are Koppel
S. Pinson, *Modern Germany: Its History and Civilization,* 2nd
ed. (New York, Macmillan, 1966), covering the period since the
1770's; vol. III of Hajo Holborn, *A History of Modern Germany*
(New York, Knopf, 1969), covering the span of 1840 to 1945;
and Allan Bullock, *Hitler, A Study in Tyranny,* rev. ed. (New
York, Harper Torchbooks, 1964). The monographs that have
shaped my interpretation most are Fritz Stern, "Gold and Iron:
the Collaboration and Friendship of Gerson Bleichröder and
Otto von Bismarck," *The American Historical Review,* Oct.,
1969; Lamar Cecil, *Albert Ballin: Business and Politics in Im
perial Germany, 1888–1918* (Princeton, N. J., Princeton University Press, 1967); Carl E. Schorske, "Politics in a New Key:
Schönerer," *The Responsibility of Power,* edited by Leonard
Krieger and Fritz Stern (New York, Anchor Books, 1969). On
the Hitler madness an outstanding work is by a group of German scholars, Helmut Krausnick *et al., Anatomy of the SS State,*
(New York, Walker, 1968); a work which I had only time to glance
at but which certainly answers the question, How could it happen
in a civilized country? is Albert Speer's memoirs, *Inside the Third
Reich* (New York, Macmillan, 1970). *Hitler's Secret Conversa-
tions 1941–1944,* with an Introduction by H. R. Trevor-Roper
(New York, Signet paperback, 1953), and Trevor-Roper, *The
Last Days of Hitler* (New York, Macmillan, 1947), are partic-
ularly useful for Nazi doctrines and attitudes and for the
characters of the Nazi leaders. Another English scholar, Gerald
Reitlinger, has written a methodical and sober account of *The
Final Solution* (London, Vallentine, Mitchell, 1953) ; Joseph
L. Lichten's essays "The Warsaw Ghetto Uprising: Legend and
Reality," *The Polish Review,* vol. VIII, 1963, and "Did Polish
Jews Die Forsaken?" *ibid.,* vol. IV, 1959, are important beyond

the bounds that their titles seem to set. Aside from Kurt Gerstein's enigmatic character, Saul Friedländer, *Counterfeit Nazi: The Ambiguity of the Good* (London, Weidenfeld and Nicolson, 1969), reveals how difficult opposition to the Nazi regime was. On post-1945 Germany see Leo Katcher, *Post-Mortem: The Jews in Germany Today* (New York, Delacorte Press, 1968), and Karen Gershon, ed., *Postscript* (London, Gollancz, 1969).

For Russia before 1917, Simon Dubnow, *The History of the Jews in Russia and Poland* (Philadelphia, Jewish Publication Society, 1916–20), is still unequalled; *The Jews in Soviet Russia since 1917*, edited by Lionel Kochan (London, Oxford University Press, 1969), is the definitive work to date; the plight of Soviet Jewry at the moment is presented by Ben Tzion, "The Jewish Question in the Soviet Union," *The New York Times Magazine*, May 3, 1970. On the situation in eastern Europe, see Paul Lendvai, *Anti-Semitism without Jews: Communist Eastern Europe* (New York, Doubleday, 1971). For the United States, I have made much use of two monographs: John Higham, "Anti-Semitism in the Gilded Age: A Reinterpretation," *The Mississippi Valley Historical Review*, Mar., 1957, and the Editors of *Fortune* Magazine, *Jews in America,* published in book form by Random House (New York, 1936); the definitive work on the Jews in America has yet to be written.

On England one cannot do better than to read George Eliot's novel of Jewish life, *Daniel Deronda* (New York, Harper and Brothers, 1876), with many re-issues since then. A good general account of the land of his birth is given by Cecil Roth in *History of the Jews in England*, 3rd ed. (Oxford, Clarendon Press, 1949); the situation in England at the turn of the century in the wake of the flood of immigrants fleeing the pogroms is well seen in Cyril Russell, ed., *The Jew in London,* with an Introduction by Canon Barnett and a Preface by James Bryce (London, T. F. Unwin, 1900). On the Balfour Declaration, the most enlightening works I have come upon are the chapter on Zionism in Julian Amery, *The Life of Joseph Chamberlain,* vol. IV (London, Macmillan, 1951); Chaim Weizmann's autobiography, *Trial and Error* (New York, Harper, 1949) Blanche E. C. Dugdale, *Arthur James Balfour,* 2 vols. (London, Hutchinson, 1936) and Frank Owen, *Tempestuous Journey: Lloyd George, His Life and Times* (London, Hutchinson, 1954). Robert

Blake's *Disraeli* (New York, St. Martin's Press, 1966), supersedes all previous studies of that fascinating personage.

On the birth of Israel, the works mentioned in conjunction with the Balfour Declaration are germane. A central text is Theodore Herzl's *The Jewish State: An Attempt at a Modern Solution of the Jewish Question,* first published in 1896 and available in several editions; his *Complete Diaries,* edited by Raphael Patai, 5 vols. (New York, Herzl Press, 1960) are as fascinating as they are important. Arthur Hertzberg, ed., *The Zionist Idea* (New York, Meridian Books, 1960), will demonstrate how deep that idea goes. Maurice Samuel, *Light on Israel* (New York, Knopf, 1968), is an intensely personal and intensely passionate account of the pre-history, birth, trials, and prospects of Israel; factually the book is impeccably accurate, but its passion raises one's suspicions about its objectivity. John Bowle's *Viscount Samuel: A Biography,* about Herbert Samuel, the high commissioner for Palestine from 1920 to 1925 (London, Gollancz, 1957), and Herbert Samuel's *Grooves of Change: A Book of Memoirs* (New York, Bobbs-Merrill, 1946), are important books because his significance as first high commissioner, and the positive role of Britain in general in the creation of Israel, tend to be ignored or denigrated by writers, such as Maurice Samuel (no relation) or Abba Eban, in the works cited above, who are more conscious of British-made obstacles in the last years before 1948. The American role in 1948 is best seen in President Harry S Truman, *Memoirs,* 2 vols. (Garden City, N.Y., Doubleday, 1955–56). A brief, calm, lucid assessment of the present situation and prospects in Palestine is Arthur Hertzberg, "Palestine: the Logic of Partition Today," *Columbia Forum,* Fall, 1970.

Index

Aaron of Lincoln, 118 n. 8
Abarbanel (Spanish Marrano), 145–146
Abarbanel, Isaac, 109–110, 113, 177
Abarbanel, Judah, 126
Abraham ben David, 96
Abraham ben Jacob, 81
Acton, Lord John, 16–17, 279 n. 8
Adams, Henry, 262
Adenauer, Konrad, 230
Adler, Felix, 260
Aggadah, 41
Akiba ben Joseph, 45–46, 47, 65
Aleichem, Sholom, 271
Alexander I (czar of Russia), 234–236
Alexander II (czar of Russia), 236–238
Alexander III (czar of Russia), 238
Alexander the Great, 28, 29
Alfonso VI (king of Castile), 103–104
Alfonso X (king of Castile), 102–103
Allenby, Edmund, General, 289–290
Alonso, Hernando, 142
America, South, Jews in, 263–264; Marranos in, 142–143
"American Anti-Semitic Association," 262
Amoraim, 47, 51
Amsterdam, Marranos in, 138–139
Anan ben David, 58–59
Anatoli, Jacob, 101
Anti-Defamation League, 9, 267
Antiochus Epiphanes, 29
Antipater the Idumean, 30
Anti-Semitism, 17–18, 88–92, 106, 159; Christian origins of, 17–18, 71–72, 115 n. 3; origin of term, 210; of socialists, 189, 207–208, 210; in Argentina, 263–264; in Austria, 212, 217, 218; in England, 279 n. 11; in France, 189–193, 275 n. 2; in Germany, 204–205, 207–208, 209–215, 217–227, 276 n. 4, 277 n. 7; in Hungary, 246–247; in New York, 242; in Poland, 245–246; in Rumania, 247–248; in Russia, 234–244; in the United States, 18, 20, 24 n. 2, 258, 259, 260, 262–264, 267; in Vienna, 212, 218
Aquinas, St. Thomas. See Thomas Aquinas, St.
Arabs, 285, 290–294
Arendt, Hannah, 279 n. 8
Argentina, Jews in, 264, 270

Arianism and tolerance of Jews, 76
Ashkenazim, 83, 84
Auto-Emancipation (Pinsker), 216, 282
Autonomy, Jewish. See Self-government and autonomy, Jewish
Averroës, 57, 61, 66, 96–97, 101, 126
Avignon, Jews in papal, 97, 108

Babylonia, Jews in, 35, 42, 45, 47–53, 64
Baal Shem Tov, 153–154, 161
Balfour, Arthur J., 283, 286–288, 290
Balfour Declaration, 204, 273, 285–286, 288–289, 290, 296 n. 5
Ballin, Albert, 214–215
Banking, prominence of Jews in. See Finance, prominence of Jews in
Bar Kochba, Simon, 37, 43, 226
Baron, Salo W., 173, 244, 257, 260
Barth, Karl, 278 n. 8
Basle, Zionist congresses at, 282–283, 287
Bea, Cardinal, 222
Belgium, Jews in. See Netherlands, Jews in
Belloc, Hilaire, 279 n. 11
Bellow, Saul, 271
Ben-Gurion, David, 234, 291, 293
Bentinck, Lord George, 252
Berek, Joselowicz, 187
Berlin, Irving, 271
Berlin, Jews in, 161, 200–201, 202, 207, 213, 216, 233; Congress of, 209
Berlin Society for the Study of Judaism, 200–201
Bernard of Clairvaux, St., 87, 90
Bernstein, Eduard, 276 n. 3
Bernstein, Leonard, 271
Besht, 153–154, 161
Bevin, Ernest, 256, 292–293
Bismarck, Otto von, 208–212, 215, 218, 232, 276 n. 4
Bleichröder, Gerson, 180, 209, 215, 276 n. 4
Bloch, Marc, 193–194
"Blood accusation," 44, 88, 92, 117 nn. 5–7, 131, 236, 237, 284
Blum, Léon, 188–189, 192, 275 n. 1
B'nai B'rith, 9, 266–267
Bohemia. See Czechoslovakia
Book of the Kahal, The (Brafman) 237, 240
Börne, Ludwig, 205–206